PROUST BETWEEN DELEUZE AND DERRIDA

Crosscurrents

Exploring the development of European thought through engagements with the arts, humanities, social sciences and sciences

Series Editor
Christopher Watkin, Monash University

Editorial Advisory Board
Andrew Benjamin
Martin Crowley
Simon Critchley
Frederiek Depoortere
Oliver Feltham
Patrick ffrench
Christopher Fynsk
Kevin Hart
Emma Wilson

Titles available in the series
Difficult Atheism: Post-Theological Thinking in Alain Badiou, Jean-Luc Nancy and Quentin Meillassoux
Christopher Watkin
Politics of the Gift: Exchanges in Poststructuralism
Gerald Moore
Unfinished Worlds: Hermeneutics, Aesthetics and Gadamer
Nicholas Davey
The Figure of This World: Agamben and the Question of Political Ontology
Mathew Abbott
The Becoming of the Body: Contemporary Women's Writing in French
Amaleena Damlé
Philosophy, Animality and the Life Sciences
Wahida Khandker
The Event Universe: The Revisionary Metaphysics of Alfred North Whitehead
Leemon B. McHenry
Sublime Art: Towards an Aesthetics of the Future
Stephen Zepke
Mallarmé and the Politics of Literature: Sartre, Kristeva, Badiou, Rancière
Robert Boncardo
Animal Writing: Storytelling, Selfhood and the Limits of Empathy
Danielle Sands
Music, Philosophy and Gender in Nancy, Lacoue-Labarthe, Badiou
Sarah Hickmott
The Desert in Modern Literature and Philosophy: Wasteland Aesthetics
Aidan Tynan
Visual Art and Self-Construction
Katrina Mitcheson
Proust Between Deleuze and Derrida: The Remains of Literature
James Dutton

Visit the Crosscurrents website at www.edinburghuniversitypress.com/series-crosscurrents.html

PROUST BETWEEN DELEUZE AND DERRIDA

The Remains of Literature

James Dutton

EDINBURGH
University Press

Edinburgh University Press is one of the leading university presses in the UK. We publish academic books and journals in our selected subject areas across the humanities and social sciences, combining cutting-edge scholarship with high editorial and production values to produce academic works of lasting importance. For more information visit our website: edinburghuniversitypress.com

© James Dutton, 2022

Edinburgh University Press Ltd
The Tun – Holyrood Road, 12(2f) Jackson's Entry, Edinburgh EH8 8PJ

Typeset in 10.5/13pt Sabon
by Cheshire Typesetting Ltd, Cuddington, Cheshire

A CIP record for this book is available from the British Library

ISBN 978 1 4744 9050 4 (hardback)
ISBN 978 1 4744 9052 8 (webready PDF)
ISBN 978 1 4744 9053 5 (epub)

The right of James Dutton to be identified as the author of this work has been asserted in accordance with the Copyright, Designs and Patents Act 1988, and the Copyright and Related Rights Regulations 2003 (SI No. 2498).

Contents

Series Editor's Preface	vi
Acknowledgements	viii
Abbreviations	ix
Introduction: Text: The Difference between Philosophy and Literature	1
1. Voice: Tracing *Restance* through the Textual Abyss	22
2. Sense: The Hollow of Experience, the Mark[ ] of *Aiôn*	46
3. Desire: Deferring a Productive Without	87
4. Love: Differentiating Groups, Faciality and the Black Hole/White Wall System	117
5. Jealousy: Absolute Knowledge as a Dream (of) Writing	145
6. Grief: The *Revenant* and the Impossibility of Mourning (Writing)	172
Conclusion: Sign: Ending Text	196
Bibliography	206
Index	216

Series Editor's Preface

Two or more currents flowing into or through each other create a turbulent crosscurrent, more powerful than its contributory flows and irreducible to them. Time and again, modern European thought creates and exploits crosscurrents in thinking, remaking itself as it flows through, across and against discourses as diverse as mathematics and film, sociology and biology, theology, literature and politics. The work of Gilles Deleuze, Jacques Derrida, Slavoj Žižek, Alain Badiou, Bernard Stiegler and Jean-Luc Nancy, among others, participates in this fundamental remaking. In each case disciplines and discursive formations are engaged, not with the aim of performing a pre-determined mode of analysis yielding a 'philosophy of x', but through encounters in which thought itself can be transformed. Furthermore, these fundamental transformations do not merely seek to account for singular events in different sites of discursive or artistic production but rather to engage human existence and society as such, and as a whole. The cross-disciplinarity of this thought is therefore neither a fashion nor a prosthesis; it is simply part of what 'thought' means in this tradition.

Crosscurrents begins from the twin convictions that this re-making is integral to the legacy and potency of European thought, and that the future of thought in this tradition must defend and develop this legacy in the teeth of an academy that separates and controls the currents that flow within and through it. With this in view, the series provides an exceptional site for bold, original and opinion-changing monographs that actively engage European thought in this fundamentally cross-disciplinary manner, riding existing crosscurrents and creating new ones. Each book in the series explores the different ways in which European thought develops through its engagement with disciplines across the arts, humanities, social sciences and sciences, recognising that the community of scholars working with this thought is itself spread across diverse faculties. The object of the series is therefore nothing less than to examine and carry forward the unique legacy of European thought as an inherently and irreducibly cross-disciplinary enterprise.

Christopher Watkin
Cambridge
February 2011

Acknowledgements

This book has been a consuming passion of mine throughout its long life. The greatest of thanks are owed to John Attridge, whose guidance has served as a constant, confidence-building foundation, and to Sean Pryor, Sigi Jöttkandt, Jasmin Kelaita and Chris Danta, whose support and insight at significant moments has proved telling. I am fortunate to have worked with such inspiring academics. I would also like to thank my doctoral supervisors, Claire Colebrook and Derek Attridge, for their exemplary scholarship that has encouraged my efforts in this work and beyond. I am grateful to Carol MacDonald – whose belief in this project made all the difference – along with Chris Watkin and the anonymous readers of this manuscript, as well as the production staff at Edinburgh University Press. In turn, Elliott Plank, Fahryn Hill, Mitchell Unger, Gareth Sciffer, Evy Wiggins and Rhys Dutton have been invaluable supports throughout this process, and their company and insights have contributed in often unexpected ways to what follows.

Earlier versions of material from this book appeared in *Textual Practice* and *Angelaki: Journal of Theoretical Humanities*, and I am grateful to their editors and publishers (https://www.tandfonline.com/) for permission to reprint this content.

Finally, this book is dedicated to Claire Keating, whose love, patience and magnanimous spirit is my daily inspiration, and to my parents, Clive and Robin Dutton: my love and gratitude for you is beyond measure.

Abbreviations

Marcel Proust
- FT *Finding Time Again* / *Le Temps retrouvé*
- GW *The Guermantes Way* / *Le Côté de Guermantes*
- PF *The Prisoner* and *The Fugitive* / *La Prisonnière*; *Albertine disparue*
- S *The Way by Swann's* / *Du côté de chez Swann*
- SG *Sodom and Gomorrah* / *Sodome et Gomorrhe*
- YG *In the Shadow of Young Girls in Flower* / *À l'ombre des jeunes filles en fleurs*

Cited page numbers for the French text refer to the corresponding volume, except for *La Prisonnière* and *Albertine disparue*, which both refer to the single, translated volume *The Prisoner and The Fugitive*. In this case, I have marked each with either *P* or *A*, respectively.

Gilles Deleuze (and Félix Guattari)
- AO (with Félix Guattari). *Anti-Oedipus: Capitalism and Schizophrenia*
- B *Bergsonism*
- DR *Difference and Repetition*
- LS *The Logic of Sense*
- PS *Proust and Signs*
- TP (with Félix Guattari). *A Thousand Plateaus: Capitalism and Schizophrenia*
- TR *Two Regimes of Madness: Texts and Interviews 1975–1995*
- WP (with Félix Guattari). *What is Philosophy?*

Jacques Derrida
- D *Dissemination*
- G *Glas*
- OG *Of Grammatology*

LI   *Limited Inc*
M   *Margins of Philosophy*
PC   *The Post Card: From Socrates to Freud and Beyond*
SM   *Specters of Marx: The State of the Debt, The Work of Mourning, and the New International*
SP   *Speech and Phenomena: And Other Essays on Husserl's Theory of Signs*
SS   *Signéponge/Signsponge*
WD   *Writing and Difference*

Introduction: Text: The Difference between Philosophy and Literature

Marcel Proust's *À la recherche du temps perdu* famously blurs the distinction between philosophy and literature. Formally, it is generally accepted to be a literary work, but its initiating strangeness – its intoxicating, obfuscating sentences, its bizarre, context-less beginning, or the fact that it is simply 'too long'[1] – points towards something more difficult, more 'philosophical', than the term 'literary' normally conveys. If the *Recherche* were a work of philosophy, there could be no justification for its digressiveness and eccentricity, unless the philosophical significance of Proust's work were found to lie in the very fact of this extensive staging: the reading-through that is different upon every re-reading, offering ever-new, richly forgettable details. Proust's novel is one that purposely inhabits the margins of genres, forcing readers to deny the categories they might seek to apply to it, and creating new ones that it will once more then defy. For Proust, a philosophical work that cogently posits its ideas as though they will remain present and unchanged is not a literary modus operandi – it is not even something that writing *can* do. Instead, the *Recherche* is a novel whose philosophical depth is always in a process of renewal, one that drives the literary to the point of its philosophical breakdown by entertaining all its infinite possibilities. Proust's novel is always in the movement of becoming-other: it remains an undecidable text.

The inability to adequately account for the *Recherche*'s generic instability – especially between philosophical and literary discourse – is a theme often broached by critics of the novel. For Vincent Descombes, 'the doctrine proposed by Proust as theorist is particularly inappropriate for narrative transposition'.[2] For Antoine Compagnon, similarly, 'Proust's novel is "out of sync" with its aesthetic doctrine.'[3] But this does not mean that these critics devalue the philosophical merit of the *Recherche*: rather, Descombes argues that a 'philosophical' reading of Proust's text 'is not the kind of study that singles out passages of a speculative character in order to probe their content';[4] Compagnon notes that it is 'in the gap between the question it asks and the question that reading the novel allows us to reconstruct' that we find the 'plurality' of the work's rich meanings.[5] The unattainable movement between these diverse possibilities of meaning – the reading of this immense work – makes the novel irreducible to any of its philosophical statements. But it is the sheer breadth of the reading that Proust's novel demands (not only in terms of its enormous material and stylistic length, but Proust's deferring desire to extend it without end) that also makes it so important an investigation of the conditions of the literary.[6] It asks something searching about attention, and what remains from our readerly encounters. In the novel's final volume, *Le Temps retrouvé*, Proust's narrator challenges the superficiality of a kind of realist literature that seeks to articulate presentable 'forms' and 'meanings': 'descriptions' which remain hermetically stable despite the temporal changes the reader undergoes in read*ing*.

> How could a purely descriptive literature have any value at all, when reality lies hidden beneath the surface of little things of the sort it documents (grandeur in the distant sound of an aeroplane, or in the outline of the steeple of Saint-Hilaire, the past in the taste of a madeleine, etc.) so that the things have no meaning in themselves until it is disentangled from them? (FT 203)[7]

> Comment la littérature de notations aurait-elle une valeur quelconque, puisque c'est sous de petites choses comme celles qu'elle note que la réalité est contenue (la grandeur dans le bruit lointain d'un aéroplane, dans la ligne du clocher de Saint-Hilaire, le passé dans la saveur d'une madeleine, etc.) et qu'elles sont sans signification par elles-mêmes si on ne l'en dégage pas ? (201)

Proust suggests that a determinate meaning is not inherent in the objects described by realism. But this passage also implies that 'meaning' can never be fully disengaged from these 'little things'. Even if a meaning is partially 'disentangled' from them, it will always bear the inextricable impression of the 'little things' it arises from – which might, in many respects, be the 'meaning' itself, in its purest form. The 'meaning' that Proust's narrator refers to here, as well as the 'little things' of descriptive experience, are never exempt from the movement of time. They are always in a process of becoming something else, further entangling themselves with other meanings and metaphors, and then incorporating the imprint of those new interactions. Proust's novel, rather than denying the work of time and becoming, shows us that the work of literature is to exemplify this process of change – like all literary works, the *Recherche* can only unfold anew across each reading. In this rebuke to realism, as we shall see, Proust is drawing attention to the paradox inherent within a logic of presentation: he is not strictly opposed to this descriptive literature, but rather, he is more interested in the depth of its 'little things', and how their significance is always interwoven with other, ineradicable, remains.

For Proust, the literary is always a process of becoming. The *Recherche* could never be a work of 'purely descriptive literature', directly stating its philosophical position along with its characters, events and morals, because the meanings that it would seek to present are always becoming entangled with other possible meanings. This process of weaving inevitably leads to a deferral of 'present' meaning, since there is always another element that will come to make up the fullness of an idea. This may account in part for why Proust chose to write not a 'purely' philosophical work but an enormous, interminable novel – one that remained unfinished on his death, and one his readers can always re-read, safe in the knowledge that its weaving will always take another kink, fray or tear. As Roland Barthes writes in *Le Plaisir du texte* (1973), 'Joy of Proust: from one reading to the next, one never skips the same passages.'[8] There can be no presentation of the 'essence' of Proust's novel, because that would mean limiting the other potential becomings that the next reading might offer. And in the same way, there can be no *presence* to the total *Recherche*, because it is always gesturing towards its other possible – but always to be deferred – meanings. How can we assign to any part of the novel a specific, present and static 'form' or 'meaning', if the greater philosophical weight of the novel lies in its dispersive *re*interpretability and functionally infinite interconnections? One of my aims in this book is to use Proust's conception of textual becoming to challenge our more general beliefs about the idea of literary presence. As Derek Attridge notes,

> [the] statement that a work is not an object but an event may be a truism, but it is a truism whose implications have generally been resisted. [. . .] We still talk about 'structure' and 'meaning,' and ask what a work is 'about,' in a manner that suggests a static object, transcending time, permanently available for our inspection.[9]

Proust's *Recherche*, the lingering remains of which always invalidates any attempt to say what it is 'about', forces its readers to contemplate the possibilities of textuality as, and only as, an event.

Towards the end of the novel, Proust's narrator refers to a book he is going to write – indicating but, despite what some hasty critics have affirmed, never confirming that this may be the book we have just read. He notes that 'the idea of my book was in my head, always the same, in a process of perpetual becoming [l'idée de mon œuvre était dans ma tête, toujours la même, en perpétuel devenir]' (*FT* 351; 347). While it takes the same, *re*cognisable form in his mind, its virtual quality renders this text always different from itself – even while it remains the same. In the novel as a whole, this notion of perpetual becoming extends to subjectivity itself – extends, that is, to the elusive character of Proust's narrator. The first voice that speaks in the novel refers to an 'I', but throughout the work's tremendous length there is little account given of who that pronoun refers to. Of course, it is the work's narrator. But what does that tell us? If the work itself, or the work-to-come that signals its closure – yet may in some ways be the work we have read – is always in a 'process of perpetual becoming', might not the 'subjectivity' that speaks for it be in that same process? Or, more radically, why should we assume there to be a coherent subjectivity at all? We are dealing with a literary work *given* by a subjectivity that now remains no more than a signature that should have been added at the end of the work, if its author had lived to do so.[10] As the work becomes something different not only in each reading, but also in the imagination of each reading, its only static remainder is the remains of language – what we might 'call' it, which also changes in its own, virtual manner. The 'I' of the *Recherche* works in the same way. Its coherence is reiterated only by that most minimal of epithets that we all use to signify (but never sign for) our different selves. And if Proust's novel deconstructs or disperses its speaking 'I', how can we assign any particular philosophy to it, or, indeed, any totalised meaning?

In this specific example, one which underlines the elusiveness of the novel itself, we can note the aporetic movement of the Proustian signature. Proust's writing denotes texts, characters, places, affects and even narrators that, while holding the same citable 'name', always return differently, often in direct contradiction to their previous iteration.[11] The *Recherche* is an exercise in the trickery of recognition, questioning the veracity of that *re*-, which is forever the same, but always different. Because perception is always moving, or always expiring, the *return* of *re*cognition weaves together the inexhaustible traces of past impressions: perception itself can never present its object, but only the jostling traces of its pasts and future possibilities. My reading will seek to resist a 'purely descriptive' interpretation of Proust's novel and treat it as an event, an incorporative production always in movement, always *re*iterating a multiplicity of possible forms, and as such, a work that disrupts a static 'what' of ontology by dislocating a present-able 'where' of presence.

In challenging the presentational logic inherent to metaphysics, especially in the form of a text that incorporates the traces of its differing pasts as its own never-fully-present becoming, the 'totality' of Proust's text – be it philosophical or literary – is always undecidable. In order to provide a description – one that remains always provisional[12] – of this quality, I draw in what follows on the work of two philosophers who are closely associated with the movement away from presence in Western thought: Gilles Deleuze and Jacques Derrida. Each of these thinkers deals with this challenge to metaphysics in different ways, but questioning the traditional primacy of presence in thought is central to both of their oeuvres.

To be sure, it is dangerous to reduce any philosopher's work to a simple label. This is especially the case with both Deleuze and Derrida, whose contributions to philosophy – like Proust's – challenge any kind of static interpretation. Deleuze's work prioritises becoming, change and movement over static form: this also goes for any attempt to define his philosophy. As Claire Colebrook writes, Deleuze 'reinvented his style and vocabulary with each project. No term in his work is capable of being defined in itself; any single term makes sense only in its relation to the whole which it helps to create.'[13] Similarly, for Derrida, the inability to determine an essential 'meaning' (or rather, the *presence* of one) for his key concepts often becomes the work of his philosophy itself: every 'presentation' of the term *différance*, for instance, is itself a gesture towards what it doesn't present. The 'field of being [*étant*],' Derrida writes, 'before being determined as the field of presence, structures itself according to the diverse properties – genetic and structural – of the trace' (*OG* 51). In what follows, I draw on a range of Derridean (non)concepts, such as the trace, *restance*, the *sumplokē*, iterability, the signature (or its *seing*) and the *revenant*, as ways of coming to grips with the deferral of presence at work in Proust's *Recherche*. In general, these terms point towards the inextricable absence inherent in apparent presence, and thus the crisis of any absolute distinction between the two. The structure that Derrida calls the 'trace' defers metaphysics' insistence on the presentation of an Idea, because that Idea is 'constituted' by an absent origin that can never be *re*inscribed as the Idea.[14] The trace, which gives form as it takes it away, moving towards its future by equally implying its different(iating) past, troubles the idea of presence as the remaining form of any concept.

Like Derrida's, Deleuze's work is often concerned with reconceptualising the idea of difference in order to challenge assumptions about Being and presence. As we will see in greater detail in Chapter 2 ('Sense'), Deleuze describes the virtual element of perception, experience and memory as a complex contraction that produces the sense of temporality, always interwoven in a formless movement of Ideality. In this chapter I suggest that, in particular, Deleuze's notion of 'dividual multiplicity' can help us to understand Proust's abyssal depiction of temporal experience. Dividual multiplicity obliges us to think of time and presence not as a present/absent binary, but as the always-incorporating contraction of experiences into experience – a totali*sing* (yet never totali*sed*) *sense* of experience that implies, yet does not present, every experience within it. The virtual contracts experiences into ever new forms that point towards their constituting differences, yet do not repeat the duration of living them. As Deleuze puts it in *Difference and Repetition*, it is the 'displacement and disguise' of difference that 'makes repetition an evolution as such' (*DR* 289–90). Repetition incorporates difference – it is always different while it remains the same; similarly, the idea of difference depends on repetition – winding both into a virtual synthesis of sense.

It is not my desire in this book to attempt to conflate the philosophical projects of Derrida and Deleuze, which have been notably, even explicitly, separated by a certain critical difference.[15] Instead, as recent work has noted, there is a productive difference essential to their work, a kind of difference that Bernard Stiegler, for instance, has described as pharmacological.[16] This *pharmakon* – a popular philosophical trope through the lineages of poststructuralism that acts as both poison and cure, answer and question – may help us to avoid metaphysical assumptions and attend to the inconsistent truths of textual inquiry. The deferring force of the *pharmakon*, where cure is constitutively entangled with *another* poison (to assume another cure, and so on), illustrates the difficulty of reading any inscription as static or self-present. Thinking with the *pharmakon* as Stiegler advocates (after Derrida and Deleuze, he notes) means unlacing the truths of formal and presentational logic – primary retentions, or immediate sense-data – and paying attention to the often contradictory readings inherent in every event of perception. Like so many of the ostensible truths held by Proust's narrator that are upturned by the most inconsequential of movements, the certainties we hold with regard to textual knowledge are always at the mercy of the event of (re)reading – an event that both re-signs and resigns our expectations on the immanent, unyielding basis of the mark.

Perhaps the most notable evidence for the difference between Deleuze and Derrida is the almost total lack of reference between the two in their written oeuvres.[17] Aside from some sporadic references to Derrida and deconstruction in his work, perhaps the most interesting comment Deleuze makes about Derrida's project emerges in response to a question he received after his presentation at the 1972 Cérisy conference – which was also attended by Derrida. 'As for the method of textual deconstruction,' Deleuze begins, acknowledging that he knows of it and admires it, but that it has 'nothing to do' with his own approach. Such 'textual commentary, or any other textual practice' is not relevant to his philosophy, he comments. Instead, his is 'about seeing what one can do with an extra textual practice that extends the text'.[18] This seemingly paradoxical 'problem' (using extra-textual practice to extend the text) should be seen as essential to Deleuze's understanding of textual machines. But equally, such inversion of 'text' and 'textual practice' is also crucial to Derrida's work, which is far from 'textual commentary' in a generic sense. Derrida sets out this excessive reading in *Of Grammatology*'s opening remarks, where he outlines some of the capacious meanings the terms 'writing' and 'language' have assumed throughout history (*OG* 8–9). Derrida works to draw attention to how every text extends itself, through a process of reading that is founded on limitless extension – or deferral – where the *difference* marked by inscription, or textual spacing (iteration or the 'practice' of the text itself), is of greatest – indeed vital – consequence.

Here, Slavoj Žižek's comment that Deleuze and Derrida both 'deploy their theories through a detailed reading of other philosophers' – in so far as, for them, 'philosophy today can be practiced only in the mode of metaphilosophy as a reading of (other) philosophers' – identifies the importance of reading to their approaches. It also illuminates the resistance to fixed methodologies shared by Derrida and Deleuze (and, indeed, by many of their 'generation'). But what it should also indicate is this pharmacological approach to reading, where a permanence of meaning is never possible. This is why Žižek can later assert, almost immediately after this comment, that 'Derrida and Deleuze speak different, totally incompatible languages, with no shared ground between them'.[19] It is precisely this incompatible, non-relational and thus *unfinishable* difference that renders the kind of metaphilosophical reading Deleuze and Derrida made indispensable to philosophical inquiry so productive. This deferral of settled categories renders every project a metaphilosophical one, every writing a meta-text – a dilemma Proust's enormous and radically unsigned text stages by its very material existence.

Perhaps the best authority on the matter of Deleuze's and Derrida's difference is their contemporary Jean-François Lyotard, who does discuss their different approaches to philosophy. Speaking of temporality, Lyotard argues that both 'Derrida's problematic of deconstruction and *différance*, Deleuze's principle of nomadism belong, however different they may be', to a conception of time and phenomenality focused on deferral. Lyotard ties this in part to the 'Judaic tradition' of reading that sees reading and interpretation as always one ephemeral passage that will itself call for further reading and interpretation. 'What this tradition calls "study" and "reading" requires that any reality be treated as an obscure message addressed by an unknowable or even unnameable agency.'[20] Here, Lyotard identifies the importance of deferral for Deleuze and Derrida, who both avow the inability to fix perception into static, unchangeable forms ('it would be presumptuous, if not criminal, for a thinker or writer to claim to be the witness or guarantor of the event', Lyotard writes[21]). It is my suggestion that, by attending to the importance of deferral in Proust's massive textual project (which was incessantly amended and extended), we can note an important, and unique, example of this approach to thinking and aesthetic creation, where 'writing' and 'reading' explode out of their fixed, repeatable forms and demand to be studied, read and written always – irrevocably – differently.

Of course, the philosophies of Deleuze and Derrida have often been distanced in critical literature, and the telling lack of engagement between both thinkers across their long careers supports this position. But, following Lyotard, as contemporary *readers* of Derrida and Deleuze (of the texts they left behind), we might begin to identify new, nomadic or deconstructive approaches to interpreting the unknowable and unnameable force of their philosophies – one that emerges from the texts that remain with us. Indeed, should the possibility that further reading and study of these texts come to generate new differences 'between Deleuze and Derrida', then, from the perspective of the productive deferral that I see as central to Proust's project, this strategy would serve us more usefully than any forced, or chance, concordance. Rather than claim a fixed methodological 'reading' of the texts I am discussing, this book will emphasise the power inscription has to reinvent itself, as well as the truths, histories and relations we rely on it to ratify. As Erin Graff Zivin notes, precursors (as well as relations) only ever arrive belatedly to alert us 'to the constitutive *unlikeness* of an author to him or herself'.[22] 'No book is autonomous,' she argues. 'Every book is open, exposed to the books that have preceded it (those written by its own author as well as others) and the books that will follow it.'[23] Using Deleuze and Derrida to examine Proust's work not only does not assume that these writers agree(d) on all (or even many) issues linking philosophy and literature – or that they will continue to be read in this way. Instead, it is the difference between each thinker's approach that, in so far as it should never be totalised, we can notice particularly productive insights – especially as we relate this difference to a text that never finishes finding differences from, and within, itself.

In this respect, it is useful to outline here, at the outset, the written connections that remain between both philosophers and Proust's text. Both Derrida and Deleuze have engaged directly with Proust's work, although in different ways and to different extents. Derrida's direct commentary on Proust is sparse.[24] What is interesting to note, though, is that one of the most detailed discussions of Proust in his published oeuvre is in the seminal early essay 'Force and Signification', a text that carves out the early movements for what will come to be called deconstruction. Here, Derrida proposes Proust (taking aim at Jean Rousset's structuralist method) as exemplary of both the popularity of narratorial 'double register' (*WD* 21) and a kind of Hegelian dialectic of literary art, where Proust's painstaking dedication to structure in the *Recherche* synthesises artist and artwork *as* its narratorial consciousness. Years before the comments of Descombes and Compagnon cited above, Derrida argued that 'Proust's aesthetics and critical method are, ultimately, not outside the work but are the very heart of his creation' (*WD* 22). However, as is often the case in Derrida's complicated engagement with Hegel, this Proustian *Aufhebung* does not form a simple, harmonic synthesis: it is complicated by inscription's survival – the remains of literature. Because Proust's literary technique is a 'practised preformationism' (in the sense that the *Recherche*'s syntheses were all planned out *avant la lettre* as part of Proust's genetic vision for his novel), Derrida draws attention to its fractal force, a pattern that exceeds the text itself. All of its elements, prior to and during composition, as well as in the reading of the text, 'are already in action in reduced dimensions': the art becomes 'conscious of its works' (*WD* 23) as it is already becoming them, where they are 'written' before they are inscribed. From Derrida's perspective, standard temporal or teleological accounts of literature are inadequate for Proust's preformationism, one that speaks over, for and through every word of his text – while this textual inscription remains nothing but 'itself'. What seems to be only a passing reference to Proust becomes an early mark of the importance of deferral (especially with respect to 'identity') in deconstructive reading. 'Writing is the outlet as the descent of meaning outside itself within itself [L'écriture est l'issue comme descente hors de soi en soi du sens]' (*WD* 29), Derrida argues at the conclusion of 'Force and Signification', underlining how writing can never present its meaning because that meaning is always inscribed in its 'own' constituting difference. We will take up the full force of Proust's narratorial 'preformationism' or deferral of a present identity in the next chapter.

Here, Derrida uses Proust's text as model to explore his exceptions with structuralism, and perhaps for this reason the full depth of his engagement with the Recherche remains elusive. It is precisely this remainder that I want to explore in this book. However, instead of trying to draw speculative conclusions from direct references, my aim is to show how the quality of deferral that writing takes on *as remains*, as marks that subsist and insist, always *différantly*, shares an essential, motivating force for Derrida as well as for Proust. For a theorist so concerned with the cultural and archival dissemination of all kinds of writing, Derrida worked to show how the influence one text, writer or signatory can have, intentionally or otherwise, on another is always nebulous and unpredictable. It is dependent on the force of remains. '*Longtemps je me suis*, for a long time I have – been interested in the biodegradable', Derrida writes towards the beginning of 'Biodegradables: Seven Diary Fragments', his text that deals most with this problem, parasiting perhaps the most persistent phrase of Proust's *Recherche* to have sunk into popular consciousness.[25] In doing so, Derrida gestures to the uncanny survival of writing – but also the uncertain paths that influence, archivabilty and verifiable truths take when all that remains of them *are* remains, that is, writing. Derrida's interest in unfinishability and the 'life' of literary deferral iterates throughout his texts (*Glas*, which begins and ends within the 'flow' of the same sentence, is one example), demonstrating how the forces of deconstruction emerge from every form of writing and text, especially those that were not his own. His oeuvre then gestures to the parasitism that engenders literary discourse, undermines authorial mastery and, for that matter, genre itself, where not only philosophy and literature, but every 'category' of writing, bleed into each other on the very basis of the mark's remains. In doing so, he is himself unfinishing, deferring – mourning – Proust's project, where the text's 'voice' begins speaking without a definitive author, authority or (in so far as it is writing) a voice. It begins – but it does not (indeed it cannot, while re-reading remains a possibility) end.

Deleuze's relationship with the *Recherche* is somewhat easier to trace – but Proust's work also has an important spectral place in relation to Deleuze's thought. Like Derrida, Deleuze also devoted attention to the *Recherche* in the formative stages of his career, in the form of an important early book. *Proust and Signs* was Deleuze's first book on a 'literary' author, and he returned to revise it twice (six and ten years after its initial publication). And again, like Derrida, in this study Deleuze does not accept the novel's stated philosophical doctrines at face value. Rather, he reads the *Recherche* as positing a theory of signs that breaks down transcendent and immanent distinctions in favour of what he was later to call the 'plane of immanence'. Deleuze rethinks the Proustian commonplace of involuntary memory by arguing that the *'essential thing in involuntary memory is not resemblance, nor even identity, which are merely conditions, but the internalized difference, which becomes immanent'* (PS 60). The production of different, involuntary iterations of sense is not attributable to memory, but rather the virtual plane of immanence that takes variant perceptions, 'envelops the one in the other, and makes their relation into something internal' (PS 60).[26] The result, as Patrick Bray points out, is an abyssal conception of the novel as 'an ever-expanding web of connections relaying the external stimuli of signs, woven blindly and unconsciously by a narrator-spider'.[27] As Deleuze observes, a 'new image of thought, or rather the liberation of thought from the images which imprison it, was what I was looking for already in Proust' (TR 303).[28] Deleuze famously treated texts and thinkers as malleable in the service of his own thought (one will remember his now ubiquitous buggery comment[29]). However, the curious latency of Proust's ideas throughout *Deleuze's* oeuvre (Jean-Jacques Lecercle notes that in the 'concordance of literary allusions in his works, the Proust entry is the longest, and allusions are present in practically all his books'[30]) suggests Proust's unfinished text remained unfinishable for Deleuze himself.[31] As with Derrida, my suggestion is that the liberating elusiveness of Proustian deferral – especially in terms of genre, style and external 'meaning' – served as a spectral image of thought for Deleuze. Therefore, my project in exploring each thinker's relation to Proust is not to make a directly genetic or hereditary argument, but to show how key concepts, like deferral, iterability, becoming and transversality can not only generate interesting accords between these three thinkers' work, but also retain and develop their productive differences (difference being, of course, perhaps the key (non)concept for both Derrida and Deleuze – in often almost irreconcilably *different* ways).

Indeed, it is in different ways that literature plays a major part in Derrida's and Deleuze's philosophical projects, which are literary in the sense that both direct attention to the unravelling of distinctions between literature and philosophy.[32] Colebrook points out that 'Deleuze was a philosopher but he also wrote in a highly literary manner',[33] where stylistic freedom afforded his concepts a necessary vehicle from which their originality could cut through. Derrida's texts, meanwhile, are celebrated for their literariness; as he himself noted, 'my most constant interest, coming even before my philosophical interest I should say, if this is possible, has been directed towards literature, towards that writing which is called literary'.[34] 'Writing' itself is privileged over these categories, but, for both philosophers, the concept of writing, and its interpretive depth, only ever reveals itself elusively. Deleuze argues that

> Writing is a question of becoming, always incomplete, always in the midst of being formed, and goes beyond the matter of any livable or lived experience. It is a process, that is, a passage of Life that traverses both the livable and the lived. Writing is inseparable from becoming.[35]

Because it is always becoming and always in movement, there can be no presence of textual meaning.[36] Ontology can only ever be appropriated as an abyss. Deleuze notes that the narrator of the *Recherche* is as iterable, as little proper, as ourselves and our readings. 'The "subject" of the *Search* is finally no self, it is that *we* without content that portions out Swann, the narrator, and Charlus, distributes or selects them without totalising them' (PS 128). *Being* a text, no thing is presented other than the text, which gives or appropriates the narrative, but is not it: it is always moving beyond its singular meaning. The graft of the text is the winding graft of the signature, an incorporation-expropriation which weaves always-another subjectivity from the reading subject that is dispossessed into it.

In Proust's work, Bray argues, '[w]riter and reader alike dissolve in the interlacing of a perpetually becoming text'.[37] In reading and writing (especially writing one's 'own' reading and reading one's 'own' writing) who signs, where, and which signature? As the proper name is *reiter*ated by its very being, or its having been, it disseminates its property. Propriety, and thus apparent selfhood, is only ever antonomasia – a term for the synecdoche that is the becoming-common of proper nouns. In *Signéponge*, Derrida writes

> You never know whether he names or describes, nor whether the thing he describes-names is the thing or the name, the common or proper name.
> The proper name, in its aleatoriness, should have no meaning and should spend itself in immediate reference. But the chance or the misery of its arbitrary character (always other in each case), is that its inscription in language always affects it with a potential for meaning, and for no longer being proper once it has a meaning. (SS 118)

For meaning to mean anything, it must appropriate repetition, which denies the active uniqueness of appropriation. The pure singularity of the subject of writing – the one who is signed for, or as – is always disseminated by writing.[38] For a signature to be fully itself, fully meaningful, its ontology would be pure singularity, that is, without the possibility of different repetition, without the possibility of meaning. Meaning itself descends down the abyss of iterability and *re*appropriation, definitively aporetic in its properties of always inaugural, repetitive difference. The 'presentation' of these differences is abyssal, deferring 'its' constituting differences further into its presentation.

By concerning itself with certain philosophical (or anti-philosophical) implications of Proust's literary text, this book engages with a major theme in Proust criticism, as I noted at the outset. Descombes's important study focuses explicitly on the 'philosophical' quality of Proust's novel, although he finds that the 'doctrine of Proust the theorist prescribes only constructions that prove to be impossible'.[39] As Erika Fülöp observes, Descombes's 'approach, distinguishing between the two faces of the *Recherche*, has become paradigmatic of the subsequent studies concerned with the novel's philosophy'.[40] For Isabelle Décarie, the novel emerges out of an 'inaugural indetermination' between philosophy and literature, which, she argues, necessitated Proust's invention of the *Recherche*'s radical texture.[41] Similarly, Bray remarks that 'Deleuze's reading would seem to amount to a problematization of the theorizing aspect of the novel, of the narrator as theorist'.[42] Joshua Landy, conversely, in a recent influential intervention in this subject, argues that 'if we employ a principle of charity rather than the hermeneutics of suspicion, we can in fact extract a consistent, powerful, and original philosophical system from *Á la recherche du temps perdu*'.[43] The philosophy of the *Recherche* is not 'present' in its literary form, but rather emerges against the permanence of that inscription. In another recent study, Martin Hägglund emphasises the importance to both the novel, and Proust's philosophy, of the fact that 'there is a succession of selves that come into being and pass away as [Proust's narrator] changes over time',[44] because only 'if something is *no longer* – that is, only if there is negativity – can there be a difference between before and after, past and present. This negativity must be at work in presence itself for there to be succession.'[45] By developing an 'image of thought' that challenges the presentation of defined, static forms (especially as such thought relates to textuality and the necessary passage of time involved in the act of reading), Proust's novel undermines this kind of 'difference' or 'succession' in favour of categories that are always undecidable.[46] It never stages a discrete present that can differentiate its before and after: it is always present and absent. This ambiguity or doubleness resembles what Fülöp calls 'the narrator's twofold perception, which at one moment makes the world appear simple and straightforward in its structure and truth, and then shows it as hopelessly multiple and ungraspable at all levels'.[47] In this book, I would like to follow this 'twofold perception' through to the logic at the end of Fülöp's comment: not only is the narrator's perception 'multiple and ungraspable' in its own right, but so is the textual concept of 'Proust's narrator' itself, weaving in and out of provisional identities in the present-less becoming of the text.

One recent critical engagement that has emphasised this force in Proust's writing is the work of Anne Simon. In *Proust ou le réel retrouvé* (2000) and *Trafics de Proust* (2016), Simon offers an innovative reconceptualisation of phenomenal experience as portrayed in the *Recherche*. She argues that Proust's project rethinks key tenets of logical appearance by prioritising a strategy of what she calls 'engainement' (roughly translated as 'sheathing', and a term she notes is employed at 'crucial' or 'central' moments in the *Recherche*[48]), over discrete subject/object dichotomies. Such *engainement* delegitimises dominant logics of presentation because it brings 'the self towards an encounter with alterity, or towards inhabiting a reality which does not reduce itself to the "sum of its lines or surfaces"'.[49] This moves the narrator's treatment of form in the novel towards 'the extreme singular and the fascinating contingency of moments of life that literature is tasked with restituting in their entirety, with all of their poly-sensorial attachments and their oneiric and desiring ramifications.'[50] The *Recherche* is an extreme singular that is not a totality: it moves *towards* totalis*ing*, but is never totalis*ed*. Proust seizes the undecidable presentation of literary becoming to emphasise the traces of form in a way that is always pointing towards its absent-present multiplicity. For Simon, 'Proust's writing promotes an overlap between the internal and the external: the outside world is implied in the body and effaces its opacity like the sun shining on horizons indefectibly interior and exterior.'[51]

Although the considerations of presence and becoming that concern me here may sometimes seem abstract, they are allied, both in Proust's novel and in Derrida's and Deleuze's writing, with the depth and *engainement* of affective, everyday life. Part of my aim in what follows is, in this respect, to emphasise that the generic undecidability of Proust's text is grounded in the rich undecidability of experience itself. My first chapter ('Voice') focuses on the difficult composition of selfhood, as it remains from inscriptions, woven out of memory and forgetting. It examines the problem of 'present-ing' presence in Proust's novel, especially as it relates to the novel's narrator and Derrida's critique of presence. 'Sense', the second chapter, considers the phenomenality of Being, utilising Deleuze's understanding of multiplicity and the virtual to analyse the paradoxical flow of sense and perception, and how this fluidity interacts with the abyssal becoming of a text such as Proust's. This chapter deals with the traditional Proustian themes of 'involuntary memory' and dreams, but aligns them with the ancient Greek time-scheme of the *aiôn*, in order to free them from a representational model of thought or textuality. The final four chapters consider what I call the *Recherche*'s 'affective arc' – that is, each of the affects that come, in an accumulative movement, to dominate the events of the novel. These chapters focus on desire, love, jealousy and grief, respectively.

Towards the end of the novel, Proust's narrator meditates upon the 'inner book of unknown signs [livre intérieur des ces signes inconnus]', the reading of which 'becomes one of those acts of creation in which nobody can take our place or even collaborate with us [cette lecture consistant en un acte de création où nul ne peut nous suppléer, ni même collaborer avec nous]' (*FT* 187–8; 185). These signs are the *inner* book of our own senses – in the always-already becoming of this book, its formlessness as a book not read, not written, but exclusively interior: they are the weaving of the trace. The tension here between inscription as material remains and the trace that always eludes its inscribed form is key to Proust's literary project, and his description of this 'inner book' helps to set out the terms for his philosophy of productive deferral – and its resistance to fixed forms.[52]

> That book, the most painful of all to decipher, is also the only one dictated to us by reality, the only one whose 'impression' has been made in us by reality itself. Whatever the idea that may have been left in us by our life, their material outline, the trace of the impression they originally made on us, is always the indispensable warrant of their truth. Only the impression, however slight its material may seem, however elusive its trace, can be a criterion of truth and on that account is the only thing worthy of being apprehended by the mind. (*FT* 188)

> Ce livre, le plus pénible de tous à déchiffrer, est aussi le seul que nous ait dicté la réalité, le seul dont « l'impression » ait été faite en nous par la réalité même. De quelque idée laissée en nous par la vie qu'il s'agisse, sa figure matérielle, trace de l'impression qu'elle nous a faite, est encore le gage de sa vérité nécessaire. [. . .] Seule l'impression, si chétive qu'en semble la matière, si invraisemblable la trace, est un critérium de vérité et à cause de cela mérite seule d'être appréhendée par l'esprit. (186)

The 'trace of the impression' is elusive – or rather, the *presentation* of the trace is elusive. For Proust, there is a critical distinction to be made between what he calls here 'reality' and 'impression' – and yet, neither can exist without the other. Each bears the inextricable trace of the other – and it is this trace that can never be presented, independent of the 'reality' or 'impression' that implies it. 'Impression' – the trace of which 'is always the indispensable warrant of truth' – can only be 'made in us' by 'reality itself': it is formed by its inaugurating difference from the reality that gives it. This difference comes from what is 'left in us by our life', that 'book' of all of our life's other impressions. Each new 'impression' of reality interacts with these traces of impressions that make up our life itself, and thus cleave reality and impression apart in the living of it. It is discerning the depth, the traces of these impressions as they impart their influence on reality – *while they are given to us by reality* – that lies at the heart of Proust's project.[53]

While 'nobody can come to take our place or even collaborate with us' in the *arche-writing* of our inner book, how does its mediation (as writing or reading) work if it, too, is always becoming? Frequently cited passages from the *Recherche* such as this one indicate why, for Simon, 'Proust more than any other author, spoke to philosophers'.[54] The interpretability of his language and ideas opens his fiction to a movement in which other signatories come to stand in for his; Proust's slow movement outside of his massive textual arborescence envelops other voices to come to speak for, and translate, his own. And as these functions 'constitute the paradoxical roots of the real world, roots creating the possibility of its manifestation',[55] these roots sprout into the varying ideas of each of his interpreters. The racinating exchange between the impressions of each interpreter's proper 'inner book' attracts philosophers who want to speak for, to theorise and elaborate, the meanings that grow out of the rich humus of Proust's work. It is from the interlacing roots of such 'books' as those signed by Deleuze and Derrida, that we can sign our own, proper, read*ing* of Proust. Their virtual integration is always becoming, germinating from the fertile ground of what these books mean to us as they become something other. The narrator concludes his novel at the precipice of the *possibility* of writing this inner book. We, the reader, are seemingly at the same edge – the edge of the in-between: we have just read a book that ends with the possibility of this book-to-come. No one can collaborate, no one can sign for us in the writing-non-writing of this book, not even its author. Proust may have never lived to sign for, or at, the end of his novel, but we will never live to sign for the end of our reading it. What remains of reading is the elusive sign of *every* reading, a memory and mark that neither we, nor 'Proust', can ever finish adding to.

NOTES

1. Pierre Bayard, *Le Hors-Sujet: Proust et la digression* (Paris: Minuit, 1996), 11. Throughout this book, when referring to texts of which there is no available English translation (such as this one), translations are my own.
2. Vincent Descombes, *Proust: Philosophy of the Novel*, trans. Catherine Chance Macksey (Stanford: Stanford University Press, 1992), 11.
3. Antoine Compagnon, *Proust between Two Centuries*, trans. Richard E. Goodkin (New York: Columbia University Press, 1992), 9.

4. Descombes, *Proust*, 1.
5. Compagnon, *Proust between Two Centuries*, 9.
6. Christine Cano notes that there 'is an extent to which all reading, but perhaps paradigmatically the reading of Proust, is defined by an extra-textual temporality that is quite simply the time a text "takes" to read'. Christine Cano, *Proust's Deadline* (Urbana and Chicago: University of Illinois Press, 2006), 1.
7. For English translations of Proust's text I have chosen to cite the recent, multi-translator Penguin Modern Classics edition over C. K. Scott Moncrieff's seminal translation. This choice was made primarily with respect to the willingness these editions show to being as faithful and direct with Proust's prose as possible (though this can at times be variable). While Moncrieff's style and creativity make his translation an artwork in its own right, his propensity to avoid literal translation, or to shift phrases in a way that works against what I will argue is Proust's particular literary-philosophical gambit, tends more often than not to work against my purposes here. Moncrieff's famous reimagining of the novel's title into *Remembrance of Things Past* is indicative of this problem: my claim is that phenomenal experience as Proust inscribes it is a more complex conjuncture – an endlessly deferring *recherche* – than an intentional 'remembrance'.
8. Roland Barthes, *Œuvres complètes*, vol. 4 (Paris: Éditions du Seuil, 2002), 224.
9. Derek Attridge, *The Singularity of Literature* (London and New York: Routledge, 2004), 59.
10. Compagnon gives an account of Proust's interlacing subjectivities between his life and novel – and asks whether a demarcation between them can ever be made. 'Tragically, in the face of death, the separation between life and the novel succumbs. Writing – for it is never a question of anything else – moves without mediation from the novel to life, and from life to the novel, until death occurs. It will not be long in coming.' Compagnon, *Proust between Two Centuries*, 110.
11. In 'Une idée de recherche', in *Recherche de Proust*, ed. Gérard Genette and Tzvetan Todorov (Paris: Éditions du Seuil, 1980), 37, Barthes calls this Proust's literary 'enantiology (discourse of inversion)'. For a discussion of the importance of this idea in the *Recherche*, see John Attridge, 'Episodic Trust: Self, Society and Sociology in *Á la recherche du temps perdu*', in *Incredible Modernism: Literature, Trust and Deception*, ed. John Attridge and Rod Rosenquist (Farnham: Ashgate, 2013), 202.
12. In this manner, I follow Derek Attridge's methodological 'claim' that, since 'literature, or rather the experience of literary works, consistently exceeds the limits of rational accounting, what I offer is less a logical argument than a report and an invitation: a report on a certain living-through of the literary'. *The Singularity of Literature*, 3.
13. Claire Colebrook, *Gilles Deleuze* (London and New York: Routledge, 2002), 4.

14. As Rodolphe Gasché points out, Derrida's thought overcomes phenomenology's bind of intentionality and origin encountered from Husserl to Merleau-Ponty by insisting that repetition itself is primordial, but since 'the notion of the primordial is necessarily linked to presence, this structure cannot be called primordial in the traditional sense'. Rodolphe Gasché, *Inventions of Difference: On Jacques Derrida* (Cambridge, MA, and London: Harvard University Press, 1994), 40.
15. For some context here, see Paul Patton and John Protevi's detailed 'Introduction' to their edited collection *Between Deleuze and Derrida* (London and New York: Continuum, 2003), 1–14, or Vernon Cisney's *Deleuze and Derrida: Difference and the Power of the Negative* (Edinburgh: Edinburgh University Press, 2018), which provides a useful list of other critics who have discussed the relationship between Deleuze and Derrida (5–6, 14).
16. See Bernard Stiegler, *The Neganthropocene* (London: Open Humanities Press, 2018), 58–59, 140, and *States of Shock: Stupidity and Knowledge in the 21st Century* (Cambridge: Polity, 2015), 30.
17. Importantly, though, there were some textual interactions between the two. Derrida notably wrote the obituary titled 'I'm Going to Have to Wander All Alone' for Deleuze, that marked out, or inscribed, his sense of their relationship and philosophies. Deleuze refers to Derrida and to the explicit complications of *différance* in *Difference and Repetition* (DR 318), while he and Guattari refer to Derrida in *Anti-Oedipus* (AO 202–3; 301–2) and *A Thousand Plateaus* (TP 417; 555).
18. Gilles Deleuze, *Desert Islands and Other Texts*, trans. Michael Taormina (London and Cambridge, MA: MIT Press, 2004), 260.
19. Slavoj Žižek, *Organs without Bodies: On Deleuze and Consequences* (London: Routledge, 2012), 42–43.
20. Jean-François Lyotard, *The Inhuman: Reflections on Time*, trans. Geoffrey Bennington and Rachel Bowlby (Cambridge: Polity, 1991), 74.
21. Lyotard, *The Inhuman*, 75.
22. Erin Graff Zivin, *Anarchaeologies: Reading as Misreading* (New York: Fordham University Press, 2020), 101.
23. Graff Zivin, *Anarchaeologies*, 9.
24. Derrida gave a seminar on Proust in his *Questions de responsabilité: le témoignage* series (1994–5) that remains unpublished, and aside from this, his attention to the *Recherche* is limited to occasional, often second-hand, references throughout his oeuvre (I discuss another of these in my 'Life Stories: How to Write Remains', *symploke* 28, nos. 1–2 (2020): 316). Despite this, Proust assumes a certain haunting quality within Derrida's work: note, for instance, the latter's tantalising (non)reference to the absent presence of the hymen that is neither 'time lost nor time regained' in 'The Double Session' (D 230–1) or how Isabelle Décarie describes the 'insistent presence' of Proust in Derrida's philosophy. Isabelle Décarie, 'Tentations proustiennes', *Études françaises* 38, nos. 1–2 (2002): 190.

25. Derrida, 'Biodegradables: Seven Diary Fragments', trans. Peggy Kamuf, *Critical Inquiry* 15, no. 4 (1989): 812.
26. Indeed, Deleuze insists that Proustian 'involuntary memory' 'does not reveal an identity between variations', but rather what he calls Proust's 'envelopes of [the] fixed' (as opposed to a 'memory' that implies a representational, returnable identity) which allow 'the *identification* of the variation, or individuation without identity' (*TR* 297).
27. Bray, 'Deleuze's Spider, Proust's Narrator', *Contemporary French and Francophone Studies* 16, no. 5 (2012): 707.
28. Deleuze avows similar motives in an interview published in 1968. 'Hume, Bergson, and Proust interest me so much because in their work can be found elements for a new image of thought. There's something extraordinary in the way they tell us: thinking means something else that what you believe.' Deleuze, *Desert Islands and Other Texts*, 139.
29. The famous comment, if one forgets, was written by Deleuze when discussing the weight of ancestrality in the history of philosophy. 'I suppose the main way I coped with it at the time', he writes, 'was to see the history of philosophy as a form of buggery or (it comes to the same thing) immaculate conception. I saw myself as taking an author from behind and giving him a child that would be his own offspring, but monstrous.' Gilles Deleuze, *Negotiations, 1972–1990*, trans. Martin Joughin (New York: Columbia University Press, 1996), 6.
30. Jean-Jacques Lecercle, *Badiou and Deleuze Read Literature* (Edinburgh: Edinburgh University Press, 2010), 68.
31. As Anne Simon points out, if 'Proust haunts the work of Deleuze, it is because he gives him a basis for possible states and escapes, those of an organic level that are perhaps also the anarchic "ventilations" of the rhythm of his asthma.' Anne Simon, *Trafics de Proust: Merleau-Ponty, Sartre, Deleuze, Barthes* (Paris: Hermann, 2016), 134.
32. To make this observation is not to assimilate their very different ways of reading literary texts. Zsuzsa Baross describes 'the divide between the voices and works of Deleuze and Derrida. Non-classifiable, itself non-nameable either by rhizomatics or by deconstruction, a veritable fault line runs between the two philosophies'. Zsuzsa Baross, 'Deleuze and Derrida, by Way of Blanchot: An Interview', *Angelaki* 5, no. 2 (2000): 18. But, as Gregg Lambert argues: 'Given that the question of writing and a certain strategy of experimentation are fundamental traits in both philosophies of difference, could we then say that the difference between Derrida and Deleuze could be reduced to the question of "style"? But then, this then begs a more preliminary question: "what is style?"' Gregg Lambert, 'The Philosopher *and* the Writer', in *Between Deleuze and Derrida*, 125.
33. Colebrook, *Gilles Deleuze*, 13.
34. Jacques Derrida, 'The Time of a Thesis: Punctuations', trans. Kathleen McLaughlin, in *Philosophy in France Today*, ed. Alan Montefiore (Cambridge: Cambridge University Press, 1983), 37. However, Derrida

notes that what 'interests' him is 'not strictly called either literature or philosophy', but rather 'something in writing which was neither the one nor the other'. Jacques Derrida, *Acts of Literature*, ed. Derek Attridge (London and New York: Routledge, 1992), 34.
35. Gilles Deleuze, *Essays Critical and Clinical*, trans. Daniel W. Smith and Michael A. Greco (London and New York: Verso, 1998), 1.
36. According to Colebrook, Deleuze teaches us that '*no* system of vocabulary is adequate to represent the flow of life. Indeed, the aim of writing should not be representation but invention.' Colebrook, *Gilles Deleuze*, 4.
37. Patrick Bray, 'Deleuze's Spider, Proust's Narrator', 706.
38. 'Constituting and dislocating at the same time, writing is other than the subject, in whatever sense it is understood. Writing can never be thought under the category of the subject' (*OG* 74). As Michael Naas argues, deconstruction approaches a text in so far as its 'every trace implies the death of its author not in some future present but already and structurally from the beginning'. Michael Naas, *Taking on the Tradition: Jacques Derrida and the Legacies of Deconstruction* (Stanford: Stanford University Press, 2003), 184.
39. Descombes, *Proust*, 52.
40. Erika Fülöp, *Proust, the One, and the Many: Identity and Difference in À la recherche du temps perdu* (London: Legenda, 2012), 1.
41. Décarie, 'Tentations Proustiennes', 192.
42. Bray, 'Deleuze's Spider, Proust's Narrator', 704.
43. Joshua Landy, *Philosophy as Fiction: Self, Deception and Knowledge in Proust* (Oxford: Oxford University Press, 2004), 8.
44. Martin Hägglund, *Dying for Time: Proust, Woolf, Nabokov* (Cambridge, MA: Harvard University Press, 2012), 43.
45. Hägglund, *Dying for Time*, 37.
46. Anna Magdalena Elsner suggests that Proustian mourning follows a Derridean template of 'affirmative incorporation' – the paradox of the impossible within the infinite, and vice versa, in productive, incorporative movement. Anna Magdalena Elsner, *Mourning and Creativity in Proust* (New York: Palgrave Macmillan, 2017), 45. This kind of reading, along with Hägglund's detailed understanding of Derrida's concept of 'autoimmunity' in *Radical Atheism* (Stanford: Stanford University Press, 2008) – as every concept always incorporating the trace of its opposite – influence how I read Proustian textual becoming in this study.
47. Fülöp, *Proust, the One, and the Many*, 2.
48. Anne Simon, *Proust ou le réel retrouvé: le sensible et son expression dans À la recherche du temps perdu* (Paris: Presses universitaires de France, 2000), 96, and *Trafics de Proust*, 128.
49. Simon, *Proust ou le réel retrouvé*, 112.
50. Simon, *Trafics de Proust*, 128.
51. Simon, *Proust ou le réel retrouvé*, 159–60.
52. Descombes asserts that with 'his myth of the inner book Proust anticipates

the whole course of phenomenology', but that if we engage in the *writing* of this inner book, while 'we were looking for an authentic experience, we soon find ourselves only with the experience of language' (Descombes, *Proust*, 222–3). Proust's solution, Descombes accords, is 'to write intensively [. . .] What is present is not reality itself, but the trace it has left, the impression it has made: already signs, or texts' (Descombes, *Proust*, 224). This reading points suggestively towards Derrida's more radical rethinking of metaphysics through the trace and *arche-writing*.

53. In *Literary Impressionism and Modernist Aesthetics* (Cambridge: Cambridge University Press, 2001), 10–11, Jesse Matz analyses this passage from the *Recherche*, arguing that the 'impression' the narrator refers to here 'prints in a foreign language' which always 'takes time to decipher' (which is the durational becoming of read*ing* the literary work). This temporal diffusion comes to produce the 'immediacy' of the sense of an impression's traces.
54. Anne Simon, 'The Formalist, the Spider, and the Phenomenologist: Proust in the Magic Mirror of the Twentieth Century', in *The Strange M. Proust*, ed. André Benhaïm (London: Legenda, 2009), 33.
55. Simon, 'The Formalist, the Spider, and the Phenomenologist', 33.

1. *Voice: Tracing* Restance *through the Literary Abyss*

In the opening to Part Two of *Of Grammatology* (in many ways the text that marks the dispersive 'origin' of deconstructive thought), Jacques Derrida works to unpick the logic of representation as it pertains to textuality. He points out how a 'text always gives itself a certain representation of its own roots', but in the reading or the living of the text, these roots will always resist an absolute metaphorization, eluding such finite capture *as* the event of every reading. In valorising this 'root system that does not end *there* and which as yet has no name' (*OG* 110), always problematising the next 'there' and every 'yet', Derrida sets out the course for his philosophy to-come, one focused on writing's power to elude, and to defer categorical, centred meaning. In doing so, one might say that Derridean deconstruction uproots the texts it encounters. It problematises a 'centre' to a text, or to the perception of it, loosening and mobilising what Adam Watt calls the 'structuralist investment in the authority of the text'.[1] In this chapter, I argue that this characteristic deconstructive strategy can map productively onto *À la recherche du temps perdu* – a text that constantly uproots itself. From the initial problem of being voiced by an indeterminate narrator, the Proustian universe expands without measure, resetting and forgetting itself throughout its narrated milieux. Deleuze has noted this movement in Proust's novels by referring to their 'transversal dimension', from which each potentially identifying root leading from the text 'bursts apart – and ends, in a cluster of small boxes'. The result of this uprooting is that these 'boxes are no longer able to communicate with each other' (*TR* 32). But such transversal movement across communicational distance occurs from the very *act of communication* in Proust's fiction, in the problem of determining who it is that narrates his text. In this regard, I suggest that Derrida's critique of the presence of writing acts as an appropriate medium to explore this aspect of the *Recherche*. This chapter will argue that the problem of assuming a 'Marcel', or even determining *who* narrates Proust's novel, is critical to understanding the novel's 'dimensions'. After briefly outlining how Derrida's critique of the relationship between *parousia* (presents and presence) and iterability opens out the dispersive quality of Proustian narration, I situate that quality across the former's concepts of *restance* and the *sumplokē* – his formulations for describing how a text weaves together being and non-being. In the final section, I consider this deferr*ing* voice in relation to Derrida's concept of the abyss, the hall of mirrors that weaves a signature amid the weft of the *sumplokē*.

'MARCEL'

The problem of narration is a classic theme in Proust criticism. Critical interest in the difficult consistency of subjectivity, not only as it pertains to the narrator's philosophy, but also to the characters he describes, has tended to reflect back onto the voice of the narrator, which simply begins 'speaking' without any apparent need of a context or motive. Whose voice is it, critics ask? A popular assumption is that the narrator evolves into Proust, but only at the end of the novel. This hypothesis invites the naming of the narrator as 'Marcel' – a tactic that seems to imply the author of the novel while ostensibly excluding him. As J. Hillis Miller has noted, the *Recherche* depends

> on the ironic discrepancy not so much between the writing Marcel and the written Marcel, Marcel now and Marcel then, as between either of those Marcel's and the smiling, effaced, invisible Marcel Proust. We identify either Marcel with Marcel Proust the author at our peril.[2]

For Jean-Yves Tadié, the 'heart of the work' is this separation between Proust and his narrator, which signifies 'the pathetic moment when an artist renounces his own self to enter into the world of the work'.[3] More recently, Michael Lucey has deftly summarised this aspect of the text: 'Proust's novel includes a careful, abstract study of impersonation, understood in a strong sense to designate the ongoing act, the ongoing practice, of assuming one's first person'.[4] For Malcolm Bowie, the narrator's 'voice contains many voices. He is a magpie and a mimic.'[5] Stable answers to these observations seem elusive.

Across the large corpus of Proust criticism, there are many studies concerned with the novel's voice.[6] Strangely, though, despite the rigorous philosophical interrogation undertaken in many of these studies, rarely do they challenge the notion of a narrator named 'Marcel'.

Among these, Joshua Landy's exemplary *Philosophy as Fiction: Self, Deception and Knowledge in Proust* (2004) stands out for its reading, and apparent resolution, of the narrator-character problem. In a detailed analysis of Proust's oeuvre, Landy classifies the ostensible characters of the Proustian narrator(s), devising a strategy by which to solidify their apparent fluidity. However, it is just this epithet of 'character', along with the notion of a strategy, that appears contentious. From the beginning, Landy refers to 'Proust's narrator – to whom, following convention, I shall habitually refer as "Marcel"'.[7] But this reliance upon 'convention' – to which Martin Hägglund, for instance, also has recourse[8] – elides certain important questions posed by the novel's narrator.

It is the prevalence of this 'standard critical practice'[9] that I wish to challenge. The assumption of a 'Marcel', who is not Proust (despite the fact these critics assume the author's name for this character, while the novel itself is rigorously elusive about naming its voice), and only partially the narrator (in so far as 'Marcel' can also stand for the Protagonist-but-not-the-Narrator, as well as Landy's 'Protagonist-Narrator') may be a convenient placeholder, but this convention is fundamentally at odds with one of the novel's major aesthetic strategies: the dispersion of subjectivity across memory and forgetting, and the essential discontinuity that constitutes selfhood.[10] As Alexander Segal points out with respect to Landy's account, such an approach risks losing sight of the 'blurring', noted by Roland Barthes, between the various narrating voices of the *Recherche*, a blurring which 'would pertain, most particularly, to Proust and Marcel'.[11] For Segal, if we focus on 'qualitative differences – between Proust and Marcel, two total selves, two different aesthetics – that privilege one term over another and exclude temporal difference',[12] we are misinterpreting this blurring, rather than appreciating it as a remarkable formal exploration of the philosophical questions Proust engages with in his novel. From this perspective, 'demarcating the *Recherche*' overlooks so much of its richness. If the various layers of Proust's narrative interweave and blur, then there is no ground for distinguishing between discrete texts, separating the *Recherche* from *My Life* or *The Magic Lantern* – Landy's 'nomenclature' for the 'three separate texts' we 'are dealing, in fact, with' when we discuss Proust's work.[13] Attempting to determine the point when we categorically inhabit any one of these fictions becomes a futile task,[14] while stopping at three seems too limiting.

To do so is to reduce a fiction whose intent is to challenge the unification of subjectivity. Early in the *Recherche*, there is an account of how the 'memories' that make it up were added to one another [and] now formed a single mass, but one could still distinguish between them [. . .] if not fissures, if not true faults, at least that veining, that variegation of colouring, which in certain rocks, in certain marbles, reveals differences in origin, in age, in 'formation'. (S 186)

Tous ces souvenirs ajoutés les uns aux autres ne formaient plus qu'une masse, mais non sans qu'on ne pût distinguer entre eux [. . .] sinon des fissures, des failles véritables, du moins ces veinures, ces bigarrures de coloration, qui, dans certaines roches, dans certains marbres, révèlent des différences d'origine, d'âge, de « formation ». (184)

Proust's monolithic text is constructed in the same way, constituted by varying times, tastes and selves that are blended together without rupturing the whole. For this reason, it is interesting to note that Landy criticises 'inadvertently eccentric claims' that 'place the mortal Marcel Proust on the same ontological level as imaginary entities, such as Doncières, Saint-Loup, and Gilberte'.[15] If the 'mortal Marcel Proust' could have remembered an entity which no longer exists, or blurred several memories together, the novel's narrator and the memories he relates are subject to the same rule. Indeed, that blurring is the very focus of the narrative, one which details the remember*ing* of lived events according to, as Gérard Genette writes, 'laws other than those of time'.[16] As though surveying his intention, the narrator asks:

given that individual entities (whether human or not) in a book are made up of a large number of impressions which, taken from many girls, many churches, many sonatas, are then used to form a single sonata, a single church, a single girl, should I not make my book in the same way[?] (*FT* 344)

comme les individualités (humaines ou non) seraient dans ce livre faites d'impressions nombreuses, qui, prises de bien des jeunes filles, de bien des églises, de bien des sonates, serviraient à faire une seule sonate, une seule église, une seule jeune fille, ne ferais-je pas mon livre de la façon [?] (340)

Demarcating 'whom' these memories specifically belong to becomes a difficult process, as Landy appreciates, noting that 'the character Robert de Saint-Loup is made up of two, or eight or ten, or sixty people combined; and he is doubtless more besides, incorporating additional features from Proust's strictly literary impulses.'[17] Proust observed in a letter that he should be 'obliged to incorporate contradictions' in his work in order to underscore the varieties of parts within wholes, the many sonatas and churches that form the single, literary version: 'I contradict myself all the time', Proust wrote to Jean Cocteau; 'I like when one shows all sides.'[18] In his discussion of this letter, André Benhaïm argues that, at most, 'one only believes partly in the distinction "Marcel"/Proust', and that the desire to show all sides 'relates to the multiplicity of the speaking subject' which we are 'given' across, or as, the novel. As such, it is important to note the key role played by the principle of contradiction, or of logical flexibility, across this novel: that 'disorder is precisely what governs the work'.[19]

Much of the critical discussion regarding the *Recherche*'s elusive narration, identity and potentially 'autobiographical' status hinges on one curious, oft-cited passage. In it, there is a description of this voice's lover, Albertine:

> Now she began to speak; her first words were 'darling' or 'my darling', followed by my Christian name, which, if we give the narrator the same name as the author of this book, would produce 'darling Marcel' or 'my darling Marcel'. (*PF* 64)

> Elle retrouvait la parole, elle disait : « Mon » ou « Mon chéri » suivis l'un ou l'autre de mon nom de baptême, ce qui, en donnant au narrateur le même nom qu'à l'auteur de ce livre, eût fait : « Mon Marcel », « Mon chéri Marcel » (*P* 67).

Refusing simply to quote Albertine as saying 'My Marcel' directly implies both the narrator's and Proust's intention to separate themselves.[20] And yet the implication of giving these identities the same name invites the possibility of error, further illustrating the blurred, composite project of Proustian subjectivity. Indeed, Gian Balsamo points out that even in 'Proust's aborted novel *Jean Santeuil*, there is one occasion where the protagonist, Jean, is called "Marcel" by his "new love" Charlotte'.[21] Of course, Marcel Proust is not his narrator – he says as much – but equally, Proust himself might, as one passing voice, indeed 'be' one of these narrators, just as any other of them might 'be' another.

Landy notes that this section

> effects a demarcation between author and narrator both in content and in form, the content explicitly noting that their names need not be alike, the form showing that their voices (and intentions) collide and conflict within the very texture of the prose.[22]

This collision and conflict aptly characterises the interweaving of narrative voices employed in the *Recherche*. Segal argues, however, that this analysis does not go far enough:

> given that the multiple voices 'collide and conflict', they are not the voices of a collective subject. Thus the sentence seems not to be ascribable to a single utterer, and to this extent it comes apart from a single utterance.[23]

The 'texture of the prose', then, is interwoven with voices that blur into each other, and as such a necessary conflation of tenses and characters consists of varied knowledges and times. Following Segal, what I want to suggest in this chapter is that the text of the *Recherche* stages a radical dispersion of subjective identity, such that each sentence potentially swarms with different selves or different points of view. These narrating characters are infinite in what each of them knows, or rather, could know, while each spliced instant lived by a 'narrator' advances the knowledge of the narrative's development. The impossibility of pinpointing the endless detail of this 'present', as well as the fact that any unified subjectivity 'comes apart from a single utterance',[24] suggest that a strategy of demarcation such as Landy's is likely to prove futile. If there is any possible 'essence' to the narrator, it must exist, as Brian Rogers notes, in 'the space between these focalisations' (an *in*-between that is always *between* before it is *in*).[25] As Landy himself points out,

> [j]ust as the 'facts' with which we are presented may really be subjective perceptions, so the 'truths' may belong to (a) the protagonist, (b) the narrator *at one or another* stage of his development, and/or (c) Proust, *there being no obvious discriminating marks between those that are spoken by each*.[26]

The narrative blurs, as does its voices. The very 'discriminating marks' that might be possible here are subverted, overwritten by the discriminating marks of language itself, which, by its very reproducibility, cannot innately identify its utterer.

This chapter, then, attempts to take account of the complex *property* of the Proustian narrator, or, more accurately, of that voice that apparently begins speaking without notice at the beginning of the work. This voice is not Proust's, nor is it exactly 'Marcel's'. If it were a 'Narrator' in the absolute sense of a transcendental proprietor, this voice could not assume the point of view of the protagonist of an event, feigning naivety with respect to its own superior knowledge, nor would it be, even fleetingly, referred to by the same name as the author. Gary Kemp's 'infinite sequence of Russian dolls'[27] that make up the voices of the *Recherche* – and their blurred relation to a narrated nucleus – would bear no relation to each other. As Tadié notes, in Proust's novel the '"I" who writes in a timeless present is no longer even an entirely personal "I"; hence, he escapes the perils of subjectivity'. Instead, Proust's assumption of a conditional, 'as if' subjectivity gains for his novel an 'entry into the imaginary'.[28] Thus, we must take this narrator as a voice that is not speaking, a writ*ing* whose presence disappears as it is read and as its author manipulates the ostensible 'place' from which we might have assumed it was narrat*ing*. We must write it, with the necessary *sous rature*, as a ~~voice~~.

PRESENT-ING DERRIDA

In this section, I want to suggest that Derrida's critique of presence provides a more adequate framework for an account of the novel's mobile narrating ~~voice~~. The general terms of Derrida's engagement with the concept of presence in Western metaphysics are well known.[29] In describing the Heideggerian project with an eye towards the history of philosophy as a whole, Derrida posits that the latter's future should be

> precisely a question of something entirely other: it is the tie between truth and presence that must be thought, in a thought that henceforth may no longer need to be either *true* or *present*, and for which the meaning and value of truth are put into question. (*M* 38)

As such, the problem of inscribed speech, of textuality, revolves on a 'hinge' [*brisure*] which 'marks the impossibility that a sign, the unity of a signifier and a signified, be produced within the plenitude of a present and absolute presence' (*OG* 75). Derrida's critique of metaphysics is grounded on this imagined possibility of present-ing presence. In challenging Western metaphysics' foundation upon onto-*logos* and presence – *ousia* and *parousia* – Derrida's reasoning also challenges the conventional possibilities of literary characterisation. In emphasising the disseminability of language, which hinges on the absence of its present, intended meaning, we can open up 'the presence-absence of the trace, [. . .] its play' (*OG* 76), the possibility of its determined-indeterminability, its *différance*. In the metaphysical delusion that language presently signifies absolute intention, we commit a 'subordination of the trace to the full presence summed up in logos, the humbling of writing beneath a speech dreaming its plenitude, [. . .] being as presence, as parousia, as life without différance' (*OG* 77). In challenging that delusion, Proust's fiction, just like Derrida's philosophy, awakens writing from the dream of plenitude, and uproots the trace from that subordination. And in doing so, they weave the trace into the constitution of its signifying absence, delegitimising questions about determined, or present, 'character'.

This problem of an absolute plenitude of *parousia* is explored throughout the *Recherche*. In *La Prisonnière* and *Albertine disparue*, for instance, the narrator's relationship with Albertine is described as an alternation between seemingly absolute presence to absolute absence. The ~~voice~~ discovers in these volumes that such plenitude is impossible; whether she is present or absent, Albertine's traces indicate the opposite: her presence if she is absent, and her absence if she is present. In each respect, the narrator notes that these fluctuating traces hinge upon the multiple subjectivities, or even different persons who 'palpitate [palpitent]' within the bodily envelope of the other. The 'desire for, the voluptuous memory of, the anxious search for so many more [le désir, le souvenir voluptueux, l'inquiète recherche de tant d'êtres]' can never be rendered fully present or true. Rather, the ~~voice~~ is reduced to 'following trails, even false ones [sur des pistes même fausses]', the various traces left by the other's (dis)appearance, forever seeking the

> plenitude of a being filled to overflowing with so many other, superimposed beings, so many desires for and pleasure-laden memories of other beings. (PF 82)
>
> la plénitude d'un être empli jusqu'au bord par la superposition de tant d'êtres, de tant de désirs, et de souvenirs voluptueux d'êtres. (P 85)

The dream of plenitude is forever aroused, or traced, in the desire for truth and presence that always defers itself. And simultaneously, the Proustian ~~voice~~, just like its subject matter, entices its readers to desire fullness from the 'overflowing' of all of its jostling traces, all the while deferring its own 'I'.

This 'superimposition' dealt with by Proust – especially that of the writing ~~voice~~ who says 'I' – invites comparison with Derrida's account of iterability (a sign's capacity for repetition and malleability), which, he argues, is not only a possibility of all written language, but its basis: 'the order of writing is the order ... of the *"parasitic"*' (*LI* 103; *OG* 58), where supplementary quoting and tracing makes definitive meaning elusive. Writing's iteration is the burgeoning trace of the trace, 'that which is remarkable in the mark, passing between the *re-* of the repeated and the *re-* of the repeating, traversing and transforming repetition' (*LI* 53). On the reverse side of this reproducibility, iterability opens the possibility of idealization: 'comprising identity and difference, repetition and alteration, etc., it renders the project of idealization possible without lending "itself" to any pure, simple, and idealizable conceptualization' (*LI* 71). Iterability idealises, but cannot be idealised itself; it is the movement of the utterance away from meaning at the very moment that it intends meaning, the impossibility to *exactly* articulate (*re*present) what one means. As such, iterability is the *source* of dissemination in language and literature, the 'palpitation' of the various selves that could speak it. The fact that the 'iterability of an element divides its own identity a priori, [...] it splits each element while constituting it' (*LI* 53), suggests that it is language itself which allows the 'property' of any selfhood in Proust's novel to 'come apart from a single utterance' as it folds back upon its very constitution. It is iterability, the operating *re-* of language, that disperses the presence of a proprietor-character across the traces that it delivers and simultaneously defers. As we will see, because it makes his impossible ~~voice~~ possible (or at least readable, which, in Proust's universe, may amount to the same thing), iterability – a fundamental element of all writing's reproducibility and, thus, remains – can help us to understand more fully Proust's radical, dispersive project in the *Recherche*.[30]

Although a number of critics have approached the *Recherche* through a Derridean lens, relatively little attention has been paid to the particular bearing of Derrida's conceptualisation of iterability and absence on Proust's narrative ~~voice~~.[31] One notable exception is Paul de Man's *Allegories of Reading* (1979), which deconstructs the Proustian text, thereby enacting a 'process of reading in which rhetoric is a disruptive intertwining of trope and persuasion'.[32] While his focus is not the problem of ~~voice~~ in the *Recherche*, de Man's interest in fluctuation, 'in the fluency of the transitions or in the numberless symmetries of the composition'[33] directs attention to the deconstructive potential of Proust's novel and its elusive textual 'presence'. De Man also draws attention to a kind of Proustian metonymy that substitutes properties endlessly, a 'natural, genetic, unbreakable' contagion of analogy that splices singular identity across contingent, essential relations.[34] Indeed, the 'improper' sense of literary inscription and its iterability, foregrounded by both Proust and deconstructive philosophy, gestures to the blurring of any trope's distinct identity among this system of substitutions that makes up reading – a key component of de Man's interpretation. By focusing on the consequences of textual materiality, one that is both present (in the written text) and absent (in ideas it implicates in the imaginative space of reading, which is never present before the reader) de Man draws out a key component of Proustian textuality – its ceaseless deferral. Deconstructive reading thus illuminates how Proust utilises the impossibility of absolute presence as the productive engine of his radical literary imagination.[35]

RESTANCE AND THE *SUMPLOKĒ*

Derrida's refusal of the idea of a totalising reading or synopsis is particularly helpful as a way of understanding the vicissitudes of the ~~voice~~ of the *Recherche*, which begins narrating without explanation. Derrida's remarks on the problem of prefaces in *Dissemination* are especially pertinent in this regard, touching as they do on the temporal problems of writing-over.

> From the viewpoint of the fore-word, which recreates an intention-to-say after the fact, the text exists as something written – a past – which, under the

false appearance of a present, a hidden omnipotent author (in full mastery of his product) is presenting to the reader as his future. (*D* 7)

This 'false' present projects the author across the possibility of *each* present of the text, not only in its writ*ing*, voic*ing* and subjective read*ing*, but in the innumerable reflections that such 'mastery', the omnipotence of the preface, imparts. As such, again, the idea of a 'place' for a possible speaking voice becomes irreconcilable with its constant transversal displacement, or its dissemination. Because

> writing as such does not consist in any of these tenses (present, past, or future insofar as they are all modified presents); [. . .] in pointing out a single thematic nucleus or a single guiding thesis, it would cancel out the textual displacement that is at work 'here.' (Here? Where? The question of the here and now is explicitly enacted in dissemination.) (*D* 7)

In the impossibility of negating dissemination when searching for 'a single guiding thesis' of a text, we thus come up against the *absolute* resistance to reduction: '– we shall call it the *restance* – of a sort of writing that can neither adapt nor adopt such a reduction' (*D* 7–8).

The quality that Derrida calls '*restance*' is what gives each text its irreducibility. Derived from the French *rester*, to remain, *restance* implies the remains of a text that could be said to make up its 'philosophy': they are the sense *given* by the text, but not the text itself. The *restance* is that durational totality, the everywhereness of a text (as it refers to itself) that cannot be reduced to an utterable synopsis without doing violence to the text itself, or writing-over it. It is a way of describing the (bio)degradable *effect* of textual remains, one that derives the shifts of culture, meaning and identity from out of what, as inscription, ostensibly doesn't change. Tellingly, an awareness of *restance* pervades Proust's fiction. The novel's ~~voice~~ often diverts a description of a percept to describe what 'remains' in it, rather than the thing's appearance in itself. For instance, he notes the 'idiosyncrasies of elocution which could be faintly detected in the speech of Bergotte [Certaines particularités d'élocution qui existaient à l'état de faibles *traces* dans la conversation de Bergotte]', which the writer eventually 'had transposed and set in prose [Bergotte avait transposé et fixé dans sa prose cette façon de traîner sur des mots]' (*YG* 129; 123–4) in his books. Such aural 'traces', transposed into literature, not only indicate the kind of faint *restance* that the ~~voice~~ describes having felt, and cannot articulate without reducing that feeling, but also typify the problematic translation of all of these various memories into a literary 'form', or rather, ~~voice~~. Indeed, the ~~voice~~'s consistent interest in atavism and genealogy reflects his perceptive interpretation of traces: essences which cannot be reduced to a name or else divest, or write-over, that essence. As such, *restance* is always deferring, unable to be placed or *present*ed.

Restance explains why we can speak of a ~~voice~~ in Proust's work, hearing it in spite of its absence. This *restance* cannot be made present in any act of reading, or identified with any particular moment of the text. Tenses themselves cannot be relied on as stable guides: as Derrida writes, 'in the indecomposable synthesis of temporalization, protention is as indispensable as retention' (*OG* 72). Tenses imply each other, they blur into each other in the 'heart of the present instead of surrounding it' (*OG* 72). If we try to take hold of an exact present, a this-very-moment-right ... now, to 'stick the point of the present into the actual moment' (*M* 303), we find that it splits – into the presence of the present tense, the future and past of the present tense. And these, in turn, split again, as the 'present' itself (whatever that might be – exponential, conditional) goes on passing, becoming *restance*. Hence, in his unravelling of Valéry, Derrida discovers an 'implication-complication, a complication of the same and the other which never permits itself to be undone' (*M* 302). This is the movement of the implex, that very escaping inherent within precision, in the possibility of its always being more precise. It is

> the impossibility for a present, for the presence of a present, to *present itself* as *a source*: simple, actual, punctual, instantaneous. The implex is a complex of the present always enveloping the nonpresent and the other present in the simple appearance of its pointed identity. (*M* 302)

Revealing the present as impossible to capture, the implex, then, is 'a nonpresence, nonconsciousness, an alterity folded over in the *sourdre* of the source' (*M* 303), and yet heaving its silent absence across the impossibility of a precise 'present'. The novel's title is a pertinent clue: the search to present the source loses itself among its overflow, and the overflow becomes the search. Hence, these overflowing narrators' ~~voices~~ remain deferred by the impossible-to-pinpoint implex. In this light, the very decentred, transversal movement of apparent textual presence, its synthesising *restance* that cannot be divided, is always in the process of deferral – of its 'place', 'time', 'character', 'identity', or anything that seeks to speak for the text that is *not it*, as it flows through reading. Proust's work, shifting through(with)out its ~~voices~~, even amid the work of a sentence, is proof of this flow.

In the *Recherche*, then, textual 'presence' is always problematic. The ~~voice~~ reasons that

> all we can turn on the spectacle of life is an infirm gaze which is abolished by oblivion at every successive moment, each reality no sooner glimpsed

than vanishing in the face of the next one, as the slides projected by a magic lantern succeed one another. (*YG* 400)

> nous n'y offrons au contraire, au spectacle de la vie, qu'une vision douteuse et à chaque minute anéantie par l'oubli, la réalité précédente s'évanouissant devant celle qui lui succède comme une projection de lanterne magique devant la suivante quand on a changé le verre. (385)

As with many of the phenomenal reflections in the novel, in this excerpt attention is paid to the transitions between being and not-being – in what arrives at the disappearance of a thing. The constant accumulation of these transitions is the work of reading; Proust's conception of reading is 'based', David Ellison writes, 'upon a potentially infinite series of erroneous, subjectively motivated transfers and substitutions'.[36] In this way, the implex is what overflows and vanishes between projections (or sentences, words, graphemes) that are seemingly present but synchronically absent in such a transfer. *Restance* implies the impossibility of determining any singularly true reality across the pressing, incompatible, but contingent truths of the 'dubious vision' of reading. The act of reading, and the associated work of memory, are a weaving of what it is, and what it is not, across their *restance*: text, which derives from *texere*, the Latin for weaving (as well as conjunction), is the meshing of differences. Derrida speaks of the 'play of difference and writing' (*D* 164) that is opened up by the rejection of *parousia* and metaphysical logic. In order to rehabilitate truth in a discourse not haunted by presence, a complex interweaving must be undertaken, an awareness of the inability to present what is 'in' a text, of its betweens.

To think of the trace, to consider such a rehabilitation of truth, Derrida turns to the philosophical origins of *present*ation in the thought of Plato. Reading *The Sophist*, he notes the extended conversation between Theaetetus and 'The Stranger', a discourse which Socrates begins, and in which he is apparently present throughout, but, after the first exchanges, participates in only as a listener. The father of logical metaphysics, of *parousia*-ontology, is thus simultaneously present and absent throughout his text – present and absent, that is, in the textual and immanent presence of a 'stranger'. The stranger presses Theaetetus on the being, or truth, of resemblance. They agree that likeness is 'not a real thing', because it only resembles that which 'really is' – what is 'true or real'. But a likeness must, at the same time, be true or real, because it *is*, it exists, but is 'only real in being a likeness'. The stranger determines that 'what we call a likeness is really unreal, and essentially not', despite its 'reality', to which Theaetetus responds: in 'what a strange complication [*sumplokē*] of being and not-being we are involved!'[37]

Derrida cites this 'strange complication', this *sumplokē* of being and not-being, because it is the same weaving 'together the system of differences, (solidarity-exclusion), of kinds and forms, the *sumplokē tōn eidōn*' (D 165) that constitutes not only discourse itself, but also Being – the weaving together of being and not-being, the denial or deferral of a total 'plenitude' of presence. Being is a *sumplokē* of being and not-being, because

> the unattainment of presence or beingness in any form, the whole surplus Plato calls the *epekeina tēs ousias* (beyond beingness or presence) gives rise to a structure of replacements such that all presences will be supplements substituted for the absent origin (D 167).

According to this reading, we can only conceive of presence or being because of its interweaving amid the *epekeina tēs ousias*, which unearths the supplements, the 'dubious vision' which engenders Being. We can conceive of textuality, of a text's coherent 'voice' or character, because of the *sumplokē* working through its *restance*, its disseminat*ing* absence, and its supplementary 'presentation' of read*ing*. Literature is inherently this *sumplokē* of being and not being, because it is resemblance. But it is also real, as real as *restance* renders the real itself. It is a constant weaving between real and resemblance, being and not being, presence and absence: this *sumplokē* is the only presence present, and it is only ever transversal, blurring in its act of productive deferral.

THE ABYSS *EN ABYME*

The idea of supplementarity brings us even further into Derrida's work, but also, I'd like to argue, into its relationship with Proust. One of Derrida's only direct textual engagements with Proust's novel occurs in an as-yet unpublished (that is, presently absent) seminar from his *Questions de responsabilité* series in 1994. J. Hillis Miller reproduces a section of it in an essay discussing the automatic, fractal reproduction of synecdoche. Miller's allusion to this seminar in this context says a great deal about the abyssal structure of iterability, and the problem of totalising a 'voice' that holds together while dispersing from any given utterance.

> Proust's 'récit de la mort de Bergotte,' says Derrida, 'is an unheard of art of composition "en abyme," that is to say of the inscription in the part of a whole smaller than its parts or of a detail larger than the whole like this little patch of yellow wall in which Bergotte is going to die as if he were falling into an abyss, inclusion of the whole in the part which subscribes oneself to mourning and even to mourning for oneself.'[38]

Bergotte sees his signature as merely a part of a greater whole, a part that is reproduced by and through this whole as it disseminates. Thus, utilising Derrida's understanding of Proust's composition 'en abyme', there is a tangled weaving apparent in this exchange between citations, creators, works and their signatories. The *sumplokē* we have here *claims* various signatories, but weaves them throughout the iterability of this quotation, and thus disseminates them 'en abyme'. Miller argues that citing the 'patch of yellow wall [pan de mur jaune]' (*PF* 169; *P* 176) in Vermeer's *View of Delft* exemplifies Derrida's capacity to examine the part acting for the whole, to locate that part and emphasise it. He quotes Derrida (above) referring to the patch of wall as Proust has it appearing to Bergotte, who understands the representative impact of Vermeer's synecdoche at the point of his death, which Derrida argues is proof of Proust's explication of a part for the whole, which Miller notes Derrida is doing in citing Proust. Who is citing who here? Which text is real, and which resemblance? The nexus of reference is overwhelming; its origin overflows into the abyss, which appropriates while disseminating these grafted signatures – the writing is all that remains.

Iterability here is further complicated by the original excerpt from the *Recherche*, in which the ~~voice~~ reflects upon what subsists after death – 'in' the transversal magnitude of the abyss. As Bergotte mourns his signature, surrendering his life for the 'little patch of yellow wall', the ~~voice~~ wonders what force moral considerations made in 'this life' by him,[39] or by any of us, can have. For there is nothing that could

> make the unbelieving artist feel compelled to paint a single passage twenty times over, when the admiration it will excite will be of little importance to his body when it is eaten by worms, like the little piece of yellow wall painted with such knowledge and such refinement by *the never-to-be-known artist whom we have barely identified by the name Vermeer*. (PF 170, my emphasis)

> il n'y a aucune raison, dans nos conditions de vie sur cette terre, pour que nous nous croyions obligés à faire le bien, à être délicats, même à être polis, ni pour l'artiste cultivé à ce qu'il se croie obligé de recommencer vingt fois un morceau dont l'admiration qu'il excitera importera peu à son corps mangé par les vers, comme le pan de mur jaune que peignit avec tant de science et de raffinement *un artiste à jamais inconnu, à peine identifié sous le nom de Ver Meer*. (P 177, my emphasis)

The great expanse of time decomposes, or devours, the signature as much as the signatory. The fractal, or the part becoming the whole, is the assumptive work of *restance* – the reason why we can produce a 'Marcel' from out of a ~~voice~~less work. But in turn, it is also why, as it fractures into the whole, we can sense the 'veining, that variegation of colouring' (S 186), as in certain rocks, implying all of its component parts and traces, both constituting and disseminating the origins of the whole. All that holds across an iterating signature is the text itself, its voiceless *restance*, and its *sumplokē* between what it is and is not, between what it ~~says~~ and does not, between its betweens. In this passage the ~~voice~~ of the *Recherche*, in its absolute omniscience regarding Vermeer, Bergotte, and the impressions that remain, 'never-to-be-known', within it, we see not only the impossibility of lining up the signatories with their signatures across the abyss of time, but also the overflow of every possible assumption of that signature: which is what we do every time we read a text, or determine its 'voice' – finding meaning in a text, forgetting, and weaving these across its deferring *restance*.

Discourse itself is woven amid the abyss, ~~in~~ the only ~~place~~ that writing – *sumplokē* – can occur. If there is no place for the abyss, for the flow of *restance* that gives writing and reading, its very existence comes into question. What is its ontology, and its truth, if it is always deferred? A question of its properties. Under the heading '*Abysses of truth*', Derrida argues that

> Finally, then, once the question of production, doing, machination, the question of the *event* [...] has been uprooted from ontology, the property or propriation is named as exactly that which is proper to nothing and no one. [...] The proper-ty of the abyss (*das Eigentum des Ab-grundes*) is necessarily the abyss of proper-ty, the violence of an event which befalls without Being.[40]

The *sumplokē* is the 'event' that befalls without Being, uprooted from ontology. In its constant deferral, the weav*ing* of the *sumplokē* uproots all of a text's possible *propre* – its property (that which goes outside of the text, like what we call its 'meaning' or the things we remember from it – its *restance*), properties (its voices or 'Marcels') and proprietors (Proust, Vermeer, Derrida). The text transverses; its signature is always signed abyssally, always-already eaten – woven or traced – by worms. Any kind of referencing across an 'I', a signature, or a purported self splits in each of its focalisations: 'the concept of supplement and writing designate, as one says so often today, *en abyme* [literally 'in abyss' – indefinite series of reflections as in a hall of mirrors – detail in a coat of arms]' (OG 177). The hall of mirrors is the perfectly abyssal image: in the blurred tangle of reference, the narrator reflects Proust, reflecting Vermeer or Bergotte, reflecting our unique imaginations of them, and so on into abyssal, absent-ing infinity, written by a ~~voice~~ that never presents its 'own' *propre*. The signature of a ~~voice~~ that is always deferring itself further away from *I*tself, from its *propre*, remains (rests) ~~in~~ the abyss.

Derrida's reading of Plato's *sumplokē* provides an instructive way of interpreting the textual *restance* of the *Recherche*. Because of the transversal absence of the voice that 'produces' the novel, the *sumplokē* of multiple narrators weaves its way into, or rather *as*, the deferring temporality of the text itself. As Tadié notes, this gap between narrating voices supposes an equal splitting in time(s) from the first 'I' that Proust writes.[41] In so far as Proust's novel becomes, according to Jo Alyson Parker, 'a work that within the static space of its pages will convey temporal flux',[42] one can note the *sumplokē* of iterability within the workings of its sentences and tenses – the written word implying varying gradations of a concept's being and not-being (its 'absent presen[ce]t'). Parker notes that the 'overall rhythm of [Proust's] text consists of an oscillation between the iterative and the singulative'[43] – and amid the *restance* of the *Recherche*, splitting the implex of such an 'oscillation between' becomes an impossible task. To illustrate this, I want to examine the temporal weaving apparent in a scene at the conclusion of *À l'ombre des jeunes filles en fleurs*, which exemplifies the kind of fluctuating narrative 'tenses' that occur typically throughout the *Recherche*. In this passage, we can notice a particular blurring, where the *sumplokē* of the ~~voice~~ divests the text of its *propre*. The ~~voice~~ informs us that

> eventually we had been obliged to leave Balbec, where the cold and the damp had become too penetrating for us to stay on in a hotel without fireplaces or heating system. Our final weeks there I *forgot almost immediately*. *When* I thought of Balbec, what came to mind almost invariably [. . .] (*YG* 529, my emphases).
>
> Il avait fallu quitter Balbec en effet, le froid et l'humidité étant devenus trop pénétrants pour rester plus longtemps dans cet hôtel dépourvu de cheminées et de calorifère. J'oubliai d'ailleurs *presque immédiatement* ces dernières semaines. Ce que je *r*evis presque invariablement *quand je pensai* à Balbec [. . .] (513, my emphases).

Here we find the kind of interstice critical to unravelling Proust's abyssal *sumplokē*. Detailing 'when' he thought of Balbec, the narrator is evoking a time and place, a presence. But *when* is this 'when' that he describes? And *when* is it, in turn, that he though*t* (past tense: passed) of Balbec? Is it in the times that he has 'immediately' forgotten those final weeks at Balbec, or is he remembering it to narrate it? Or does it *remain* forgotten (like the novel itself, never totally, but always *potentially*, remembered)? The futility of the answers, alongside the pressing validity of these questions, draws attention to the way that the ~~voice~~ in Proust's text is always deferring any precise present.

No 'presen[t]ce' of narration exists but that given by the ~~voice~~ itself. There are, throughout the entirety of this narration, only in-betweens of its passing, imagined 'presents'. It is a logic of shadows – of almosts, or betweens, woven together to appropriate the real. To return to our passage:

> what came to mind almost invariably was the morning moments at the height of summer, when, because I was going out with Albertine and the other girls in the afternoons, my grandmother made sure I obeyed the doctor's instructions that I should stay in bed and lie there in complete darkness.[44] (*YG* 529)
>
> ce furent les moments où *chaque matin*, pendant la belle saison, comme je devais l'après-midi sortir avec Albertine et ses amies, ma grand'mère sur l'ordre du médecin me forçait à rester couché dans l'obscurité. (513, my emphasis)

Here, we have a depiction of a forgetting, or what this narrator 'remembers' instead, when confronted with a forgetting of these last weeks at Balbec. The description of the Balbec that he has 're-seen [revis]' confronts us with an aporia: a *sumplokē* of remembering and forgetting, reality and semblance. The narrator cannot have completed this exact, complex, detailed 'morning' that he goes on to describe at length, 'every morning [chaque matin]'. In the same manner, weeks 'immediately' forgotten, but narrated to us in various cadences of their re-memory, are reconstituted through the textual *sumplokē* of expiring ~~voices~~.

Such an analysis calls to mind Genette's reading of Proust's narrative iteration, and his analysis of the 'pseudo-iterative' – occasions when the iterative narration of recurrent events blurs into the singular. Genette argues that this device shows that 'the writer himself sometimes "lives" such scenes with an intensity that makes him forget the distinction of aspects'.[45] In the case above, though, what we read is a 'forgetting' that enters directly into the narrative, as evidenced by the narrator describing what he *forgot in remembering* Balbec – its traces. Rather than an 'intoxication with the iterative',[46] by referring explicitly to the events he has just described as forgotten, in 'following trails, even false [or forgotten] ones, [sur des pistes même fausses]' (*PF* 82; 85), the ~~voice~~ is refuting the notion that he may have forgotten. It is doing something only 'writing' can do: marking down that which will be forgotten, to remain there as if it isn't. This section weaves being (a unique past event), not-being (iterative, that is, the synthesis of different memories into one, along with fictional ones) and forgetting together. Attempting to discern the moment that the iterative becomes the pseudo-iterative illustrates the futility of identifying an implex from which the *sumplokē* could be unpicked: the text weaves together other selves, fictions and forgotten memories down an abyss of property – a constant deferral. In reconsidering *parousia*, Derridean iterability affirms a reading of the

Proustian *sumplokē* that transcends the stable categories of Genette's structuralist iteration in favour of a more radical, transversal textuality.

Hence, amid this description of *an* 'every morning [chaque matin]', the ~~voice~~ guides us through what he anticipates customarily *would* occur, and as this narrative develops, he slips into a specific past tense, describing what 'Albertine would say that evening [me disait le soir Albertine]' (*YG* 530; 514). The conditional form of this phrase inscribes the synthesising texture of memory almost imperceptibly: surely Albertine did not say exactly the same thing at exactly the same time *every* day? As the ~~voice~~ marks it here, the event, as it splices through memory, spreads itself across multiple days, disavowing its singularity. Indeed next, after predicting that 'the concert always broke out at ten o'clock [À dix heures, en effet]' (*YG* 530; 514), the ~~voice~~ returns to a specific event, that his 'things had not been laid out, and the impossibility of getting up and dressing began to make [him] lose patience [Je m'impatientais qu'on ne fût pas encore venu me donner mes affaires pour que je puisse m'habiller]' (*YG* 531; 514). Surely this event, too, did not occur *every* morning? And suddenly, weaving the iterative out of the specific past, this description is again synthetic, describing that 'unvaryingly bright [si éclatant et *si fixe*]' Balbec which, 'for months on end [pendant des mois de suite]', had provided '*the same* expanse of sunlight folded into the angle of the outside wall [*le même* pan de soleil plié à l'angle du mur extérieur]' (*YG* 531; 514, my emphases) of the room. After describing how Françoise would have 'pulled her pins out of the transom and peeled off the extra layers of cloth, then drew back the curtains [Et tandis que Françoise ôtait les épingles des impostes, détachait les étoffes, tirait les rideaux]', he adds how 'the summer's day that she uncovered seemed as dead and immemorial as a mummy [le jour d'été qu'elle découvrait semblait aussi mort, aussi immémorial qu'une somptueuse et millénaire momie]' (*YG* 531; 514). Proust underlines the 'unliving' character of a day which insists, in the *sumplokē* of what is and isn't, on remaining. The 'dead' day exhumed in narrative is expired both because it has already been lived in the narrator's imagination (that is, the narrator who is the character being remembered, as the protagonist of a synthetic 'Balbec morning'), and also because it was never lived in the first place, being a mixture of all of the remembered days from this first trip to Balbec recounted as one, rather than a single 'lived' morning. Precisely because it is a mixture means that it cannot have been: the morning narrated is the weaving together of various iterations, all attached to a common, synthetic heart, 'embalmed in its vestments of gold [embaumée dans sa robe d'or]' (*YG* 531; 514). In so far as we cannot accurately describe this present-less *sumplokē* as either the 'Balbec morning' or 'Balbec mornings' – because the text weaves both together to give us the story – let me propose instead 'Balbec morning[ ]', where the gap '[ ]' signifies an absent 's' that remains, but is never present.⁴⁷ This marked, present-absent plurality signifies the deferring potentiality inscription invokes as it intersects with the imagination, where the latter interweaves and defers endless, irreducibly different iterations, like this morning the ~~voice~~ describes. In this case, the present absence of the '[ ]' draws attention to the possible other mornings that contribute to the one being narrated. From this point on, the '[ ]' formulation will indicate this kind of indeterminately singular-plural *sumplokē*, one where plurality gives the woven iterability writing otherwise marks as singular.

This self-referentially 'forgetful' narrative weaves events together from divergent tenses, thereby presenting an absent ~~speak~~*ing* ~~voice~~. Determinate intention cannot be ascribed to the narrator of such a text. There is no way to determine when the iterative 'Balbec morning[ ]', divulged as the narrative that was 'every morning' in Balbec (including those later to be forgotten) dissolves into a specific past, that of the 'ten o'clock' when the concert would begin, or used to begin. The ~~voice~~ is written into this critical *restance*, which is its absent, or deferred, origin. As Derrida notes, 'the source (of the)– I is often described as a glance, as the sight of the glance' ('quand *je revis* Balbec') which faces 'everything that is presented to it which is not present to itself' (M 284). The source describes its content, but can never be present there, for this content is always in the process of dissemination, of iteration, of incorporating the traces of what might have been forgotten. Even in the most direct of utterances ('I am here, I am writing this'), there is a cleft. '[T]he source is produced only in being cut off from itself, only in taking off in its *own* negativity' (M 285) – it takes off in the irreducible deferral of its implex, reflecting its *own* negative as it reflects another, further down the hall of mirrors that is its woven, abyssal becoming.

Thus, we can witness in the 'Balbec morning[ ]' the multiplying implex of a narrative that depicts, in such a cleft, both *a* particular morning and *those* mornings, which assume one form in memory. They multiply as they weave through other mornings that *might* have happened, but that *are also* this iterative 'morning', as an endlessly tertiary category of the 'morning[ ]' narrated. Because they interweave memory with its other, their *propre*, or the *propre* of 'the morning[ ]', is the abyss, the abyss that is the abyss of all property. Balbec, Delft, a patch of yellow wall among them, cannot be a property, have property, belong *as* property, if all of these properties disperse the moment they are inscribed. This is the 'precise' quality of the *sumplokē* that is articulation, the weaver's movement of elaboration:[48] the incorrigible weaving of infinitesimal but crucial degrees of absence, across a ~~voice~~ that pretends presence, always more precise in its deferral.

In this way, Derrida's abyssal *sumplokē* helps us to understand why Proust's narrative ~~voice~~ is so elusive of conventional categories. In always taking off from its own negativity, and thus weaving the present-deferral of the implex into all of the negatives that sign across its abyss, the *sumplokē* incorporates its being and not-being as the 'precise' deferral of presence – the alienation that is apparent 'representation'. The *sumplokē* escapes standard metaphysics, the logic of presence which is in fact the logic of everything but presence: it 'installs oneself in the evidence of the distinction between presentation and representation, within the effect of this scission' (*OG* 322). It is this 'scission' between presence and re-presence, absence and forgetting, that is the abyss of reading Proust's *sumplokē*. The implex of the text's iterations, its ~~voices~~ and its absence[ ], actively formulates this kind of alienation, because it reminds us that we are always presenting our reading before such a scission, a 'Marcel'-shaped hole that has always departed the moment we seek to present it. And yet, concurrently, we are reading this abyss, the weaving through which our own reading has scissioned the holes of our own identity.

Because of this, we can notice a deferring plurality in the *sumplokē*, not simply textually, but within the word itself, the grapheme, and discourse more broadly. In the context of the iterability of utterances, language is always in the process of rendering itself a metaphor-catachresis, 'the twisting return to the already there of a meaning' (*M* 257). Language is catachresis, always misinterpreting itself, across a nexus of meanings that 'parasitise' each other. The structure of parasitism comes to consume Derrida's project: it is what he notes he has 'tried to analyze everywhere, under the names of writing, mark, step [*marche*], margin, *différance*, graft, undecidable, supplement, *pharmakon*, hymen, *parergon*, etc.' (*LI* 103). Of course '*etc.*' This list could go on, endlessly adding to, parasiting and catachresing itself: repeating, (mis)interpreting, and re-rooting the next term[ ] that it is becoming. Because all of these terms 'have a double, contradictory, undecidable value that always derives from their syntax' (*D* 221), they are tied to their movement between every text and its *restance*.

This disseminating movement of textuality is nowhere more evident than when it is dispersed from, or rather *as*, a ~~voice~~ that uproots itself, that disseminates its *propre*. Derrida's philosophy enlightens us to the iterability of language; Proust's text acts as a radical example from which to analyse this restless, *restant* movement of literary becoming, one that points us towards the limits of subjectivity. To respond to the opening contention of this paragraph – 'the root system which has no name' – this name, if a name might be possible, is dissemination: that is, a process that departs the moment we think we can name it. Dissemination is *différance*, an alternative to ontology that is always leav*ing*, haunt*ing*, disseminat*ing* its absent presence – incorporating, acting as, but at the same time in contradistinction to, roots. The dissemination of a text never reveals its genealogy, but always implies it – text is always text[ ], because it can never include all of the sources that make it up. It interweaves its being and not-being together: dissemination is its own genealogy, just as, implectically, abysmally, the ~~voice~~ that 'is' *À la recherche du temps perdu* speaks from where it is not.

NOTES

1. Adam Watt, *The Cambridge Introduction to Marcel Proust* (Cambridge: Cambridge University Press, 2011), 108.
2. J. Hillis Miller, 'The Other's Other: Jealousy and Art in Proust', *Qui Parle*, 9, no. 1 (1995), 128.
3. Jean-Yves Tadié, *Proust et le roman* (Paris: Gallimard, 1971), 22.
4. Michael Lucey, *Never Say I: Sexuality and the First Person in Colette, Gide, and Proust* (Durham and London: Duke University Press, 2006), 26.
5. Malcolm Bowie, *Proust among the Stars* (London: HarperCollins, 1998), xvi. Bowie in turn notes that 'the modern, secular, psychological *moi*, launched upon its spectacular European career in the sixteenth century, reaches in Proust a moment of extraordinary power and authority'. Malcolm Bowie, 'Proust's Narrative Selves', *Moy qui me voy: The Writer and Self from Montaigne to Leiris*, ed. George Craig and Margaret McGowan (Oxford: Clarendon Press, 1989), 131.
6. A selective sample of the vast possibilities might include: Serge Doubrovsky, *La Place de la madeleine: écriture et fantasme chez Proust* (Paris: Mercure de France, 1974); Antoine Compagnon, 'Le narrateur en procès', *Marcel Proust 2: Nouvelles directions de la recherche proustien*, ed. Bernard Brun (Paris: Minard, 2000), 309–4; Jean Milly, 'Phrase, Phrases', *Marcel Proust 3: Nouvelles directions de la recherche proustien 2*, ed. Bernard Brun (Paris: Minard, 2001), 197–216; Nicole Deschamps, 'La voix proustienne', *Inconvenient: Revue littéraire d'essai et de création*, 11 (2002): 15–24; Eugène Nicole, '"Quel Marcel!" (And Other Oddities of the Narrator's Designations in *À la recherche du temps perdu*)', in *The Strange M. Proust*, 36–44.
7. Landy, *Philosophy as Fiction*, 5.
8. 'Following convention, I refer to Proust's narrator and protagonist as "Marcel"'. Hägglund, *Dying for Time*, 172. While his work is (rightly)

held in enormously high regard by contemporary critics, Malcolm Bowie's persistent rejection of this 'convention' is often overlooked.

9. Hägglund, *Dying for Time*, 172. In addition, Roger Shattuck notes that he favours this convention. 'Lost and Found: The Structure of Proust's Novel', *The Cambridge Companion to Proust*, ed. Richard Bales (Cambridge: Cambridge University Press, 2001), 84. Howard Moss goes beyond a mere assumption: he emphasises, as though it is reinforced throughout the text, that the 'narrator of Proust's novel is named Marcel'. *The Magic Lantern of Marcel Proust* (London: Faber, 1963), 14. Adam Watt replies that, if this is the case, such an assumption 'asks a brief moment of the novel to bear a great deal of critical weight'. *The Cambridge Introduction to Marcel Proust*, 5.
10. Deleuze and Guattari call the *Recherche* a 'schizoid work par excellence' (*AO* 43).
11. Alexander Segal, 'Demarcating the *Recherche*: Joshua Landy's *Philosophy as Fiction: Self, Deception, and Knowledge in Proust*', *Journal of the Australasian Universities Language and Literature Association*, 116 (2011): 116.
12. Segal, 'Demarcating the *Recherche*', 116.
13. Landy, *Philosophy as Fiction*, 43. For Landy, *My Life* is 'Marcel's' memoir or autobiography, whereas *The Magic Lantern* is the fictionalised novel 'Marcel' hypothesises writing at the end of the *Recherche*.
14. Indeed, as Brian Rogers argues regarding the Proust/narrator problem: 'Why should we care? The reader must take on trust what the Narrator chooses to tell us about himself. He has no name, we have no idea what he looks like. For long stretches of his book he disappears from view, [... the voice is] a disembodied presence unlike that in any novel before.' Brian Rogers, 'Proust's Narrator', in *The Cambridge Companion to Proust*, 98.
15. Landy, *Philosophy as Fiction*, 16.
16. Gérard Genette, *Narrative Discourse*, trans. Jane E. Lewin (Oxford: Basil Blackwell, 1980), 157.
17. Landy, *Philosophy as Fiction*, 17.
18. Proust, cited in André Benhaïm, 'Preamble', *The Strange M. Proust*, 6.
19. Benhaïm, 'Preamble', 7.
20. Later in the novel – indeed, in its final 'scene', though one we now know was probably composed long before this 'My Marcel' episode – the narrator directly, and awkwardly, suppresses his name: 'I was also assured that the servants of the house had recognized me. They had whispered my name, and even, one lady told me, "in the way they put it" she had them say "There's old father..." (this expression was followed by my surname). [Et on assura que le personnel m'avait bien reconnu. Ils avaient chuchoté mon nom, et même « dans leur langage », raconta une dame, elle les avait entendus dire : « Voilà le Père... » (cette expression était suivie de mon nom.)]' (*FT* 237; 235). Much earlier in the novel, the narrator describes how Gilberte refers to his 'first name [nom de baptême]' (*S* 406; 396) and

then to his 'family name [nom de famille]' and how this seemed to 'strip [dépoiller]' (S 407; 396) him of his name – one he doesn't give us.
21. Gian Balsamo, 'The Fiction of Marcel Proust's Autobiography', *Poetics Today*, 28, no. 4 (2007): 577.
22. Landy, *Philosophy as Fiction*, 23.
23. Segal, 'Demarcating the *Recherche*', 105.
24. Segal, 'Demarcating the *Recherche*', 105.
25. Rogers, 'Proust's Narrator', 97.
26. Landy, *Philosophy as Fiction*, 134, my emphases.
27. Gary Kemp, 'Proust on Art and the Value of Living', *European Journal of Philosophy*, 15, no. 2 (2007): 275.
28. Tadié, *Proust et le roman*, 32–3.
29. For one of the best readings of this critique, see Rodolphe Gasché's *The Tain of the Mirror* (London and Cambridge, MA: Harvard University Press, 1986), especially ch. 6, 'Beyond Reflection: The Interlacings of Heterology', which argues that Derrida's 'heterology' focuses 'in a nondialectical manner on the ways in which truth compounds with nontruth, [and] on how principles and nonpresence are welded together' (100). Elsewhere, Gasché asserts that Derrida's thought reveals how 'self-consciousness, presence and, finally, meaning must cohabit with a certain nonpresence, nonidentity and lack of intention'. Rodolphe Gasché, 'Deconstruction and Hermeneutics', in *Deconstructions: A User's Guide*, ed. Nicholas Royle (Basingstoke: Palgrave, 2000), 138.
30. Antoine Compagnon devotes much attention to this problem, concluding his reading of etymologies in the novel by noting that the 'meaning that was originally present for those who heard "Eudes le Bouteiller" in Douville or "stream of the valley" in Balbec has been lost. History is experienced as a loss of meaning, a falling off.' Compagnon, *Proust between Two Centuries*, 227. And of course, this loss, or falling off, could not be more presently absent than in what the title 'Princesse de Guermantes' becomes, or can be 'cited' as, by the end of the novel.
31. See Stephen Gilbert Brown's *The Gardens of Desire: Proust and the Fugitive Sublime* (New York: State University of New York Press, 2004) and Anna Magdalena Elsner's *Mourning and Creativity in Proust*.
32. Paul de Man, *Allegories of Reading: Figural Language in Rousseau, Nietzsche, Rilke, and Proust* (New Haven and London: Yale University Press, 1979), ix.
33. De Man, *Allegories of Reading*, 69.
34. De Man, *Allegories of Reading*, 62.
35. Hägglund's *Dying for Time* and Jennifer Rushworth's *Discourses of Mourning in Dante, Petrarch and Proust* (Oxford: Oxford University Press, 2016) have also provided more recent deconstructive approaches to Proust, illuminating the undecidable temporalities and structures (Rushworth's focus on the figure of the promise, in particular) of the *Recherche*.

36. David Ellison, *The Reading of Proust* (Oxford: Blackwell, 1984), 74.
37. Plato, *The Dialogues of Plato*, trans. Benjamin Jowett (Oxford: Clarendon Press, 1875), 454.
38. Jacques Derrida, quoted in J. Hillis Miller, 'Derrida and Literature', *Jacques Derrida and the Humanities: A Critical Reader*, ed. Tom Cohen (Cambridge: Cambridge University Press, 2001), 77.
39. Whosoever this citation might instantly signify here, in this fractured context: be it Bergotte, the narrator, Proust, me, Derrida, *Sarl*, Hillis Miller, Derrida, Vermeer.
40. Jacques Derrida, *Spurs: Nietzsche's Styles/Éperons: Les Styles de Nietzsche* (Chicago and London: University of Chicago Press, 1978), 119.
41. Tadié, *Proust et le roman*, 32.
42. Jo Alyson Parker, *Narrative Form and Chaos Theory in Sterne, Proust, Woolf, and Faulkner* (New York: Palgrave Macmillan, 2007), 63.
43. Parker, *Narrative Form and Chaos Theory*, 71.
44. The translation cited here skates over a phrase that is important to my reading, that of 'every morning [*chaque matin*]', which is rendered more accurately by Scott Moncrieff: 'when I thought of Balbec were the hours which, every morning during fine weather'. Marcel Proust, *Remembrance of Things Past: Volume One*, trans. C. K. Scott Moncrieff (London: Wordsworth Editions, 2006), 850.
45. Genette, *Narrative Discourse*, 123.
46. Genette, *Narrative Discourse*, 123.
47. As Derrida notes, 'polysemia is marked, moreover, in the letter *s*, the "disseminating" letter *par excellence*'. Derrida, *Positions*, trans. Alan Bass (London and New York: Continuum, 1981), 96.
48. Derrida asks in *Glas*: 'Isn't elaboration a weaver's movement?' (G 208).

2. *Sense: The Hollow of Experience, the Mark[ ] of* Aiôn

Having considered the problem of ~~voice~~ in Proust's novel in the first chapter, I want now to focus on the picture of temporal experience the novel provides. I have identified the relevance of the trace to the construction and concomitant dispersion of the Proustian text, especially with regard to questions of the self. But how do these traces come to be sensed in the first place, through the perceptual overlap of other differing/deferring traces – and how does Proust's novel portray divergent senses or traces as a unified entity (as a 'woven' text)? This is, in a broad sense, a phenomenological question, in so far as phenomenology is concerned with the analysis of lived experience and its temporal nature. As Proust describes the flow of temporal experience – as horizons that defer its present-able being in an incessant becoming – the novel's perceptual interest is directed towards the manifold, indescribable traces that constitute and inform it. A literary transposition of these motile, superimposed phenomena seems impossible, but my argument is that Proust's attention to the multiplicities inherent in experience (like the endless, productive deferral generated from attention to inscription) allows him to capture these fundamental *senses* of perception.

In what follows, I will use Deleuze's ideas of virtual contraction, dividual multiplicity and intensity to characterise Proust's portrayal of Being. At the same time, I want to locate this discussion in relation to the phenomenological tradition itself – a tradition that Deleuze critiques, but with which he also engages. By situating Deleuze in relation to phenomenological approaches to time and perception (especially those of Edmund Husserl, Maurice Merleau-Ponty and Mauro Carbone), I want to tease out how these phenomenological thinkers can be seen differently through the lens of Deleuze's account of becoming. Central to this chapter will be an interpretation of the ancient Greek time-scheme of the *aiôn*, especially as it is interpreted by Carbone. I take this idea as a guiding trope for thinking about Proust's interest in the multiplicity of sense[ ] latent in every perception – the enveloping *thinking* of every mark – where, animated by the undecidable *sumplokē*, distinctions between subject and object blur. Like the previous chapter, this one aims to set in place a theoretical vocabulary that subsequent chapters will draw upon.

'REAL WITHOUT BEING ACTUAL, IDEAL WITHOUT BEING ABSTRACT'

The first chapter reflected on the problem of 'who' speaks in the *Recherche*. I would like to begin the present chapter by assessing 'why' this voice speaks. In light of the problem of prefaces, origins and *restance* outlined in the previous chapter, how can any novel begin? As Derrida notes, the '*pre* of the preface makes the future present, represents it, draws it closer, breathes it in, and in going ahead of it puts it ahead. The *pre* reduces the future to the form of a manifest presence' (*D* 7). The preface is an impossible textual presence which would over-write the story to come: it loses itself in the abyss of its intended beginning. Proust himself derided the 'insincere language of prefaces and dedications' in which

> writers talk about 'my reader'. In reality each reader, when he is reading, is uniquely reading himself. (*FT* 219–20)

> L'écrivain ne dit que par une habitude prise dans le langage insincère des préfaces et des dédicaces « mon lecteur ». En réalité, chaque lecteur est quand il lit le propre lecteur de soi-même. (217)

For Proust, the problem of *restance*, especially regarding beginnings, is acute: how to portentously insert *his* story amid the total story of the reader, which comes to consume and appropriate the former? He is aware that his readers read his beginning through their own beginnings. As such, in his work there is no insincere pretence towards accounting for its origin. It simply begins.

This is why this ambiguous and yet determined beginning is so curious. A voice begins narrating without offering any account of its origin. From the first paragraph, the voice asks questions about the complexity of consciousness. He has not even the time to notice that he is no longer awake: suddenly, he is woken by the thought that, paradoxically, it is time for him to go to sleep. And in the sleep that he insists overcame him when he 'did not have time [je n'avais pas le temps]' to acknowledge either its imminence, or its presence, he 'had not ceased while sleeping to form reflections on [je n'avais pas cessé en dormant de faire des réflexions sur ce que je venais de lire]' (S 7; 3) the book he had been reading. So, at some point, the durational stretch of this ~~voice~~'s perception has known and made sense of the book he was reading, but not known *when* he left it as the instant or 'point' he falls asleep. He then describes how his 'reflections had taken a rather peculiar turn [ces réflexions avaient pris un tour un peu particulier]' (S 7; 3). His conscious experience merges with the imprecise twilight of sleep until he can no longer separate his own subjectivity from what he is reading, to the point that he himself 'was what the book was talking about: a church, a quartet, the rivalry between François I and Charles V [j'étais moi-même ce dont parlait l'ouvrage : une église, un quatuor, la rivalité de François Ier et de Charles-Quint]' (S 7; 3). This 'belief [croyance]', he notes, 'lived on for a few seconds [survivait pendant quelques seconds]' after he wakes, without disturbing him, only to 'lay heavy like scales on [his] eyes [pesait comme des écailles sur mes yeux]' until it again, imperceptibly, becomes 'unintelligible [inintelligible]', leaving him 'free to apply [himself] to it or not [j'étais libre de m'y appliquer ou non]' (S 7; 3). What exactly is occurring here, in this unintelligibility? This ~~voice~~, even before it has introduced a personality, is describing a scenario in which subjectivity degrades (that of falling asleep, and the implex in which it has both almost begun and almost concluded). In lieu of a preface, this subject-less ~~voice~~ describes a moment in which subjectivity disperses, in which one momentarily loses all trace of who one is.

One cannot write a beginning, or form a '*pre*' that would *pre*cede a reader's prior existence (that the book becomes a part of), so Proust works the other way – he questions the continuity of that possessive apostrophe. What is it that remains with us from our experience, and is it this that makes us return, apparently always, to the self that we believe we are? The narrator posits that a

> sleeping man holds in a circle around him the sequence of the hours, the order of the years and worlds. He consults them instinctively as he wakes and reads in them in a second the point on the earth he occupies, the time that has elapsed up to his waking. (S 9)
>
> Un homme qui dort tient en cercle autour de lui le fil des heures, l'ordre des années et des mondes. Il les consulte d'instinct en s'éveillant, et y lit en une seconde le point de la terre qu'il occupe, le temps qui s'est écoulé jusqu'à son réveil. (5)

Proust's sleeper 'reads' from all of the times of his life in order to project reality before him – he 'instinctively' projects the abyss of his entire life into that 'second'. The only recourse the subject has to determine his subjectivity – why he is not a new person entirely – is the living remains of the times he has experienced, compressed into that instant of awakening. And by contracting these experiences in an atemporal 'origin' – the indeterminate instant of waking that can only be 'presented' after the fact – the narrator portrays how immediate perception supervenes upon apparently objective, measurable temporality. Because it is an implex, we can never dissect perception, or be able to 'distinguish', according to the narrator,

> the various suppositions of which it was composed, any better than we isolate, when we see a horse run, the successive positions shown to us by a kinetoscope. (*S* 11)

> je me trouvais ne distinguait pas mieux les unes des autres les diverses suppositions dont elle était faite, que nous n'isolons, en voyant un cheval courir, les positions successives que nous montre le kinetoscope. (7)

In this sense, caught as he wakes in the durational shift of chronological time, the narrator describes his waking moments as their *sumplokē*, without paying heed to any specific 'present'.

Read in this light, the novel's beginning is a deferral: it is a movement (or weaving) between various places, none of which it prioritises. The narrator describes his waking as a superimposition of interwoven scenes.

> I had seen sometimes one, sometimes another, of the bedrooms I had inhabited in my life, and in the end I would recall them all in the long reveries that followed my waking. (*S* 11)

> j'avais revu tantôt l'une, tantôt l'autre, des chambres que j'avais habitées dans ma vie, et je finissais par me les rappeler toutes dans les longues rêveries qui suivaient mon réveil. (7)

The 'reveries' of these composite-yet-singular bedrooms that 'present' the present-less opening of his novel indicate the transversal movement of the narrative to come. But Proust also implies that consciousness works in this way more generally. The novel can stage this seemingly bizarre movement through a whole series of different scenes – these 'bedrooms' – which are only narrated under the proviso that they are not 'the' opening scene, because it is this constituting synthesis that underlies all temporal experience. The mind perceives becoming, movement and deferral, rather than a distinctive, totalised plenitude of any 'present' percept.

This aspect of Proust's novel, heralded by these passages from its opening section, strongly evokes Deleuze's idea of the virtual – a key component of his philosophy of becoming, especially with regard to perception and sense. 'The Method of Dramatization', a talk given before the Société française de philosophie in 1967, contains a succinct account of this idea as the mode of differentiation:

> Virtual is opposed to actual, and therefore, possesses a full reality. We saw that this reality of the virtual is constituted by the differential relations and the distributions of singularities. [. . .] The Idea is an image without resemblance; the virtual actualizes itself not through resemblance, but through divergence and differentiation.[1]

The virtual is the intensive sense of perception that utilises all its multiple temporalities to generate its sense. Elsewhere, in *Difference and Repetition*, he considers that the 'virtual must be defined as strictly part of the real object – as though the object had one part of itself in the virtual into which it plunged as though into an objective dimension' (*DR* 209). The virtual is the movement of the real to the outside of the actual – the Ideal that crosses immanent temporalities as sense, without abstractly 'presenting' them.[2]

Viewing Proust's insistence on the multiplicity manifest in perception from the perspective of Deleuze's concept of the virtual allows us to draw out the complexities of becoming in the novel – as perception described in the text, but also as a reader's perception *of* this multiplying text. Perception as described in Proust's novel contends with the virtual contraction of temporality, but is narrated with such dexterity that it purposefully unravels the conventional categories of perception – particularly those of immanence and transcendence, actuality and abstraction. In this way, it rejects the idea of 'presence' affirmed by these traditional categories in favour of a more nuanced depiction of the *sumplokē* of becoming as it is perceived, or, rather, *sensed*. Deleuze's own repeated citation of Proust's phrase 'real without being actual, ideal without being abstract [réels sans être actuels, idéaux sans être abstraits]' (*FT* 181; 179; *DR* 208; *WP* 22) – itself a marker of the virtual force inscription produces in the always-unique event of every reading – underlines the closeness with which the *Recherche* shadows this aspect of his thought.

In particular, it is the role of memory that goes beyond itself, in so far as it produces these instants in a synthesis as described by Deleuze, that delivers this unintelligible sense. In *Difference and Repetition*, he defines the imagination 'as a contractile power: like a sensitive plate, it retains one case when the other disappears' (*DR* 70), which renders this kind of synthesis sensible. When consciousness makes sense of the world, the imagination 'contracts cases, elements, agitations or homogeneous instants and grounds these in an internal qualitative impression endowed with a certain weight' (*DR* 70). The 'flash' of subjectivity described by the narrator is an example of this contractile power of consciousness. Deleuze is quick to point out that contraction 'is by no means memory, nor indeed an operation of the understanding: contraction is not a matter of reflection. Properly speaking, it forms a synthesis of time' (*DR* 70). What Deleuze calls contraction thus takes time outside of itself and allows the subject to sense perceptions in an intense instant, no longer bound by their progressive duration. This synthesis can recover an entire subjectivity by contracting long moments of experience into a 'momentary glimmer [lueur momentanée]' (*S* 8; 4); in Proust's narration, they do so all at once, as the sense of his sleepy bedroom[ ]. Contraction is the necessary signifying, sensible function of memory contending with repetition. This sense of temporality accords with Derrida's, for whom a 'limitless memory would in any event be not memory but infinite self-presence. Memory always therefore already needs signs [syntheses, flashes] in order to recall the non-present, with which it is necessarily in relation' (*D* 109). Synthetic 'reading', the contraction that *produces* sense endlessly, in turn produces this non-present. The durational extension of communicating, and of living time in the external world, can be interpreted in a series of similar, momentary glimmers, located at the limits of – but always deferring – total presence. For Deleuze, it is this synthetic process that forges the experience of time out of a succession of instants:

> A succession of instants does not constitute time any more than it causes it to disappear; it indicates only the constantly aborted moment of its birth. Time is constituted only in the originary synthesis which operates on the repetition of instants. (*DR* 70)

The imagination relates to times only as it can interpret them as their syntheses, which consciousness performs instantly in determining the immanent sense of differentiation.

When we describe this kind of instant in terms of duration, we can see the full expression of this contractile power, and the role that signifying productions of perception undertake. The 'imagination', Deleuze writes in *Bergsonism*, goes about contracting the durational experience of lived chronology, because 'there must be a difference in kind between matter and memory, between pure perception and pure recollection, between the present and the past' (*B* 55). But at the same time, subjectivity itself actualises an original encircling of divergent instants with duration, so that the pure present and pure past intermingle. Thus, for Deleuze, our ordinary understanding of this difference in kind is backward: when 'we believe that the past is no longer [. . . w]e have thus confused Being with being-present' (*B* 55). Rather than think that the present is present, and that each instant that passes can be ruled off as a past which is no longer being lived as a present, we should affirm that what we imagine as 'the present *is not*; rather, it is pure becoming, always outside itself' (*B* 55). The present – *parousia* – is active; it is the metaphysical delusion of plenitude and being-there, but it *is not*, as far as its essence is never available to us. It is always experienced as the form of the implex, interwoven as all of its passing presents, which gives the illusion of an apparent presence.³ 'The past, on the other hand, has ceased to act or to be useful. But it has not ceased to be. Useless and inactive, impassive, it IS, in the full sense of the word: It is identical with being in itself' (*B* 55). Proust's observation that we are 'totally steeped [il nous baignent tout entiers]' (*SG* 380; 374) in our past mirrors this account of being and presence. The past not only makes up all of our being, but it *is* all of our being, in so far as this 'IS' appropriates the actualisation of those divided-up instants of pasts that *are* in the present that *is not*: its virtuality. The divisible nature of an unfolding present is owed solely to the possibility of the virtual in consciousness. Subjectivity contracts duration in order to remember and thus make sense of its reality without actively and constantly reliving it. As such, 'the subjective, or duration, is the *virtual*. To be more precise, it is the virtual in so far as it is actualized' (*B* 42).

For Deleuze, the power of the virtual in subjectivity marks itself as a multiplicity on the operation of memory. 'The whole of our past is played, restarts, repeats itself, *at the same time* on all the levels that it sketches out [sur tous les niveaux qu'il dessine]' (*B* 61). Our past's inscription is virtual: all the levels it sketches out are sensible, but their immediate presence is deferred *as the sense of* this sense. Even if the sensible appears entirely in each instant, it still plays out in duration and within the tension of the past which IS, but cannot be living, and the present that *is not*, but is all living. The past must be actualised in the present, which is actively unavailable to us. Duration and the instant, movement and the virtual, go hand in hand; each *produces* the other. Such is the horizon (or cone, as Deleuze describes it) of perception, which inscribes the entirety of a subject's past within itself, but stretches along what is immediately sensible, rendered 'temporal' as it is projected back into the world. The virtual gives the present its past, and all of it at once. It is in this sense, I want to suggest, that we should read the concluding image of the *Recherche*, where the ~~voice~~ describes the bell at his parents' front gate as 'still ringing in me [cette sonnette qui tintait encore en moi]' (*FT* 356; 351):

> It must be therefore that this tinkling was always there, and also, between it and the present moment, the whole of the past, unrolled indefinitely, which I did not know that I was carrying. (*FT* 356).

C'est donc que ce tintement y était toujours, et aussi, entre lui et l'instant présent tout ce passé indéfiniment déroulé que je ne savais pas que je portais/ (352)

This 'between' of the present and the past is the virtual *sumplokē* of Being itself – the sense of the present[ ] enveloping the sense of the past[ ].

DIVIDUAL MULTIPLICITY

Deleuze's understanding of the virtual opens up a much greater problem of how, in the concept of identity, a metaphysics structured on presence and *parousia* conceives of difference and contrariety. If perception contracts a percept to incorporate all its variant traces – which in many respects deviate from, or even contradict, the essence of the given percept itself – how can that percept have any identifiable being? The virtual nature of contraction holds difference and contrariety as intrinsic properties of perception itself, in so far as nothing is fully given as present, but only as a constant, deferring movement, a becoming-other that retains each qualitative difference – which is an imperative element of its constitutive identity.[4]

My suggestion is that virtual multiplicity is crucial to the deferral of *parousia* that structures Proust's fiction. His narrator problematises changes of quality brought about by divergent lines, of wholes within wholes as the sense of a constantly productive, rather than *re*presentative, memory. In doing so, he challenges the notion of distinct or discrete individualities, particularly with regard to time*s* and *re*cognition*s* across the aporetic 'present' of duration. This accords with Deleuze's argument that 'it would be a serious mistake to think that duration was simply the indivisible': rather, in 'reality, duration divides up and does so constantly: that is why it is a *multiplicity*' (B 42). These plural or multiple wholes of duration are actualised constantly and extensively across the horizons of virtual consciousness. Proust's sleepy bedroom[ ] illustrates for us how the virtual does not divide up, but multiplies in kind, as endlessly diversified sense[ ]. Sense can never exist in a void – it relies on its interwoven *engainement* with inscription (in the Derridean sense: not only written or signifying language, but the materiality of a signifying, haptic or 'textual' external world), such as the *Recherche*'s ~~voice~~ 'becoming' the subject of his book in falling asleep. Hence, reading exemplifies this sense-producing *engainement*, because inscription motivates the sense[ ] that is constantly deferred, producing new, dividual Ideas. Inscription is never definitively read: it always invites re-reading[ ]. Matter sets off varied and intensively illimitable contractions

– like the Balbec morning[ ], never complete in its iterability – which manifest as varieties of sensibility for the chronologically bound, immanently perceiving subject.

Deleuze affirms that duration 'does not divide up without changing in kind'. Rather, 'it changes in kind in the process of dividing up: This is why it is a nonnumerical multiplicity [...] There is *other* without there being *several*; number exists only potentially' (B 42).[5] This analysis of nonnumerical multiplicity is key to the kind of *productive difference* that harmonises the instant and duration across Proust's depiction of subjectivity. In *Cinema I*, Deleuze uses affect as an example of this kind of productive movement, a kind of parallax where not only duration, but concepts themselves, always change qualitatively – as nonnumerical multiplicity – rather than quantitatively. He notes that 'affect is indivisible, and without parts; but the singular combinations that it forms with other affects form in turn an indivisible quality, which will only be divided by changing in quality (the "dividual")'.[6] The dividual thus describes this kind of qualitative *productivity* of difference in place of quantitative homogeneity[7] – the kind we find in the ungraspable 'sense' of reading inscription[ ]. In delivering sense from the instant of an undivided whole of his past, the Proustian narrator treats his perceptual life – of affects, of temporalities and experiences – as just such a dividual production: the Méséglise way becomes the Guermantes without overwriting either. Antoine Compagnon notes that this kind of dividual movement is an integral, guiding structure for the narrator's perception of the world. He refers to a draft from Proust's notebooks which compares Vinteuil's sonata to the septet it becomes, a work that is 'completely different, as original as the sonata, so that the sonata, which had seemed to [the narrator] to form a totality, was now nothing more than a unity, and [he] could now go beyond the notion of the one and understand multiplicity'.[8] This unity that allowed the narrator to understand multiplicity is dividual – it is an accorded diversity, a difference immanent to its apparent similarity. The contraction of duration, of lived temporality as it appears to subjectivity, is a multiplicity in which the folds that render its 'transcendental' quality occur not as definitive, divided affects, times, or presen[ce]ts, but as constantly new, 'immanent' combinations. Thus, to Deleuze, durational temporality, as a

> nonnumerical multiplicity by which duration or subjectivity is defined, plunges into another dimension, which is no longer spatial and is purely temporal: It moves from the virtual to its actualization, it actualizes itself by creating lines of differentiation [en créant des lignes de différenciation] that correspond to its differences in kind. (B 43)

This is a purely temporal dimension, as Bergson notes that every 'distinction between body and mind must be established in terms not of space but time'[9] – a time actualised by a self that *senses* varied lines of differentiation, all 'inscribed' on the 'mystic writing pad' of the imagination. Applying this Freudian–Derridean concept (one otherwise foreign to Deleuze's philosophy) allows us to think the productivity of the dividual, which is 'real without being actual, ideal without being abstract'. The virtual 'writing' or 'sketching out' of nonnumerical multiplicity gives a transversal materiality to literary inscription, like a 'contractile power' or 'sensitive plate' (*DR* 70) that signifies only in so far as it defers its presence or meaning[ ]. Lyotard was perceptive to point out the productive difference between Deleuze and Derrida on this point,

> [b]y showing that one is always and everywhere dealing with differing/deferring. This critique is called 'grammatology' when it emphasizes that nothing is that is not inscribed, 'written' in the sense that Derrida gives to this term. Or, following Deleuze's path, that there is no difference that does not presuppose repetition. An ontology of differing/deferring necessarily involves the avowal of inscription always already there, of a pre-inscription revealed after the event and a mourning of presence.[10]

Lyotard's incisive reading draws attention to the productive force of inscription's nonnumerical multiplicity, differently generated by Derrida and Deleuze. In focusing on the irreducibility and infinity of differing/deferring, both note inscription's vitalism (or force). It is precisely because the sense of inscription is always differed/deferred that sense 'itself' can never be made present, even as it is (always-already) inscribed. Dividual multiplicity inscribes the forward movement of duration, time and imagination as the fractal generation of inclusive difference, like Proust's enormous text that, materially, never changes, but always escapes our grasp in any one moment – a 'writing' that is always different in so far as it remains the same.

PHENOMENOLOGY, *PHANTASIEVORSTELLUNG* AND DELEUZE'S *NOĒTEON*

As I indicated at the beginning of this chapter, the questions considered so far bear an unavoidable relation to phenomenology. In the following section, I situate this analysis of sense, especially as it relates to Deleuze's reading of the virtual and dividual multiplicity, in relation to a phenomenological reading of similar questions of perception. In doing so, I want to point towards continuities between phenomenological analyses of experience and Deleuze's 'image of thought', but also to underline the restrictions imposed on phenomenological reasoning by its insistence on a plenitude of presence, or the presentation of the Idea (and) of thought.[11] Derrida's rethinking of *parousia* is also an important strand in this section of my argument, as providing an account of phenomenology's unwillingness to accept the movement and deferral of thought – the deferral that 'produces' (in the Deleuzian manner) sense. As Derrida notes with respect to memory, a 'boundary (between inside and outside, living and nonliving) separates not only speech from writing, but also memory as an unveiling (re-)producing a presence from re-memoration as the mere repetition of a monument' (*D* 108–9). Memory is separated from itself, from its total present plenitude, by what Deleuze calls the virtual – the present-lessness of sense, the always dividually becoming, the endlessly deferring. As Éric Alliez notes, the 'important thing is to be able to situate oneself with regard to phenomenology, which claims to grasp perception as the originary mode of the givenness [*donation*] of things themselves'.[12] Because of its concern with presence, phenomenology casts a significant shadow across the reading of sense as virtual and being as becoming (and text as *restance*).

Deleuze notes that his work on Bergson can be read as an 'attempt to repair Bergson's harsh treatment at the hands of the phenomenologists'.[13] But the restitution Deleuze contemplates here also implies a link: phenomenology encounters similar questions of multiplicity and sense to the ones raised in Bergson's work. There are key elements to phenomenological thought which 'dividually' continue into the kind of post-phenomenological reading of perception as a present-absent, virtual *sumplokē* that interests me here.[14] Critically, these emerge only after we overcome certain phenomenological theories' insistence on intentionality – the classical approach that takes consciousness as being always a consciousness 'of something', which invokes *parousia* in presenting '*some-thing*'.[15] If phenomenology cannot divorce thought from its origin as perception, it is because it relies on an 'objective' presentation of matter at the inauguration of the *epoché*: by untethering thought from this reliance on presence or presentation, we can conceive of a mobility of the trace that defers 'objectivity' as the sense of constitutive, nonnumerical multiplicity. With this in mind, I would like to insist on phenomenology's interest in *Phantasievorstellung*, or 'phantasy-idea' – a term which Husserl introduces in *The Phenomenology of Internal Time-Consciousness* (1928). There is an active multiplicity inherent in Husserl's belief that, once the stimulus of a sensation 'disappears, [...] sensation itself now becomes *productive*. It produces a phantasy-idea [*Phantasievorstellung*] like, or nearly like, itself with regard to content and enriched by a temporal character'.[16] Husserl's

Phantasievorstellung implies that, even for phenomenology, sense involves a dividual split, a multiplication of an Idea in its formless trace. From the point of view of the *sumplokē*, initiating presence is always deferred, an impossible-to-point implex; the original presentation that gives the *Phantasievorstellung* is always-already woven into it: presence *is* absence. Therefore, appearance [*phainesthai*] is always the *sumplokē* of what the 'thing' is (as present) and isn't (as Ideality).

With this in mind, I would like to take a moment to consider the similarities between this understanding of phenomenology in light of multiplicity, and the rethinking of *parousia* that I am suggesting. Husserl describes perception as a '*synthesis*, a mode of combination exclusively peculiar to consciousness'.[17] As the subject perceives an object through this synthesis, Husserl argues that the object is first 'given continuously as an objective unity in a multiform and changeable multiplicity of manners of appearing, which belong determinately to it'.[18] While consciousness makes sense of an object, the object stands as a 'synthetic unity pertaining to a multiplicity of manners of appearance'. As such, the multiplicity of various modes of appearance that 'give' an object or idea *become* the thought-image of that object, rather than the object remaining an 'undifferentiated blankness'.[19] Our perception of objects interlays the various multiplicities that constitute an object's mode of appearing (its lines of differentiation) to render it *sensible*: an intentionality as 'presentification' that 'reproduces at every moment a flux of the present, and in totality a flux of the present'.[20] Our perception, not only of objects, but all that constitutes the intellectual process (our ideas of affects, abstract concepts, memories), is made up of horizons of these lines of sense – 'an intentional *horizon of reference* to potentialities of consciousness that belong to the process itself'.[21] But in being given as multiple appearances, the presentation of an object or idea involves a virtual synthesis. The given thing is always a synthetic form of all of its imperceptible differences, a *sumplokē* of what it is (in 'any' infinitesimal 'present') and isn't (what is *was* or *will be*, across the other 'presents').

In *The Phenomenology of Internal Time-Consciousness*, Husserl suggests that intentionality becomes a flux, 'knit together into a constitutive whole in which we are conscious of an intentional unity, the unity of the remembered'.[22] Across the multiplicity of 'presence', a determinable thing is liable to change, to incorporate its varying forms that make up its Idea. Thus, its first appearance is shown to be 'mere hallucination'. It 'does not exist in the "real" objective world. The objective relation which was previously thought of as really subsisting is now disturbed.'[23] Of that first perception, '[n]othing remains but the perception; there is nothing *real* out there to which it relates'.[24] From this 'phenomenological standpoint', the reality aroused by that original percept contributes to the ongoing virtual quality of the Idea perceived (that is, the *sumplokē*: the unity of all perceptions that we are able to note *become* the same object). Only one perception appears to be *immanently real*, but all were 'real' at one time. Therefore, the object envelops multiple realities: sense, even a *Phantasievorstellung*, is all that remains, or *rests*.

Classical phenomenology is bound to this 'presentification' of form and naming. By contrast, we should emphasise this horizon-quality of sense, and its incorporative, resting *Phantasievorstellung*, an ontology more adequately described as a dividual *restance*, which can't be named or totalised. The presentlessness of the always-extending-further horizon defies the finitude of any determinate identity, because there is always another deferral, always more, to it. The sense of any perception, or even the sense of sense, is given by the 'modes of intentional flux that pertain to' it, the 'horizons and the intentional processes implicit in their horizons'.[25] These are the 'horizons' of the present-absent *sumplokē*, as the flux of experience that is sensible, but resists totalisation and defers its fullness the moment it is given any kind of ontological form. When considering sense or signification, Derrida writes, it is not possible

> to rest upon the copula. Coupling is a mirror. The mirror is traversed of its own accord, which is to say that it is never traversed at all. This being-traversed is not something that happens by accident to the mirror – to the West–; it is inscribed within its structure. This is as much as to say that, forever producing itself, it never comes to be. Like the horizon. (D 353)

The horizon *rests* across any possibility of nominal, ontological signification – disqualifying while mirroring itself. While external *Phantasievorstellungen* seem to be traversed in appearance (in the *parousia* of form), sense incorporates the abyss of signification, the infinite regress of mirroring. As such, form only disseminates into the incorporation of *Phantasievorstellungen* across the transversal *sense* that runs a priori to form (or is 'pre-inscribed', in Lyotard's formulation, only ever to be revealed after the event of perception), supplementing its absent origin. In this regard, the virtual extension of sense is underwritten by the trace: its 'protowriting', Derrida notes, 'is at work at the origin of sense' (SP 85). But because the origin of sense *and* signification is always absent, repeatable and deferr*ing*, it runs along a temporal axis that extends infinitely. Sense, 'being temporal in nature, as Husserl recognized, is never simply present; it is always already engaged in the "movement" of the trace, that is, in the order of signification' (SP 85).

The trace is the *restance* of sense, but, like the entire horizon, it is never present, only sensible as a deferring dividuality.

By reading Ideas in this way, absolved from the clamping anchor of *parousia*, rather than thinking of concepts as finite, nameable and present forms, we can consider them as horizons – aggregates which are transversal, which sense essence without ever presenting its trace. In *A Thousand Plateaus*, Deleuze and Guattari describe Husserl's 'tendency to make the vague essence a kind of intermediary between the essence and the sensible, between the thing and the concept' (*TP* 408). We can read this kind of 'vague essence' as the depth of these horizons, incorporating the trace[ ] that constitutes Ideal differentiation. Essences express themselves vaguely, *as sense*, and nomadically, as constantly productive lines of difference. Indeed, the continual exploration and engagement with ever-widening horizons that are sensed, but never formalised (striated), is the essence of Deleuze and Guattari's nomadology, which rethinks the *parousia*-bind of phenomenology. Sense is never striated, or else it would be entirely present-able meaning, *Bedeutung*. Thus, when Deleuze and Guattari affirm Husserl's 'discovery' of 'fuzzy aggregates' (*TP* 407), they are upturning the presence *of* presence in perception, arguing for the fuzziness of a non-explicated *Sinn* (sense) over the impossible plenitude of a 'fully present' *Bedeutung*, or meaning. They are advancing Husserl's phenomenology by detaching it from its bind to presence.[26]

Deleuze's reading of the *noēteon*, or that which can be thought, extends his rewriting of phenomenological presence by emphasising the elusive duration (or the deferring dividuality) of sense. Deleuze notes that the transcendental memory of sense

> forces thought to grasp that which can only be thought, the *cogitandum* or *noēteon*, the Essence: not the intelligible, for this is still no more than the mode in which we think that which might be something other than thought, but the being of the intelligible as though this were both the final power of thought and the unthinkable. (*DR* 141)

Deleuze emphasises how *noēteon* is instantaneous and can only be explicated as it reveals itself in deferring inference. Like the virtual's 'lines of differentiation', the *noēteon* is inscribed in thought, but it cannot be presented. In this way, it evokes the trace of sense that is never explicated, because, as what is *only* thinkable, the *noēteon* is the formless, *aisthetic* 'image' of thought, that cannot be reduced to any concrete image or form. When Deleuze describes 'transcendental memory' as 'not a contingent past, but the being of the past as such and the past of every time' (*DR* 140), we can treat this 'image' of thought, its 'final power', as the transversal, fractal, ultimate power of a thought liberated from the presentation of its static image. The *noēteon* is the superimposition of the thought's traces, an image wrought by traces that not only do not present themselves, but defer their very being in favour of the strictly unintelligible sense of their trace[ ]. In Derridean terms, the 'trace must be thought before being' (*OG* 51), but this conception is multiple, iterable and abyssal: it *is* thought before it is (a) being, while the trace must be thought before Being *is*.

Deleuze's *noēteon* is thus a way to describe the deferring *movement*, but not the presentation, of a thing. Because the *noēteon* acts as 'the being of the intelligible as though this were both the final power of thought and the unthinkable' (*DR* 141), this hybridity is the natural being of thought without presence, a final, totalising power of an interactive unity of difference[ ], an IS that incorporates its *is not* as another of its qualities: 'both its "nth" power and the paradoxical element within transcendental exercise' (*DR* 141). Indeed, as Bergson notes, 'there is no perception that is not full of memories. With the immediate and present data of our senses we mingle a thousand details out of our past experience':[27] these memories cannot be described, or even thought, without inviting a thousand more. Such is the totality, the present-absent conflation of the 'image of thought' – a non-image image. The *noēteon* reroutes the expectations we have of thought as presence, or those expectations which 'present thought', by allowing us to consider thought as its own final power, thought as and including what is 'unthinkable' – a thought unbound to presence.

Rather than attempt to narrate a totalised 'present image', Proust's novel focuses upon the kind of residuum of perception that this formula of the *noēteon* allows us to think. Through his narrator, Proust drives an overt subjectivity to its essential limits, knowing full well the impossibility of bridging the gap between the *noēteon* and the *noēton* (that which can be thought; and that which can be described). His narrator writes of a certain 'permanence of the elements that compose' a person's soul, and notes that they are integral to our desire for self-expression. But there is a limit to these

> elements, this final residue which we are obliged to keep to ourselves, which speech cannot convey even from friend to friend, from master to pupil, from lover to mistress, that this inexpressible thing which reveals the qualitative difference between what each of us has felt and has had to leave on the threshold of the phrases which he uses to communicate to others. (*PF* 236)

> éléments, tout le résidu réel que nous sommes obligés de garder pour nous-mêmes, que la causerie ne peut transmettre même de l'ami à l'ami, du maître au disciple, de l'amant à la maîtresse, cet ineffable qui différencie qualitative-

ment ce que chacun a senti et qu'il est obligé de laisser au seuil des phrases où il ne peut communiquer avec autrui. (*P* 246)

The duration necessarily utilised by narrative, by these 'phrases' used to communicate, cannot be qualitatively inclusive of all of the *noēteon*'s traces. However, a work of art allows the artist to

> manifest in the colours of the spectrum the intimate make-up of those worlds we call individuals, and which without art we should never know. (*PF* 236)
>
> extériorisant dans les couleurs du spectre la composition intime de ces mondes que nous appelons les individus, et que sans l'art nous ne connaîtrions jamais. (*P* 246)

Thus, because Proust's novel extensively produces the intensive features of a subjective whole, the narrative action *traces* this 'spectrum' of *noēteon*: the sensed past[ ] lost by chronological lived-experience, but which IS as 'the past of every time' (*DR* 140), in so far as the pure present from which he perceives the past *is not* – and is always becoming upon every (re)reading.

POST-PHENOMENOLOGY

The idea of 'sense' that we need in order to do justice to this kind of subjectivity is one that combines the *noēteon*, the *aisthesis* of perception, and the constituting work of the trace. When I mentioned in the above section my desire to consider sense as an absent-present abyss rather than the defined work of its intentional *Bedeutung*, it was in the hope of considering the multiplicity at work in the abyss of sense, which I take to be 'that which can only be thought', or *noēteon*. The importance of the *noēteon* is that it allows us to move towards a potential or thinkable difference between sense and presence (or the intended presence presented by meaning). In order that sense might sense any*thing* (or the becoming and deferral of any*thing* sensible) it must resist the distinguishing work of any copula that attempts to pin down Being. This is one of the fundamental difficulties that confronts Proust's narrator. As perception is constantly produced in consciousness, there exists an extensive gap between what occurs (what is sensible and inferred as sensible in *noēteon*) and that which can be made intelligible. The trace[ ] *is* the concept: or rather, it weaves as it defers whatever we *think* we can think.

Consider again the passage evoked at the beginning of this chapter, in which the narrator notes the disintegration of boundaries between the actual, the sensible and the temporal as he is falling asleep – as well as during that sleep, and those that subsist after he wakes. As the abyss of sleep appropriates 'his' *propre*, he notes that the essential configurations set by the sensible and temporal world begin to wane: he fails to notice whether or not he is asleep, whether or not he is himself, the subject of his book, or some fold between the two. Deleuze uses the terms 'differen*t*iation' and 'differen*c*iation' to distinguish between virtual and actual forms of difference: we 'call the determination of the virtual content of an Idea differen*t*iation; we call the actualization of that virtuality into different species and distinguished parts differen*c*iation' (*DR* 207). In this example, the narrator is following the horizons of sense through the traces which constitute his *propre*, which is constituted, and projected into sense, as differen*t*iation. The production of the percepts he has described (his books, its subjects, the objects in his room, himself) expands, and, dividually, intermingles and *produces further*. The sense *of* sense crosses the boundaries rendered by the intelligible, affirmed by his absolute extensity: time, or more specifically, the chronological aspect of time, is diverted by the enveloping solipsism that sleep, and its dreams, actuates. The possibility of multiple, superimposed yet different forms is constantly produced and actualised in his immanent 'reveries'. The narrator senses a form of himself *as* François III, Charles V, or his lampshade, as well as a 'fuzzy aggregate' of the all of these, and all of their various qualities.[28]

Proust locates this degradation of form in the extra-sensible environment of dreams, but the novel as a whole must also contend with the iterability of its literary expression: how to write the territorialisations of sense that he wants to share in repeatable and disseminable language? Let us consider another example from the novel. When the narrator describes his grief for his grandmother's death, he dwells upon the virtual problem of remembering the original times (all of the traces) of an appearing Idea, distinct from their transcendental unification.

> I clung to these sorrows, however cruel they might be, with all my strength, for I felt indeed that they were the effect of my memory of my grandmother, the proof that this memory which I had was indeed present in me. I felt that I truly remembered her only through sorrow, and would have wished the nails to be driven yet more firmly home that had riveted her memory inside me. (*SG* 161)

> Ces douleurs, si cruelles qu'elles fussent, je m'y attachais de toutes mes forces, car je sentais bien qu'elles étaient l'effet du souvenir de ma grand-mère, la preuve que ce souvenir que j'avais était bien présent en moi. Je sentais que je ne me la rappelais vraiment que par la douleur, et j'aurais voulu que s'enfonçassent plus solidement encore en moi ces clous qui y rivaient sa mémoire. (156)

He senses a 'presence' of 'the effect of his memory', but notes the metaphysical delusion of presenting it 'in' his consciousness. That effect is grief – which, as described here, accords with *restance*, those sensible remains of the trace. He seeks to drive this 'effect', or rather this *affect*, further into his 'present' 'consciousness' or 'recall', though it remains there in the dividual horizon of all of these already.

The narrator's account of this grief, particularly the attitude that he takes to intellectualising and remembering it, epitomises the attempt to extend the sensible through the intelligible to its true, virtual inscription[ ] – the *noēteon*. He describes the 'memory' of a person as we usually understand it: when this person is 'separated from us but [...] knows us and remains joined to us by an indissoluble harmony [séparé de nous mais qui, resté individuel, nous connaît et nous reste relié par une indissoluble harmonie]' (*SG* 161; 156), their *restance* extends across the horizons of our senses – their trace[ ] remain[ ]. This *restance* is made up of all the traces produced by that person's various modes of appearance, and thus constitutes the 'fuzzy aggregate' of that person's possible *noēteon*. The narrator's grief in this instance is his desire to retain the property of all his recognitions of his grandmother without moving towards the one 'present' of her, for this would see her finally consigned to the past, and as such, finally dead.

> I was anxious not to suffer only, but to respect the originality of my suffering such as I had suddenly endured it against my will, and I wanted to continue to endure it, in accordance with its own laws, each time this strange contradiction between survival and oblivion, intersecting within me, returned. (*SG* 161)

> je ne tenais pas seulement à souffrir, mais à respecter l'originalité de ma souffrance telle que je l'avais subie tout d'un coup sans le vouloir, et je voulais continuer à la subir, suivant ses lois à elle, à chaque fois que revenait cette contradiction si étrange de la survivance et du néant entre-croisés en moi. (156)

The narrator thus locates the multiplicity active in his virtual contraction, the lines of differen*t*iation crossing one another in producing his sense of grief. This state of grief is triggered by his recognition of one particular moment from his past *across* that of his 'present': in untying his boots, he remembers performing the same act at a distinct moment when his grandmother was alive, which suddenly brings her memory back to him, as if she were still present. But as he attempts to continue this crossing of 'survival and contradiction, intersecting within' him, to exemplify the relation of times across multiple channels of sensibility, he notes that the recognition of two symmetrical times comes

> from this same impression, so particular, so spontaneous, which had been neither traced by [his] intellect nor inflected or attenuated by [his]

pusillanimity, but which death itself, the abrupt revelation of death, had hollowed out in [him], like a thunderbolt, in accordance with some inhuman, supernatural diagram, like a double and mysterious furrow. (SG 161–2)

> ce ne pourrait être que d'elle, si particulière, si spontanée, qui n'avait été ni tracée par mon intelligence, ni atténuée par ma pusillanimité, mais que la mort elle-même, la brusque révélation de la mort, avait, comme la foudre, creusée en moi, selon un graphique surnaturel et inhumain, un double et mystérieux sillon. (156)

The production of dividual *noēteon* 'hollowed' out in him by the 'thunderbolt' of recognition seems 'supernatural' or 'inhuman', because of the very 'double' nature of its furrow. While the 'double' or multiple makes up the virtual of perception, its present actualisation is elusive because it occurs as, and across, its horizons of sense. To actualise this 'double' moment would be superhuman, because the time-scheme of Western metaphysics is that of chronology, of *chronos*, which is structured around the discrete presentation of identity and contrariety. But Proust's narrator is gesturing here towards a more complex temporal 'impression', one 'so particular, so spontaneous', that it circumvents this presentational logic: it 'hollows out' in him another time-scheme, the supernatural time-scheme of the inhuman, the present-absent being of Being that *is* reflection only in so far as it *is not*.

FORGETTING, THE *AIÔN* AND THE HOLLOW

This kind of strange temporality is integral to the novel's portrayal of sensible multiplicity. In the next section of this chapter, I situate Deleuze's reading of this alternative model of time alongside the work of two phenomenological interlocutors – Maurice Merleau-Ponty and Mauro Carbone – in order to suggest that temporal experience and the *thought* of temporality can be unwound from a presentational logic of *parousia*. Deleuze's reworking of temporal order and structuration in favour of difference and becoming mirrors the organisation of temporal experience in Proust's novel – especially in scenes like that of the grief-stricken narrator untying his boots.

In discussing the poetic possibilities of the sensible, Mauro Carbone uses themes from Greek mythology to describe a kind of 'mythical time', in which forgetting becomes sense. He characterises remembering as an

> initiation [which] consists in the contact with primordial time, with the time of the '"always" which is used to define the life of the gods.' The faculty of recollection, indistinguishable from the poetic function, offers the experience of a very specific time that the Greeks called *aiôn*.[29]

Carbone's *aiôn* is conceived as the exhaustion of forgetting. Memory cannot simply arrive at this exhaustion, but rather does so within this time of the 'always', that is the life of the gods. For Jean-Pierre Vernant, whose work Carbone relies on in developing this idea, the *aiôn* 'no longer means the perpetual rebeginning of that which ceaselessly renews itself by returning to its beginnings, [but] comes instead to signify permanence in an eternally immobile identity'.[30] I would like to suggest that this 'immobility' should be thought of in the same manner as *noēteon*: as an 'image of thought', a present-absent *restance*. The *aiôn* is because it '*has been*' – in the sense of an appropriating event.[31] For Carbone, the '*has been*' of the *aiôn* is the inevitable weaving-through of the unintelligible, yet sensible trace[ ]. The '*has been*' is the eternal *is*, occupying appropriable multiplicities of subjectivity, but to the point that the sensible becomes all of what Being *is*, constantly occurr*ing*.

The *aiôn* is thus a time of deferred presence: the 'mythical discourse', as Derrida puts it, 'in which difference would be erased' (*D* 303).

> If account be taken of what divides it, cuts it up, and folds it back upon its very triggering, then the present is no longer simply the present. It can no longer be named 'present' except through indirect discourse, in the quotation marks of citation, storytelling, fiction. It can only go out into language by a sort of ricochet. (*D* 303)

The '"present"' can only go *out in*to language. In folding back upon its triggering, the present works into language by intensifying its differences, by translating while erasing them, into a sensible multiplicity. In this way, *restance*, the trace and *noēteon* can all be seen as devices for underlining the present-less present of the *aiôn*, which is the infinite intensity of sense, a sensible iteration in which each reflection in the abyss opens *out in*to another abyss.

Carbone's discussion of the *aiôn* echoes Deleuze's invocation of this term in *The Logic of Sense*, where he, too, uses the concept of the *aiôn* to rethink chronological temporality. For Deleuze, *aiôn* designates a time that is 'infinitely subdivisible', rather than strictly infinite: the 'Aion' is 'the essentially unlimited past and future, which gather incorporeal events, at the surface, as effects (Aion)' (*LS* 61). Deleuze's 'Aion' draws attention to the difference between the idea of infinity itself, and something which is infinitely subdivisible. If a time is infinitely subdivisible, his analysis implies, that subdivision's infinity extends throughout any comparative '*other/any*' division: its infinity transcends the terms of infinity itself. This difficult notion allows us to think of an '*essentially unlimited past and future*': an infinity that is essentially thinkable, but cannot be represented. Just as Derrida argues that the 'possibility

– or the potency – of the present is but its own limit, its inner fold, its impossibility – or its impotence' (*D* 303), then these '*essentially unlimited*' time*s* are exactly those (such as 'subdivision') that challenge the extension of infinity by opening out into the intensity of *aiôn*. Like Carbone, Deleuze defines the *aiôn* in the context of the Stoic knowledge of the mutual 'necessity' and 'reciprocal exclusion' (*LS* 61) of *aiôn* and *chronos* – *aiôn* is a dividual multiplicity of the present-able time*s* of chronology, appropriating and multiplying their degrees of identity and contrariety. *Aiôn* is the time of time[ ], where infinite subdivision is its *essential*(ly unlimited) quality. The quotidian folds of chronology, its possibility of tensions and relaxations, are operative due to the absorbing quality of the *aiôn*, encircling and impressing its textures upon experience, memory and dividuality.

It is for this reason that Carbone goes on to characterise the *aiôn* as 'our always operative and never thematized experience of time, that is to say our operative temporality'. Despite its 'never thematized experience', this temporality is always organised as the trace, and therefore is 'why it seems possible to recognize in the sentence "I did not know" and "I have always known it" the formula of the passage from operative intentionality to act intentionality'.[32] In the 'presentation' of chronological time, to feel as though we have forgotten a memory, we must first have experienced it, and then remember this experience: it must re-member itself to us in order for us to re-cognise that it *was* forgotten, but is no longer. Of the expression 'I did not know', Carbone notes that 'this formula seems also to designate the *grafting* of chronological time (to the extent that "I did not know" in reality implies "until *now*") onto that of the *aiôn*'.[33] Forgetting can only come about in chronological time, despite the aporia that we can never *know*, or rather *present* forgetting. If we did so, it would no longer be itself, no longer be forgetting, because it would lack the essential quality of being forgotten. Forgetting thus traces the very structure of *noēteon*'s sense, in so far as it is the intensive extension of the literary, or the tracing of the trace. If we follow the horizon of sense far enough, if we roll over again in bed, it is possible that we would *re*write another *Recherche* through every trace we forget.

By locating the specificity of forgetting in chronology, we can see the evocation of a kind of 'mythical time' in subjective Being. It is the sense of the forgotten which, 'by mapping onto chronological time what pertains to mythical time, with all the equivocations this graft inevitably generates',[34] makes the virtual sensible, by evoking its trace, its forgetability. As these phenomenal elements and myriad impressions come to be 'forgotten' in chronological time, they are sensible from the totality of *aiôn*, and they de/reterritorialise the multiple traces of time that are the *is* of the past. Whatever it was that the narrator thought he had 'forgotten' about his grandmother is certainly sensible in the 'grafting' of memory across the chiasm of the 'double' time he senses while tying his boots.³⁵ These varied and remembered grandmothers are sensible only because she has first been forgotten, a state of forgetfulness that was

> nothing more than a negation, an enfeeblement of the mind, incapable of re-creating an actual moment of life and obliged to substitute it for conventional and indifferent mental images. (SG 162)

> rien qu'une négation, l'affaiblissement de la pensée incapable de recréer un moment réel de la vie et obligée de lui substituer des images conventionnelles et indifférentes. (157)

Despite this seemingly absolute oblivion, there is a complex, atemporalising appropriation operating here. The work of sensible appropriation collapses the potentially infinite time of forgetting in the instantaneous graft of remembering – of weaving together the trace[ ] of sense.

The narrator cannot ask for the truth, the real life or real time of his grandmother and his relationship with her, because it exists in a state of forgetting, which is an 'enfeeblement of the mind' to the extent that it substitutes 'conventional and indifferent mental images' for the living of them. But in the remembering that is constituted by the possibility of forgetting her, these images are anything but 'conventional' or neutral: they are the soil, the content, of his existence. And as such, the forgetting that presents itself as a negation does not present itself at all, or else it would reveal – or remember, and thus not forget – these images. Forgetting itself is something essentially unnameable, since to 'know' a forgotten thing is not to know the forgetting, but rather to remember some*thing* that *was* forgotten: the forgotten thing is divested of its forgetting. Forgetting is a *sumplokē*; it *is* only as it *is not*.³⁶

In this scene, it is not until what the narrator has forgotten can be located and determined *as* forgotten that he fully accesses the *noēteon* of his grandmother's death. The traces of this forgetting impart sense,

> now that the instinct for self-preservation, or the intellect's ingenuity in shielding us against sorrow, was beginning to build on the still smoking ruins, to lay the first foundations of its useful but ill-starred building-work. (SG 162)

> l'instinct de conservation, l'ingéniosité de l'intelligence à nous préserver de la douleur, commençant déjà à construire sur des ruines encore fumantes, à poser les premières assises de son œuvre utile et néfaste. (157)

The time of this unconscious building-work, the innumerable traces relative to the varied dividual productions of the object grieved-for, is the *aiôn*. For Carbone, if '*aion* manifests itself as the temporality operative within the unconscious, understood as "undividedness of feeling," it seems possible to define Mnemosyne as the memory operative *within feeling itself*.'[37] Mnemosyne here plays the role of *noēteon*. If

> its essential poietic power makes Mnemosyne the faculty of eidetic creation, always operating within experience, Mnemosyne also reveals itself on the other side – the other side of the *same* – as the *faculty of eidetic recognition*, which in its turn never ceases to operate within experience. Therefore, Mnemosyne corresponds to the 'double formula of the unconscious': 'I did not know' and 'I have always known it.'[38]

It is the essential creative power of memory, as incorporated by Mnemosyne, that combines the totality of penumbras of forgetting, their inscription and actualisation in memory as an 'always known'. It is as Mnemosyne applies this abstract creativity that sense becomes 'always known', the very instantaneousness of the instant, and the sensible reality of forgetting. Thus, 'Lethe proves not to be the opposite of Mnemosyne, but rather its *reverse* (and complementary) *side*: namely, the side in virtue of which Mnemosyne can exercise its eidetic creativity.'[39] In a *sumplokē*-like arrangement, Mnemosyne uses forgetting to create virtual sense. Carbone quotes Merleau-Ponty at this juncture, noting that 'the unconscious' should be understood as

> the feeling itself [. . .] since feeling is not the intellectual possession of 'what' is felt, but a dispossession of ourselves in favor of it, an opening toward *that which we do not have to think in order that we may recognize it*.[40]

What is evoked here, I want to suggest, are the sensible horizons of forgetting that 'give' *noēteon*. It is as the virtual 'unconscious' goes about rapidly deriving eidetic possibilities that the nature of *form* ebbs away, and the full capacity of the *aiôn* is evident. Therefore, because this 'feeling itself' of the sensible is not an intellectual 'possession', deriving its sense from the horizons given by the synthesis of forms that exist freely and entirely in the *aiôn*, their expression in this time scheme must operate somehow in, or through, consciousness. In Carbone's reading of Merleau-Ponty, this is the present-absent being of Being. It is possible for us to have 'an architectonic past', but '[t]his "past" belongs to a mythical time, to the time before time, to the prior life'.[41]

Much as Proust's narrator describes sensible multiplicity as a 'mysterious furrow [mystérieux sillon]' (*SG* 162; 156), Carbone, via Merleau-Ponty, likens 'brute being' to a '"hollow," hollowed out precisely by the woof of sensible being's differentiations'.[42] Carbone and Merleau-Ponty thus reconsider the phenomenological *epoché* as a (pre)originary interweaving: it is the virtual contraction of consciousness which fills the 'hollow' of brute being, as the native activity of sensible consciousness interprets the horizons of sensibility given by brute being and 'filled' by intentionality. We thus have a twofold activity, one which requires experience in order to initiate these hollows that are the brute sense of Being, but at the same time must be emptied by chronological, differenciating 'forgetting'. This kind of hollow, or concavity, is to Carbone the very material of Being itself. He cites Merleau-Ponty's statement that 'I am not even the author of that hollow that forms within me by the passage from the present to the retention, it is not I who makes myself think any more than it is I who make my heart beat.'[43] Intentionality is not a thoroughly active process, but is rather an *aisthesis*, that chiasm between intuitional and brute sensibility, encouraged, forced into itself by the filling of the 'hollow' of experience compiled within the constantly occurring *aiôn*, the always.

In Carbone's reading of Merleau-Ponty, to be is to form horizons, to activate a constant, infinitive and always occur*ring* chiasm between brute Being and intellectual sense. For Deleuze, as this chiasm divides up into its various multiplicities, as it *produces* being, it progresses along an 'oriented line of the present, which "regularizes" in an individual system each singular point which it takes in'. To this 'system' of 'point[s]', 'the line of Aion is opposed' (*LS* 77). The *aiôn* which produces, possesses and always enacts Being, is a line which, rather, 'leaps from one pre-individual singularity to another and recovers them all, each one of them within the others' (*LS* 77). It is pre-individual in so far as it *is* this hollow of brute being, the forgotten exorcised of its forgetting, the pre-individual of the narrator's 'reveries' in which he is encircled by the years, before the instantaneous 'thunderbolt' of his *restance*. Thus, in its infinity, the *aiôn* is not a line, not even the Borgesian straight-line-labyrinth that Deleuze evokes to describe it (*LS* 62). For geometric lines and circles still operate upon a plane of differenciation, a representational image in a chronological present which IS, comparable next to that which it *is not* – an idea of *parousia*. Rather, the *aiôn is this very hollow of subjective being*, the essential quality of the self; Mnemosyne dreaming, submerged under the river Lethe, possessing and haunting what might possibly be forgotten by the self who lived it.

I would like to consider an example from the novel to illustrate this notion of a 'pre-individual singularity' – the *aiôn*'s trace[ ]. Proust's novel, as we have seen in relation to the narrator's 'un-forgetting' of his grandmother, is highly attuned to this 'hollow' of subjective Being, guided by 'forgetting'. The *Recherche* shows how percepts have woven into their sense constituent, 'forgotten' traces, to the point that the very movement of the narrative comes to be possessed by the integration of this superimposition. The 'present' moment being narrated disperses, or is deferred, in the interest of capturing and interweaving the various 'lines of time' that are operative of the hollow – the pre-individual singularity – of sense. Consider this example, in which Albertine's laugh

> at once summoned up the pink carnations, the perfumed walls against which it seemed to have just brushed and from which, pungent, sensual and revealing as the scent of geraniums, it seemed to be transporting with it a few almost ponderable, irritant and secret particles. (SG 196–7)

> évoquait aussi les roses carnations, les parois parfumées contre lesquelles il semblait qu'il vînt de se frotter et dont, âcre, sensuel et révélateur comme une odeur de géranium, il semblait transporter avec lui quelques particules presque pondérables, irritantes et secrètes. (191)

Albertine's laugh is not a presentable thing for many reasons – but especially because its intensive, microscopic, constituent particles are abyssal: they defer their '*almost* ponderable, irritant and secret' *noēteon* into other lines of differentiation. On a similar occasion, the narrator suspects Albertine of infidelity, and notices a young woman gazing at her. 'You would have said she was signalling to her, as if with the aid of a lighthouse [On eût dit qu'elle lui faisait des signes comme à l'aide d'un phare]' (SG 250; 245). The implex of these glances, of their interpretive meanings, provides impressions which unlock innumerable lines of time, both from that moment of illumination and from pasts both actual and hypothetical. The constituting pluralism of these lines evokes a weaving, in which seemingly discrete temporalities fuse and *re*-fray down the dividual abyss.

> It was perhaps because Albertine had already yielded to her desires or to those of a friend that the latter felt free to address these dazzling signals to her. They were doing more then than demand something for the present, their authority for that had come from good times in the past. (SG 250–1)

> C'était peut-être parce qu'Albertine avait déjà cédé à ses désirs ou à ceux d'une amie que celle-ci se permettait de lui adresser ces brillants signaux. Ils faisaient alors plus que réclamer quelque chose pour le présent, ils s'autorisaient pour cela des bonnes heures du passé. (245)

The distinction between types of time becomes indiscernible, and irrelevant. The narrator signals, much later in the novel, that this kind of multiplicity is a guiding principle of temporality as he imagines it. In turn, we can read the narrator's excursive style itself as an example of this kind of immanent multiplicity, of the hollow that gives sense from the *aiôn*.

> It seems that events extend further than the moments in which they happen, and cannot be completely contained within them. Certainly, they spill over into the future through the memories we retain of them, but they also demand space in the time that precedes them. Certainly you will say that at that time we do not see them as they will actually be, but are they not also changed in our memory of them? (*PF* 371)

> Il semble que les événements soient plus vastes que le moment où ils ont lieu et ne peuvent y tenir tout entiers. Certes, ils débordent sur l'avenir par la mémoire que nous en gardons, mais ils demandent une place aussi au temps qui les précède. On peut dire que nous ne les voyons pas alors tels qu'ils seront ; mais dans le souvenir ne sont-ils pas aussi modifiés ? (*P* 386)

In spilling across present-able temporal borders, events blur the stability of times into formless intensities. Proust's deferring fiction is a *sumplokē* of these times, an Idea enacted only by reading through its *restance*, deferring essence in the multiplicity of time[ ] operative in its reading.

If sense is only ever *deferred*, even in Proust's literary accounts of perception, why do we feel that sense can be 'present' to consciousness? Deleuze argues that Plato's determination of the 'being *of* the sensible [. . .] rests upon intensive qualities, but recognises these only in the course of development' – as they are differen*c*iated as 'empirically' sensible, one quality differing from another – 'and for that reason, it assigns both the being of the sensible and contrariety to qualities' (*DR* 236). This determination of intensity as the qualities or 'being *of* the sensible' informs the imagined 'presentation' of sense. For Deleuze, the error here lies in holding contrariety to be an essential element of the being of the sensible. He argues that

> while the contrary-sensible or contrariety in the quality may constitute sensible being *par excellence*, they by no means constitute the being *of* the sensible. It is the difference in intensity, not contrariety in quality, which constitutes the being 'of' the sensible. (*DR* 236)

For Deleuze, to think, to know something, is not to work through all its component parts over again: intensity is the *sense* of the virtual. Intensity, which gives quality but never presents its fullness other than deferring sense, is the compounding, dividual becom*ing* of the trace, as it elaborates down the abyss. Because the trace can never be fully presented in chronology or external expression, it is not 'articulable' as the differences known by contrariety.

> It is intensity or difference in intensity which constitutes the peculiar limit of sensibility. As such, it has the paradoxical character of that limit: it is the imperceptible, that which cannot be sensed because it is always covered

by a quality which alienates or contradicts it, always distributed within an extensity which inverts and cancels it. (*DR* 236–7)

Sensibility constitutes the limit of itself, which is why it has been evident throughout our enquiry that the 'imperceptible' within it (which appears to directly contradict it) *contributes* to its perceptibility. Difference itself, not merely contrariety but that of intensity, 'pursues its subterranean life while its image reflected by the surface is scattered' (*DR* 240): as the empirically sensible image is superimposed throughout its scattering in the *aiôn*, difference goes on rendering intensities as totally inferred *noēteon*. Ultimately, '[t]he expression "difference of intensity" is a tautology. Intensity is the form of difference in so far as this is the reason of the sensible' (*DR* 222). The totality of identity cannot be presented because of its constitutive, deferring difference – but it can be sensed in the formless trace of intensity.

SLEEPING, DREAMING AND THE *AIÔN*

Equipped now with a lexical and conceptual armoury with which to think of thought outside of the limitations of presence, let us return to the figuration of this deferring sense in Proust's novel. As I have suggested, the narrator notes the sensible *restance* of his pasts in the experience of sleeping and waking. And he is explicit about this being, firstly, a temporal consideration. Describing the phenomenon of deep sleep, or *sommeil de plomb*, he specifies that the

> time that elapses for the sleeper, in sleep of this kind, is utterly different from time in which a waking man's life transpires. (*SG* 376)

> Le temps qui s'écoule pour le dormeur, durant ces sommeils-là, est absolument différent du temps dans lequel s'accomplit la vie de l'homme reveille. (370)

This 'utterly different' time resembles the temporality that Carbone calls the *aiôn*. Carbone notes that in

> sleep, as in the dimension of brute being, where subject and object are not yet constituted, where activity and passivity are undifferentiated, where space and time lose their distinction, the present is enveloped, in fact, by a past which is farthest away, a past [. . .] as 'indestructible,' as 'intemporal.'[44]

This description seems to correspond to the narrator's drifting, transversal sense of Being when he describes himself falling asleep. The past which is 'farthest away' envelops the state of sleep, without ever reaching the fullness of presentation. Because sleep arouses the *aiôn* to tell its stories, a trace may be produced across multiple, divergent lines of articulation and association, and still possess what we may try to call, afterwards in waking recollection, a concept.

When we are awake, the narrator notes, 'we can claim that there is only one time, for the futile reason that it is by looking at the clock [on peut prétendre qu'il n'y a qu'un temps, pour la futile raison que c'est en regardant la pendule]' (SG 378; 372) that we measure its passing. But the world of sleep utilises the *aiôn*, the 'always' of both times and forms. Its currency is the extended, equally sensible perception of every *noēteon* that makes up each concept. In attempting to interpret these as the waking-actual, as *noēton*,

> at the moment when we confirm it, we are of course a man awake, plunged into the time of waking men, we have deserted the other time. Perhaps even more than another time: another life. (SG 378)
>
> au moment où on le constate, on est justement un homme éveillé, plongé dans le temps des hommes éveillés, on a déserté l'autre temps. Peut-être même plus qu'un autre temps : une autre vie. (372)

'[A]nother life', or, rather, other lives: the *restance* of all of the other selves that we appropriate in Being, in signing, that we feel to be forgotten entirely. The absolute intermingling of the lines of multiplicity within the *aiôn* is too large for chronology or the pure present: but they are not entirely negated, for they rest, in inference, as *noēteon*. That is why, to the narrator,

> [w]ere we to include the pains and pleasures of our dreams (which generally vanish very quickly on waking) in a budget, it would not be that of our everyday life. (SG 378)
>
> Souffrances et plaisirs du rêve (qui généralement s'évanouissent bien vite au réveil), si nous les faisons figurer dans un budget, ce n'est pas dans celui de la vie courante. (372)

The *restance* of these pains and pleasures is never present in the budget, but is invested silently into the balance of payments.

The *aiôn* traces the 'always' of perception(s), but it can also incorporate differences of intensity which simultaneously compile inferences. Proust's fiction grapples with the role played by intensity-as-difference. This project is especially evident at moments where 'subject and object are not yet constituted',[45] in sleep and dreams. The narrator describes a number of dreams to us, and in them it is possible to locate an idea of experience which does not *constitute* any subject or object, but can sense differences in intensity. In the episode related above, in which the narrator describes wishing to 'cling' to the grief he feels for his grandmother's death, he describes his mind's 'shielding' him from grief by building on its 'still smoking ruins'. Immediately after this thought, he notes the sense of its impression.

> [A]s soon as I came to fall asleep, at that more truthful hour when my eyes were closed to the things without, the world of sleep (on the threshold of which, my intellect and my will, momentarily paralysed, could no longer contend with the cruelty of my genuine impressions) reflected, refracted the painful synthesis of survival and nothingness, in the organic depths, now become translucid, of the mysteriously illuminated viscera. (SG 162)
>
> dès que je fus arrivé à m'endormir, à cette heure, plus véridique, où mes yeux se fermèrent aux choses du dehors, le monde du sommeil (sur le seuil duquel l'intelligence et la volonté momentanément paralysées ne pouvaient plus me disputer à la cruauté de mes impressions véritables) refléta, réfracta la douloureuse synthèse de la survivance et du néant, dans la profondeur organique et devenue translucide des viscères mystérieusement éclairés. (157)

While his every intellectual effort may be towards preserving the individual perceptions of his grandmother, the synthesising act of consciousness applies itself in sleep, where it can totalise the actual from the time scheme of the always, of the *aiôn*. As I noted with respect to the very beginning of the novel, sleep deterritorialises multiple folds of thought. In falling asleep, the extensive differen*c*iations taken up by the narrator's intellectual understanding – in reading his book – fall away into varied forms of differen*t*iation: Ideal intensity. The sleeping consciousness occupies many of these possible determinations, and weaves each of them into its fluctuating *sumplokē*. Hence, as the body, and the organs, are the only constant aside from the very hollow of his experiences, the narrator describes them as constituting the only activity of his being. In 'order to travel along the arteries of the subterranean city [pour y parcourir les artères de la cité souterraine]' (*SG* 162; 157) – Carbone's 'dimension of brute being in which subject and object are not yet constituted'[46] – 'we have embarked on the dark waves of our own blood, as if on the sixfold meanders of some internal Lethe [nous sommes embarqués sur les flots noirs de notre propre sang comme sur un Léthé intérieur]' (*SG* 162; 157). The narrator here attests that our bodies constitute the essence of 'brute being': our own blood is the river by which sleep engenders forgetting in us. At the same time, he outlines the multiple, differen*t*iated environment which marks the trace of the *aiôn* in sleep and dreams: difference itself is mitigated by its differen*t*iation *as* consciousness itself, in a purely sensible intensity.

Sleep gives the narrator access to the *aiôn*, but he cannot make this experience present in his waking life. In one dream, the narrator remembers that he has, for many weeks, forgotten to write to his grandmother. He asks his father to take him to her, a request his father refuses, consoling him with the assurance that she is being looked after well. He then 'thought' that he could remember that she had said some consoling words to him, 'shortly after she died [je crus me rappeler qu'un peu après sa mort]' (*SG* 163; 158). Suddenly, as his grandmother's kind words fade into a conversation with his father in which he is told that he can no longer visit her (though his father promises to leave for the narrator her 'exact address'), the narrator replies: 'You know very well though that I shall always live near her, stags, stags, Francis Jammes, fork [Tu sais bien pourtant que je vivrai toujours près d'elle, cerfs, cerfs, Francis Jammes, fourchette]' (*SG* 164; 159). It appears that at this point the dream diverts into nonsense, but not so: rather, the narrator, in attempting to translate the intense 'words' (which, in a dream, of course, are not spoken, but rather subsist Ideally) into the intelligible environment of his wakefulness, cannot extend the horizon that incorporates the trace between these seemingly disparate Ideas. The extra-sensibility of the dream has lost its currency in the practical sense of the everyday. In waking, by which the narrator already 'had recrossed the river with its gloomy meanders, [. . .] had come back to the surface, where the world of the living opens out [Mais déjà j'avais retraversé le fleuve aux ténébreux méandres, j'étais remonté à la surface où s'ouvre le monde des vivants, aussi si je répétais encore]' (*SG* 164; 159), the words which made perfect sense in his dream lose the very signifying differen*t*iation that presented them to him as a natural Ideal connection.[47]

Just as another language may appear to be nonsensical to a non-speaker, so the networks of sense bestowed as *noēteon* in dreams have no correlative in the intellectual world. If we could present the full, immanently sensible extension of a horizon, its difference would appear to be erased – this very differen*c*iation that separates it from other Ideas, and as such defines it, would depart. But in the totality of the *aiôn*, the totality in which the sensible extends across its horizons so that the virtual is real but not actual, Francis Jammes and a fork are relevant, indeed integral (as vague peaks of the 'fuzzy aggregate' captured upon waking) to grief for one's grandmother. In this way, the dream illustrates how forgetting *remains* in the novel, both remembered so that it could be written into it, and forgotten as its *restance* – the perceptive *sumplokē* that extends beyond or behind any concept.

Consider another example, related much earlier in the novel. Again, the dream occurs at a moment when a character is experiencing profound grief, though, on this occasion, it is Swann coming to terms with Odette's rejection of his love. Indeed, he appears to be entertaining the same kind of desire as the narrator grieving for his grandmother: to 'cling' on to as many 'presentations' of that beloved person as possible, and reject the apparent passing of time.

> Having in the past often thought with terror that one day he would cease to be in love with Odette, he had promised himself to be vigilant and, as soon as he felt his love was beginning to leave him, to cling to it, to keep hold of it. (S 379)

> Jadis ayant souvent pensé avec terreur qu'un jour il cesserait d'être épris d'Odette, il s'était promis d'être vigilant, et dès qu'il sentirait que son amour commencerait à le quitter, de s'accrocher à lui, de le retenir. (371)

Proustian irony signals that it is inevitable that Swann should eventually change in time, and lose contact with the fertile links to his love. This is why, to the narrator, 'it is so difficult to duplicate oneself and give oneself a truthful display of a feeling one no longer has [il est si difficile d'être double et de se donner le spectacle véridique d'un sentiment qu'on a cessé de posséder]' (S 379; 371), because a 'truthful display' is always in constant, deferring, becoming. As such, Swann invariably gives up on these attempts to imagine all these different, challenging Odettes, instead convincing himself 'that it would be better to rest a little [qu'il valait mieux se reposer un peu]' (S 379; 371).

The dream that Proust inserts into the text at this moment, however, points towards a different possibility. In 'the twilight of a dream', Swann finds himself

> walking with Mme Verdurin, Doctor Cottard, a young man in a fez whom he could not identify, the painter, Odette, Napoleon III and [the narrator's] grandfather, along a path that followed the sea and overhung it steeply, sometimes very high up, sometimes by a few metres only, so that one climbed and descended again constantly; those who were descending again were already no longer visible to those who were still climbing, what little daylight remained was failing and it seemed as though darkest night was about to descend on them at any moment. (S 380)

> Ce fut en dormant, dans le crépuscule d'un rêve. Il se promenait avec Mme Verdurin, le docteur Cottard, un jeune homme en fez qu'il ne pouvait identifier, le peintre, Odette, Napoléon III et mon grand-père, sur un chemin qui suivait la mer et la surplombait à pic tantôt de très haut, tantôt de quelques mètres seulement, de sorte qu'on montait et redescendait constamment ; ceux des promeneurs qui redescendaient déjà n'étaient plus visibles à ceux qui montaient encore, le peu de jour qui restât faiblissait et il semblait alors qu'une nuit noire allait s'étendre immédiatement. (372)

Without wishing to analyse the dreams depicted in the novel (which Proust seldom does, instead letting descriptions of these dreams simply remain, in all their strangeness, in the novel), this passage seems to describe a distinctly vague and 'fuzzy' perceptual environment. The defined 'presentation' of the scene is obscured: there is a description, but it blurs into the implex of its 'scene'. Swann *is* 'walk*ing* with' a group of people (whose constitution and position 'with' Swann surely changes by degrees) through environs 'that one climbed and descended again constantly' – 'constantly' one thing and then its opposite.

After the painter informs the group that Napoleon III has left with Odette because she is his mistress, Swann attempts to console the young man in the fez, who has burst into tears. But thus

> did Swann talk to himself, for the young man he had not been able to identify at first was also himself; like certain novelists, he had divided his personality between two characters, the one having the dream, and another he saw before him wearing a fez. (*S* 381)

> Swann se parlait-il à lui-même, car le jeune homme qu'il n'avait pu identifier d'abord était aussi lui ; comme certains romanciers, il avait distribué sa personnalité à deux personnages, celui qui faisait le rêve, et un qu'il voyait devant lui coiffé d'un fez. (373)

Swann is simultaneously himself and other: sensing this contradiction only intensifies – rather than disqualifies – it. And in the same movement of superimposition, Swann 'realises' that Napoleon III was, equally, in fact Forcheville. Swann confuses one for the other via

> a vague association of ideas, [. . .] but in reality, and in everything which the character in the dream represented to him and recalled to him, it was indeed Forcheville. (*S* 381)

> quelque vague association d'idées [. . .] mais en réalité, et pour tout ce que le personnage présent dans le rêve lui représentait et lui rappelait, c'était bien Forcheville. (373)

The same dream figure can be both Napoleon III and, simultaneously, Forcheville, because the logic of the dream, like the fully expanded perceptions of a *noēteon* (as with grief, Francis Jammes and a fork), produces and portrays the nonnumerical multiple as the total.

In describing the unusual events depicted here, it would be fine to say that the production and recollection of phenomena occurs differently in dreams. But what constitutes this difference? As a present second also represents 'many hours', and a domineering woman remains exactly and immanently herself while sprouting a heavy moustache, the narrator portrays the sensibly residual, multiple intensities that occur simultaneously in dreams. In such an environment, the inherent differen*t*iations within Ideas are exposed as a fully sensible multiplicity. The fact that a dream is only ever thought means that *it possesses no actual*, but only virtuality. As Deleuze notes,

> [the] virtual is opposed not to the real but to the actual [. . .] *The virtual is fully real insofar as it is virtual.* Exactly what Proust said of states of resonance must be said of the virtual: 'Real without being actual, ideal without being abstract'; and symbolic without being fictional. (*DR* 208)

None of the contents of these dreams are abstract, or 'purely' fictional, for they are comprised of the very content of the subject's lived experience: the hollow of Being.

Because every production in dreams is a full sense-giving *noēteon*, Swann can portray himself to himself as another. In consoling the fez-capped man – himself – Swann can externally perceive himself, because this virtual, intensive 'person' is made up of the elusively symbolic elements, the deferring *noēteon*, of what he might possibly think about himself, and nothing more. He cannot transcend his subjectivity even when he is awake, but in the dream it, and all of its 'symbolic' differences, are *fully immanent*, without the contradictions or spacings imagined by presentational or chronological form. Because there is no need for a form of himself, because the dream can articulate feelings without having to present or actualise them, or even give them form, Swann 'knows' that Napoleon III 'is' Forcheville, as much as he 'is' the young man in the fez. He is concurrently experiencing Carbone's '"I did not know" and "I have always known it"'. Here, the gap between the *noēteon* and its *noēton* is brought to its own illimitable conclusion:

> with the warmth that he felt in his own palm [Swann] modelled the *hollow* of a strange hand which he thought that he was clasping, and from feelings and impressions of which he was not yet conscious, devised peripeteias of a sort which, through their logical linking, would produce just at the right moment in Swann's sleep the person required to receive his love or prompt his awakening. (*S* 381, my emphasis)

> avec la chaleur sentie de sa propre paume il modelait *le creux* d'une main étrangère qu'il croyait serrer, et de sentiments et d'impressions dont il n'avait pas conscience encore, faisait naître comme des péripéties qui, par leur enchaînement logique, amèneraient à point nommé dans le sommeil de Swann le personnage nécessaire pour recevoir son amour ou provoquer son réveil. (373, my emphasis)

Swann is not yet conscious of these impressions, and, in many respects, he never shall be: but they are modelled by the 'hollow' that remains. By reducing them to a form, by describing these to himself upon awakening, the residuum that acquired intensive equity in the dream defers along the horizon of sense. Therefore, these 'feelings and impressions', in their synthesis in the awakened world, become conscious, but also compress the virtual-real of the dream into the virtual of chronological consciousness. They still retain the horizon of sense which any *noēteon* contracts or compresses in itself. The contraction is what marks the difference between this and the full, extensive actuality of the virtual given by the *aiôn*, sensed in and by the dream.

CONCLUSION: 'NOTHING, SORRY, I'M HALF ASLEEP.'

To conclude, let us consider one final, illustrative example of the aporia of sense in Proust's novel – one which shows his interest in the traces of sense injected *back* into the iterability of signification and language. During the course of an argument towards the end of the novel, Albertine stops short one word before the end of her sentence, blushing and bringing her hands to her mouth. The narrator guesses that she has almost revealed something untoward about her nature, something that she wanted to keep hidden. She goes on trying to suppress the aborted sentence, offering excuses and distractions, but the narrator's focus remains on the unspoken final word.

> But as she talked, my mind was still pursuing, in the waking, creative sleep of the unconscious (a sleep in which things which first passed us by almost unnoticed now take full shape, in which our sleeping hands grasp the key to secrets hitherto sought in vain), the search for the meaning of the interrupted sentence whose intended conclusion I wished to discover. (*PF* 313)

> Pendant qu'elle me parlait, se poursuivait en moi, dans le sommeil fort vivant et créateur de l'inconscient (sommeil où achèvent de se graver les choses qui nous effleurèrent seulement, où les mains endormies se saisissent de la clef qui ouvre, vainement cherchée jusque-là), la recherche de ce qu'elle avait voulu dire par la phrase interrompue dont j'aurais voulu savoir quelle eût été la fin. (*P* 326)

The 'creative sleep' of his unconscious grasps the 'key' to what he senses, because the presence-less 'thought' of his mind operates like that of his dreams. The narrator's awareness of Albertine's censored word *rests* as the traces of that sensed, but deferred, revelation.[48]

Not only does this horizon overlay the instant suppression of the guilty word, as she 'blushed crimson, [and] looked heartbroken [sa figure s'empourpra, elle eut l'air navré]' (*PF* 312; *P* 324), but it also reminds him of an 'angry look when [he] offered her a gift of money to give a grand dinner [son regard excédé quand je lui avais proposé un don d'argent pour donner un beau diner]' (*PF* 313; *P* 326) shortly before. The *noēteon* of these impressions reveals that the key to rendering intelligible the missing word is not in the literal, the given, and as such the *noēton* (the word 'break', which was the last word uttered by Albertine before cutting off). Rather, the sense that reveals its missing word reveals an extra context, a horizon, to the word he was hanging on to.

> And suddenly, the sight of her shrugging her shoulders as I made my offer took me back to the earlier words of her sentence. And I realized that she had not said '*casser*' but '*me faire casser*'. Horrors! (*PF* 314)
>
> Et tout à coup, le retour au regard avec haussement d'épaules qu'elle avait eu au moment de ma proposition qu'elle donnât un dîner me fit rétrograder aussi dans les mots de sa phrase. Et aussitôt je vis qu'elle n'avait pas dit « casser », mais « me faire casser ». Horreur ! (*P* 326–7)

In turn, the narrator (and indeed Proust himself), chooses not to fully explicate, or even fully cite the depths of her 'revolting expression [affreuse expression]' (*PF* 314; *P* 327). Albertine has revealed, in active sensibility, the depth of her interpretable character: and yet it only opens out into more frightening possibilities and doubts. Her excuse: 'Nothing, sorry, I'm half asleep [Non rien, je m'endormais à moitié]' (*PF* 312; *P* 324). Her undecidable sleep traces both *her* and the narrator's sensible hollows. Albertine's probable intended phrase – 'se faire casser le pot', a slang expression for anal sex – points towards an unknown sex life, and thereby activates the narrator's jealousy. As we will see in more detail in Chapter 5, jealousy in the novel marks a particular subset of the structure I am describing here, in which unknowable horizons multiply – or defer – towards infinity. It is altogether to the point that Albertine does not finish her sentence, because there is no end, no final revelation, in Proustian jealousy – and nor is there in the deferral of sense.

More than any *petit madeleine* episode, this scene seems to me emblematic of Proust's enterprise in the *Recherche*, a text concerned primarily with the incompletable traces of sense. To complete it, to finalise and fix Albertine's revelation[ ], would be to lose it. So instead, the narrator writes a version of it that breaks off, keeping all of its possibilities intact. What remains is, then, the bind *and* possibility of writing and inscription, the sense that must only ever be deferred so that it can – and will – go on. Characteristically, the scene commences with a premonition:

> she answered with a look of disgust and, to tell the truth, using words which I did not perfectly understand (even her opening ones, as she did not complete her reply). I was only able to supply them all a little later once I had guessed her meaning. One can hear retrospectively once one has understood. (*PF* 311)
>
> la réponse qu'elle me fit d'un air de dégoût, et dont, à dire vrai, je ne distinguai pas bien les mots (même les mots du commencement puisqu'elle ne

termina pas). Je ne les rétablis qu'un peu plus tard, quand j'eus deviné sa pensée. On entend rétrospectivement quand on a compris. (P 324)

The narrator splits the implex, dives through lines of time to *re*iterate Albertine's utterance into the text, which immediately *re*-disseminates as it is read. We 'know' things after we have *known* them: the 'I did not know' as mirror image of the 'I have always known it'.

Proust folds rhetoric back upon itself by injecting the infinity of sense into its possibly infinite description, still asking at which point he is ever truly awake. Indeed, in his reflections at the end of the novel, the narrator distinctly defines how important have been the *restance* of extraordinary, but in many senses inarticulate, correspondences in the virtual to his sense of the world. He had learned from M. de Charlus, to a greater extent than he did in his love affairs, 'how utterly neutral matter itself is, and how thought can give it any characteristics it wants [combien la matière est indifférente et que tout peut y être mis par la pensée]' (*FT* 219; 217). Human consciousness renders, across the varied lines of multiplicity and the virtual, the instant variation and Ideality that are added to the mere 'material' of perception. The 'astonishment [étonnement]' that he felt at each varied perception of his different loves proved that

> a memory persists only in a direction which diverges from the impression with which it originally coincided but from which it becomes increasingly remote. (*FT* 219)

> un souvenir ne se prolonge que dans une direction divergente de l'impression avec laquelle il a coïncidé d'abord et de laquelle il s'éloigne de plus en plus. (217)

This is the constant graft of the *noēteon* across chronological time, the inherent change instantly sensible across Ideas. It is this residuum which, without 'prolonging' the memory, renders it ever more differentiated in its deferral.

This may be why, in the paragraph that follows the one cited above, the narrator makes his well-known observation that,

> [i]n reality, each reader, when he is reading, is uniquely reading himself. The writer's work is only a kind of optical instrument which he offers the reader to enable him to discern what without this book he might not have perhaps seen in himself. (*FT* 219–20)

> En réalité, chaque lecteur est, quand il lit, le propre lecteur de soi-même. L'ouvrage de l'écrivain n'est qu'une espèce d'instrument optique qu'il offre au lecteur afin de lui permettre de discerner ce que, sans ce livre, il n'eût peut-être pas vu en soi-même. (217–18)

By chasing the fleeting yet 'forgettably' rich impressions of his narrator, Proust is bringing the possibility of the *noēteon* as close as possible to the intelligible, to its *noēton*, from which these impressions immediately disseminate. Merleau-Ponty describes 'this circularity, this intentional implication in a circle' that multiplies across the horizon, that senses *and* disseminates the trace. 'We will close the circle after the study of logos and history as Proust closes the circle when he comes to the moment where the narrator decides to write. The end of a philosophy is the account of its beginning.'[49] No wonder Proust's novel is so long: encircling, sensing or tracing even a single horizon might indeed go on for ever. In this sense, he is alerting his reader to pay attention to the *restance* of the residuum, the horizons which remain (as the deferring 'inscription') in every act of perception. He is asking the reader to question what exactly is sensible, and how far the trace of that sensible Idea, how far its essence, what is sensible *in* the sensible, might extend. This is why his narrator has 'always been so interested in the dreams we have while we are asleep, [. . .] because, making up in potency what they lack in duration, they help you better to understand the subjective [Si je m'étais toujours tant intéressé aux rêves que l'on a pendant le sommeil, [. . .] parce que, compensant la durée par la puissance, ils nous aident à mieux comprendre ce qu'a de subjectif]' (*FT* 220; 218),[50] the virtual, the synthesised sense lived, and resting across every 'sense'. 'The subjective' here is better understood in the potent, but durationally vague world of dreams precisely because, like the 'subject' of the book the voice is becoming at the opening of the *Recherche*, they take on the infinitely subdividable quality of the *aiôn* – they compensate duration with intensity. In dreams, subject and object[ ] are indistinguishable in their *engainement*, the operative intentionality that, once deferred as sense, makes chronology possible. Thus the narrator notes how, in his dreams, he had

> often seen in one night, in one minute of one night, remote periods of time, consigned to those vast distances at which we can no longer distinguish the feeling we had then. (*FT* 220–1)
>
> N'avais-je pas vu souvent en une nuit, en une minute d'une nuit, des temps bien lointains, relégués à ces distances énormes où nous ne pouvons presque plus rien distinguer des sentiments que nous y éprouvions? (218–19)

In dreams, he can sense the *restance* of all these horizons, all of the intensity of differen*t*iation, at once. In the enormous, virtual project of his novel, Proust traces the 'always' of the *aiôn* throughout the long horizon of each of 'our' deferring senses – a trace that is inscribed and that we can dream of, but can never, no matter how many times we may re-read it, make present.

NOTES

1. Deleuze, *Desert Islands*, 101.
2. See also Gilles Deleuze, *Cinema II: The Time-Image*, trans. Hugh Tomlinson and Robert Galeta (London and New York: Bloomsbury, 2013), 83–4, which refers to the 'purely virtual images which have been constantly preserved in time' of 'deeper and deeper circuits which are themselves virtual, which each time mobilize the whole of the past'; also *What is Philosophy?*, which proposes that in 'general, a state of affairs does not actualize a chaotic virtual without taking from it a *potential* that is distributed in the system of coordinates. From the virtual that it actualizes it draws a potential that it appropriates' (*WP* 122). The virtual organises temporalities that are not actual into an appropriated potential: that is, as the horizon of sense.
3. As Derrida notes when discussing the implex, '[p]resence is never present. The possibility – or the potency – of the present is but its own limit, its inner fold, its impossibility – or its impotence' (*D* 303).
4. Deleuze's thinking here follows that of one of his great philosophical influences, Henri Bergson. When he speaks of duration, Bergson notes that its 'so-called quantity is really a quality, [. . .] which we cannot curtail by an instant without altering the nature of the facts which fill it'. Henri Bergson, *Time and Free Will: An Essay on the Immediate Data of Consciousness*, trans. Frank Lubecki Pogson (London: Allen & Unwin, 1910), 197–8.
5. Bergson argues that generative change in a conceptual whole across duration 'alters the nature, the appearance and, as it were, the rhythm of this whole; without this interpenetration and this, so to speak, qualitative progress, no addition would be possible. Hence it is through the quality of quantity that we form the idea of quantity without quality.' Bergson, *Time and Free Will*, 123. The whole is never re*placed*: its developmental totality assumes and defers any question of presence.
6. Gilles Deleuze, *Cinema I: The Movement-Image*, trans. Hugh Tomlinson and Barbara Habberjam (London and New York: Bloomsbury, 2013), 110.
7. This sense of qualitative productivity is a key element of Deleuze's philosophy, but it is one with a long history, particularly in the various lineages of Neoplatonism. See Éric Alliez, *Capital Times: Tales from the Conquest of Time*, trans. Georges Van Den Abbeele (Minneapolis: University of Minnesota Press, 1996), 26–73. Pseudo-Dionysius, a notable Christian Neoplatonist, notes how light can be dispersed from distinct sources but still forms an uninterrupted unity, demonstrating how there is 'distinction in unity and there is unity in distinction'. Peter Sloterdijk discusses this analogy in *Spheres, Volume 1: Bubbles: Microspherology*, trans. Wieland Hoban (London: Semiotexte, 2011), 589–99.
8. Compagnon, *Proust between Two Centuries*, 52. Compagnon also shows how Vinteuil's *petite phrase* changes in Swann's perception of it, its traces

becoming dividually new. 'The new alloy, Swann-and-Odette, the uneasy merging of a self constituted by affect made intelligible, yet tortured by inexorable uncertainty, exacts instability to exist.' Compagnon, *Proust between Two Centuries*, 92.
9. Henri Bergson, *Matter and Memory*, trans. Margaret Paul and W. Scott Palmer (London: Allen and Unwin, 1912), 294.
10. Lyotard, *The Inhuman*, 147.
11. As Paul Patton notes, Deleuze's 'rejection of the representational image of thought' is one 'of the most fundamental commitments upheld throughout his philosophy' – along with 'his long-standing interest in the mobility of philosophical concepts'. This challenges Husserlian phenomenology's unwavering reliance on the *epoché* and its origin in situated, present-able intentionality. Patton, *Deleuzian Concepts* (Stanford: Stanford University Press, 2010), 21.
12. Éric Alliez, *The Signature of the World, or, What is Deleuze and Guattari's philosophy?* trans. Eliot Ross Albert and Alberto Toscano (London and New York: Continuum, 2004), 66.
13. Gilles Deleuze, quoted in François Dosse, *Gilles Deleuze and Félix Guattari: Intersecting Lives*, trans. Deborah Glassman (New York: Columbia University Press, 2010), 407.
14. As Colebrook argues, in 'addition to his creative response to structuralism and psychoanalysis Deleuze's work can also be seen as a radicalization of phenomenology'. Colebrook, *Gilles Deleuze*, 6.
15. Elizabeth Grosz describes how this epitomises 'Deleuze's disagreement with phenomenology', because '[s]ensations are mobile and mobilizing forces, not quite subjective or experiential [...] and yet not fully objective or measurable in a way that material objects are'. *Chaos, Territory, Art: Deleuze and the Framing of the Earth* (New York: Columbia University Press, 2008), 57.
16. Edmund Husserl, *The Phenomenology of Internal Time-Consciousness*, trans. James Churchill (Bloomington, IN: Indiana University Press, 1964), 32, my emphasis.
17. Edmund Husserl, *Cartesian Meditations: An Introduction to Phenomenology*, trans. Dorion Cairns (The Hague: Nijhoff, 1960), 39.
18. Husserl, *Cartesian Meditations*, 39.
19. Husserl, *Cartesian Meditations*, 40.
20. Husserl, *The Phenomenology of Internal Time-Consciousness*, 75.
21. Husserl, *Cartesian Meditations*, 44.
22. Husserl, *The Phenomenology of Internal Time-Consciousness*, 75.
23. Edmund Husserl, *Ideas: General Introduction to Pure Phenomenology*, trans. W. R. Boyce Gibson (London: Allen &Unwin, 1932), 259.
24. Husserl, *Ideas*, 259.
25. Husserl, *Cartesian Meditations*, 51.
26. As Drucilla Cornell notes, Derrida also bases his critique of phenomenology on 'the deconstruction of the distinction between *Sinn/Bedeutung*

upon which Husserl relied to justify the very concept of a transcendental signifier'. Drucilla Cornell, 'Where Love Begins', in *Derrida and Feminism: Recasting the Question of Woman*, ed. Ellen K. Feder, Mary C. Rawlinson and Emily Zakin (New York and London: Routledge, 1997), 163.

27. Bergson, *Matter and Memory*, 24.
28. Bray notes that Proust begins the novel with the 'metaphysically troubling experience of a dreamer who awakens without being able to "reenter" the body'. Patrick M. Bray, *The Novel Map: Space and Subjectivity in Nineteenth-Century French Fiction* (Evanston: Northwestern University Press, 2013), 102.
29. Mauro Carbone, *An Unprecedented Deformation: Marcel Proust and the Sensible Ideas*, trans. Niall Keane (Albany: State University of New York Press, 2010), 64.
30. Jean-Pierre Vernant, *Myth and Thought among the Greeks* (London: Routledge & Kegan Paul, 1983), 90.
31. As Proust's narrator observes in the single explicit reference to Bergson in the novel, we 'possess all our memories, if not the faculty of recalling them [. . .] we are totally steeped in them [Nous possédons tous nos souvenirs, sinon la faculté de nous les rappeler [. . .] ils nous baignent tout entiers]' (*SG* 380; 374). The focus of the reflection is, however, on the property of memories. If we cannot answer for 'a memory we cannot recall [qu'est-ce qu'un souvenir qu'on ne se rappelle pas ?]' (*SG* 380; 374), then these memories that were our lived experience, and which we have forgotten are no different from someone else's lived experience we might also have forgotten – an experience we haven't lived but equally 'cannot recall'. The aporia of forgetting is moreover the aporia of *appropriating* subjectivity ('becoming' the subject of the book we are reading as we fall asleep), which is always in a fractal process of dispossession.
32. Carbone, *An Unprecedented Deformation*, 65.
33. Carbone, *An Unprecedented Deformation*, 65.
34. Carbone, *An Unprecedented Deformation*, 65.
35. Indeed, here it is more important than ever to recognise Bergson's injunction never to spatialise (or present) time. These chiasmata are the various meetings of times dividually, as ever new productions. A concurrently multiple chiasm of varied lines seems impossible in chronological differenciation, but this is the crux of the *aiôn*, an infinity that transcends its very terms.
36. As a final word on the difficult ontology of forgetting, consider Derrida's remarks on Nietzsche's note 'I have forgotten my umbrella' in *Spurs*: 'as a trace which has been marked in what *remains* of this nonfragment, such an account would withdraw it from any assured horizon of a hermeneutic question' – to conjure the forgetting is to give it, to appropriate it, which is not to forget it. Derrida, *Spurs*, 127.
37. Carbone, *An Unprecedented Deformation*, 66.
38. Carbone, *An Unprecedented Deformation*, 66.

39. Carbone, *An Unprecedented Deformation*, 64.
40. Merleau-Ponty cited in Carbone, *An Unprecedented Deformation*, 66. Carbone's emphasis.
41. Maurice Merleau-Ponty, *The Visible and the Invisible*, trans. Alphonso Lingis (Evanston: Northwestern University Press, 1968), 243.
42. Carbone, *The Thinking of the Sensible*, 11. Simon also refers to the 'sillon' mentioned in this passage as that which 'defines vision as *engainement*, and style as founded on the "coils" which represent a primordial "metaphor"' – the operative hollow of sense. Simon, *Trafics de Proust*, 61.
43. Merleau-Ponty, *The Visible and the Invisible*, 221.
44. Carbone, *The Thinking of the Sensible*, 12.
45. Carbone, *The Thinking of the Sensible*, 12.
46. Carbone, *The Thinking of the Sensible*, 12.
47. Elsner draws on Derrida to describe the how dreams present forms without presenting them, as an 'image without a model', or a deferring in-between. 'Imagination and reality become so intricately intertwined [in dreams], that all differences seemingly fade away and what emerges is a "milieu", an in-between state.' Elsner, *Mourning and Creativity in Proust*, 112.
48. On this scene, see Malcolm Bowie, *Freud, Proust, and Lacan: Theory as Fiction* (Cambridge and New York: Cambridge University Press, 1987), 72–3, in which he refers to this exchange as an example of Proust's depiction of Freudian 'failed performances (*Fehlleistung*)' that, although rare in the novel, 'provide the narrator with a direct route to the realm of unconscious motivation'.
49. Merleau-Ponty, *The Visible and the Invisible*, 177.
50. Moncrieff's translation is more useful here: 'If I have always been so interested in dreams, is it not because, compensating duration with intensity they help us to understand better what is subjective?' Proust, *Remembrance of Things Past, Volume Two*, trans. C. K. Scott Moncrieff (Ware, Hertfordshire: Wordsworth Editions, 2006), 1181.

3. Desire: Deferring a Productive Without

This book has so far studied the dividual flow of Proust's text, its harnessing of the temporal and phenomenal peculiarities of literature to challenge finite conceptions of presentational logic. In the following chapters, I suggest that the affective arc that shapes the novel's development is a fitting way to examine the productive *restance* of the *Recherche*. By this point, we can begin to interpret the complexities of Proust's narrative project, both in the sense of his transversal narrative voice, and how it is applied to horizons of sense across the chiasmata of the work's narrators. This chapter focuses on how desire, as depicted by the narrator in the early volumes, disseminates this difficult tension between difference, sense, deferral and apparently unifying form. In order to develop a model of Proustian desire, which is a much-discussed theme of the *Recherche*,[1] I adopt certain concepts outlined by Deleuze, especially in his work with Guattari. In particular, their reading of schizophrenic desire in *Anti-Oedipus* provides a productive perspective on the deferring sense of Proustian desire, which operates in the novel as a motivating principle to explore the present-less trace of Being itself. My method here will be to adduce a series of passages from the novel in which this pattern can be traced – the pattern, that is, of a dispersive desire without a determinate object, the origin of which is always absent. The lack of this specific, identifiable and formal object of desire, and the productiveness of this 'without', will be key to my reading. The prioritization of the movement of sense over the presentation of form in Proustian desire is figured, in the examples I will discuss, by the idea of place, and of a kind of *genius loci* as an unpresentable object of desire.[2]

DESIRING THE BOIS, FOREIGN TO ITSELF

To begin with, I would like to consider a passage at the end of the first volume, *Du côté de chez Swann*, in which the narrator describes the iterative walks he used to take through Paris's Bois de Boulogne in his youth. Although this section is not one of the parts of the novel that we immediately associate with the themes of sexuality and desire, it provides a good example of how Proustian desire is motivated by fractal difference-in-unity. In this section, the narrator describes 'the complexity of the Bois de Boulogne which makes it an artificial place and, in the zoological or mythological sense of the word, a Garden [Cette complexité du Bois de Boulogne qui en fait un lieu factice et, dans le sens zoologique ou mythologique du mot, un Jardin]' (S 424; 414) – a varied, complex arrangement of harmonic differences. As he wanders through the Bois, he notes the tremendous variety and vibrancy of the colours and shapes of its plants and trees at this particular time of year, observing that the 'different parts of the Bois, merging so completely in summer in the thickness and monotony of their green, were now separated [Les différentes parties du Bois, mieux confondues l'été dans l'épaisseur et la monotonie des verdures, se trouvaient dégagées]' (S 426; 415). The Bois is constituted by its differences: it changes not only from tree to tree, but also season to season. In particular, on this day the narrator was aware that it

> was the hour and it was the season in which the Bois seems perhaps the most manifold, not only because it is more subdivided, but also because it is subdivided differently. (S 425)

> C'était l'heure et c'était la saison où le Bois semble peut-être le plus multiple, non seulement parce qu'il est plus subdivisé, mais encore parce qu'il l'est autrement. (414)

As such, the difference itself, 'subdivided' in an unusual manner, draws to the narrator's attention the variety of intensities within the disseminating 'name' Bois de Boulogne.

This is a Bois whose constitutive features (the trees, their leaves, an ampelopsis or orange-red chestnut) seem to trace for the narrator a certain eddying truth. All of these conjunctive differences contingently and interdependently constitute this Bois: while they necessarily *are* this Idea, they cannot be presented to him at once. In this example, Proust's narrator not only contends with the phenomenological problem of presenting form, but also engages with the presence of particular places: how can the very environs before him offer a sense of themselves without originating each component part – and how to divide up these infinitesimal, unifying differences? Because the 'present' Bois is indistinguishable from an abyssal whole rooted in its own difference, we can note a parallel with the deferring ~~voice~~ of the narrator's differing selves, which are seemingly united in the novel, their various temporalities incorporated in a whole that defers its parts while constituting them. The racinating function that presents and absents these narrators as one reads further into the implex of their utterance is the same function that uproots the difference of the Bois that this narrator senses, and attempts to depict.

In describing the resplendent, unique points of difference provided in separation *within* the Bois, the narrator notes that, from these 'distinct parts [différentes parties]',

> [o]pen spaces made visible the entrance to almost every one of them, or a sumptuous bit of foliage marked it like a banner. One could distinguish, as on a coloured map, Armenonville, the Pré Catalan, Madrid, the Race Course, the shores of the lake. From time to time there would appear some useless construction, a fake grotto, a mill for which the trees parted to make room or which a lawn carried forwards on its soft platform. One sensed that the Bois was not merely a wood, that it fulfilled a purpose foreign to the life of its trees. (S 426)

> Des espaces plus éclaircis laissaient voir l'entrée de presque toutes, ou bien un feuillage somptueux la désignait comme une oriflamme. On distinguait, comme sur une carte en couleur, Armenonville, le Pré Catelan, Madrid, le Champ de courses, les bords du Lac. Par moments apparaissait quelque construction inutile, une fausse grotte, un moulin à qui les arbres en s'écartant faisaient place ou qu'une pelouse portait en avant sur sa moelleuse plateforme. On sentait que le Bois n'était pas qu'un bois, qu'il répondait à une destination étrangère à la vie de ses arbres. (415)

The more the narrator senses the Bois, and with each 'entrance' to it that his perception makes 'visible', the greater, the more complex the Idea – and even the name – of the Bois, becomes. Such a description of the Bois is a dividual production comprised strictly of nonnumerical multiplicity. It describes each 'sumptuous bit' as deriving from *and* constituting 'distinct parts' that are present and absent as the stubborn remainder, the *restance* of the unity that the singular name appropriates, or writes over. Just as each tree transcends (while immanently constituting) its many leaves and component parts, so does the Bois itself: it can mean anything from 'a piece of yellow Persian masonry patterned in blue [une jaune maçonnerie persane à dessins bleus]' to 'a tree clothed in Japanese ivy [un arbre habillé de vigne vierge]' (S 426; 415), which represent and 're-absent' these constituent features. The plenitude that might be the presentable, definable 'Bois de Boulogne' the narrator describes defers itself even as he thinks its definition can be taken from one of those distinct elements. The most interesting concept in this section for my purpose here is the attempt of the ~~voice~~ to describe such a sensible multiplicity. In noting that the Bois existed beyond the purpose of these components, 'for a purpose foreign to the life of its trees', he signals a desire to uncover the constitutive traces that the sense of this place offers to him. In following the networks given as sense towards what I have called its *noēteon* – the unintelligible horizon of its sensible multiplicity – the narrator is attempting to trace the trace, to tie down its deferring, essential differen*t*iation, which seems to be an impossible task. The example of the Bois indicates the simultaneity of possible 'presentations' that any place gives him, without ever forming a totalised, present, presence.

But the motivation for describing this is not aesthetic, or abstract. Immediately following the above extract, the narrator emphatically reveals the feeling that evoked his pleasure among this autumn Bois:

> the exhilaration I was experiencing was not caused merely by an admiration for autumn, but by some desire. The great source of a joy which the soul feels at first without recognizing its cause, without understanding that it is motivated by nothing outside. And so I looked at the trees with an unsatisfied tenderness that passed beyond them and went on without my knowing it towards that masterpiece of lovely strolling women which they enclose each day for several hours. (*S* 426)

> l'exaltation que j'éprouvais n'était pas causée que par l'admiration de l'automne, mais par un désir. Grande source d'une joie que l'âme ressent d'abord sans en reconnaître la cause, sans comprendre que rien au dehors ne la motive. Ainsi regardais-je les arbres avec une tendresse insatisfaite qui les dépassait et se portait à mon insu vers ce chef-d'œuvre des belles promeneuses qu'ils enferment chaque jour pendant quelques heures. (415–16)

It is to desire that this overwhelming sense is attributed. Or does the overwhelming sense motivate the desire? The difficult order of attribution here attests to how this passage, as with countless others from the novel, frays its temporalisation even as it asserts it. This ~~voice~~ attributes his 'exhilaration' to 'some desire' – but one which he *felt* 'without recognizing its cause'. The feeling precedes its own cause, or origin. And most critically, because the ~~voice~~ attributes this to desire without being able to acknowledge its origin, this desire *exists*, is thought and sensed, before it can be presented as an object, as a thing or form – as a 'representational image of thought'. Multiple narrators or ~~voices~~ can lay claim to the sense of this desire because its *noēteon* is sensible before it can be called desire; this instituting repetition, which gives the multiplicity of ~~voices~~, also gives this desire – or, more accurately, gives it without a giving that can be presented or formalised.[3] As each attempt to define this desire, after it has been sensed, chases every other down the abyss in search of its presentation, the *sumplokē* of the text defers that origin, noting only that this 'unsatisfied tenderness' is due to what 'passed beyond' its stimuli. The key to the excerpt is 'his' (any of these narrators, sensible as or by textual *restance*) having felt the desire without being conscious of it. No one part of this multiplicity can be singly *named* as the cause, yet the name of each thing contributes to it. Thus, while perceiving the trees themselves, he is as far as possible towards not perceiving them at all: a perception which 'passed beyond them' relies on them to produce the incorporative, nonnumerical absences that are the differen*t*iation of this longing. There is a unity here that is not intelligible; it *is*, but *isn't* – it is present-able only as a *sumplokē*, without its, or any, presence.

Deleuze and Guattari's notion of schizophrenic desire can help us explicate the unconsciously motivated desire depicted in this passage, and, as I will argue, in Proust's novel more generally. Schizophrenic desire is marked by the same kind of transversal movement of many of Deleuze's philosophical concepts.[4] In *Anti-Oedipus*, Deleuze and Guattari examine the binding difference that precedes representation in sense and desire.[5] They understand that the 'full body is the unengendered, but filiation is the first character of inscription marked on this body' (*AO* 154): sense is the absent origin of perception that delivers correspondence and difference – filiation and variety – before perception 'itself', before its formalised, 'representational image of thought'. This accords with a breakdown of the phenomenological transcendental-immanent distinction: the full body is seemingly present, but its presence implicates the various absences of the filiations it presents. As Deleuze and Guattari write, we already 'know the nature of this intensive filiation, this inclusive disjunction where everything divides, but into itself, and where the same being is everywhere, on every side, at every level, *differing only in intensity*' (*AO* 154). This is the Bois itself, dividual, with its various emergent percepts – the Pré Catalan or a 'beautiful strolling woman' – tracing their way *towards* their full presentation, only ever to be deferred. The 'same included being traverses indivisible distances on the full body, and passes through all the singularities, all the intensities of a synthesis that shifts and reproduces itself' (*AO* 154). In arguing that the intensities of desire are sensible prior to (or rather *always*, from the multiplicity of the *aiôn*) its originating form or intelligibility, Deleuze and Guattari describe an atemporal, transversal sense of desire as a schizophrenic process rather than a constructed, hierarchised model which formalises its 'causes' (which are intensities, and therefore sensible *at once*). While Michel Foucault, notably one of the strongest supporters of *Anti-Oedipus*,[6] nonetheless refused its hypothesis of productive desire, arguing that desire can only ever relate to a lack,[7] Proust, via Deleuze and Guattari, can teach us that desire is instead the *lack of lack*, in so far as it is the manifestly productive sense of the trace, modelled throughout the hollow of Being itself. The sense of desire precedes its causes, origins and presentation as intensity, tracing an *aiôn* that gives this sense without giving it – a lack that lacks only its lack. And to 'present' this lack, to 'present' the trace, would only present a(nother) deferral. Once desire is thought of outside of a metaphysics bound to presence, we can note its abyssal function as the work of the trace. Desire lacks only the trace, and can only ever move towards that trace's productive deferral, *ad infinitum* as the very movement of Being, or desire, as the narrator's object-less desiring in the Bois scene indicates.

In *Anti-Oedipus*, Deleuze and Guattari affirm R. D. Laing's definition of the schizophrenic process as 'a voyage of initiation, a transcendental experience' (AO 84). While they are referring here to hallucination or delirium, we can note that the same process applies to sense in consciousness more generally, 'that there is no reason to oppose an interior voyage to exterior ones' (AO 84). In that manner, we might describe Proust's narrator's passage through the immanent-transcendent Bois as the lack of that 'outside' which had so little to do with the 'great source of joy' rendered by his soul. Like the *sumplokē*, this Bois *is* to the narrator, precisely because it incorporates its 'is not'. It is more than the life of its trees – the 'purpose' that programs his desire – but only because their actuality presents various virtual absences to him. This is the desire that is sensed in its contractive flash by the narrator's 'soul', motivating him 'without [his] knowing'. As Deleuze and Guattari put it,

> [this] is not a case of an hallucinatory experience nor of a delirious mode of thought, but a feeling, a series of emotions or feelings as a consummation and a consumption of intensive qualities [. . .] The intensive emotion, the affect, is both the common root and the principle of differentiation of deliriums and hallucinations. (AO 84)

This 'delirium' arises from the integration of these intensive qualities *as* the contentious present plenitude of *restance*. Just as in this passage the narrator notes that the expression 'Bois de Boulogne' is an insufficient articulation of the purpose it held for him, and as the trees themselves are an inadequate signifier for the *sumplokē* of associations they conjure and disseminate, so do the signifiers 'feeling' or 'affect' compress the intensive absences of sense.

It is for this reason that Deleuze and Guattari argue that the 'schizophrenic process' is what is reached towards in the desiring act: it is the movement of this fully virtual contraction that can be made present only by absenting its formal multiplicity. For them, schizophrenic desire is this process of encoding while decoding sense, the movement of the self towards the various forms of becoming that are of the 'intense and intensive order' which cannot be explicated in full, knowable presentation (*AO* 85). Desire comes about in the schizophrenic transversal of multiplicity, of a metaphysics of becoming opposed to presentable 'form'. In the same way, Proust's narrating ~~voice~~ describes his desires as following the flows of a *noēteon* that infers the multiplicities of lost time – using literature to attempt to trace a trace. It is thus crucial that Proust's narrator should describe this sensation (that becomes a narrated event) as he does in the above extracts: he notes that not only was he staring at the trees 'with an unsatisfied tenderness that passed beyond them', but that this longing became directed towards 'that masterpiece of lovely strolling wom*en*'. The iterability of this last expression is noteworthy. Just as the Bois 'fulfilled a purpose foreign to the life of its trees', so does the narrator direct his description of this sensed *noēteon* towards *some*thing that should not be defined, that should remain abstract and multiple so as to defer at the very point that it might be defined. In its iterability, language is as schizophrenic as desire.

The narrator's feeling about the Bois may not be one of the novel's most important meditations on the theme of desire, but it importantly foregrounds the movement that concerns me here. The tension between the Bois and its individual trees, parts or any deferring properties, works like the tension between the different temporal moments of narration in the novel, creating a structure of *restance* or the trace. The key point for me to emphasise here, moreover, is that the atemporal, present-absent movement of this indistinction between the one and the many, the particular instance and the dividual whole, mirrors the repetition that characterises, for Deleuze and Guattari, the sense of desire. In the following section, I will highlight the way that desire in the novel is motivated by a sense of overweighing, unpresentable multiplicity, from a theoretical perspective. Following this theoretical discussion, I will return to the link we have begun to explore between desire and a certain sense of place, which is never totalised, always more extensive, and multiple.

DESIRING (WITHOUT) ITSELF

Proustian desire operates along the same lines as this model developed by Deleuze and Guattari: it is motivated by decoded flows of dividual intensity, at the breakdown of the immanent/transcendent distinction. In this model, the objects of desire are never static, but rather always deferring: weaving themselves tighter into their *noēteon*. As Deleuze and Guattari suggest, the 'reality of the object, insofar as it is produced by desire, is thus a *psychic reality*' (AO 26): its immanent reality is inextricably transcendent, even as it appears. Desire 'is the set of *passive syntheses* that engineer partial objects, flows, and bodies, and that function as units of production. The real is the end product, the result of the passive syntheses of desire as autoproduction of the unconscious' (AO 26). Desires emerges, desire *desires*, because of the necessary passive synthesis of difference – textual *and* temporal – as the deferral of intelligible, and thus iterable, form or differen*c*iation. Desire is always for what exceeds the present. In this sense, desire in Proust's oeuvre finds itself bound within the primordial order of the trace: temporality, property and priority are broken down across the *noēteon* that disperses presence. Approaching the motif of desire in Proust's novel from this perspective challenges conceptions of unity, and the *presence* of those conceptions, in the work. In turn, it reopens the aporetic nature of Proust's specifically literary project – the *sumplokē* of his text that is real, present and whole only in so far as it is none of these things.

One of the most influential accounts of desire in the *Recherche* is René Girard's reading of the novel in *Deceit, Desire and the Novel* (1965). For Girard, all desire is an act of mimesis: the subject's imitation of a mediator, who acts as 'a veritable artificial sun, [from whom] descends a mysterious ray which makes the object shine with a false brilliance'.[8] This approach allows Girard to refute the 'symbolist' reading of Proustian desire. Girard takes the example of the narrator's desire to see the great Berma in the role of Phèdre, which seems not to be mimetic because, as he notes, 'the narrator has never seen her. Nor is it memory of previous performances; the child has had no direct contact with the dramatic art.' But as far as Girard is concerned, the 'symbolist' argument falls apart here because 'the narrator has not *invented* the great Berma' but rather, has heard of her excellence through Bergotte: someone who is not only an artist, but a figure who holds a revered position within the Swann family circle, or, as Girard puts it, those who 'are the priests of a religion of which Bergotte is the God'.[9] Thus, Bergotte is a mediator for the narrator's desire: he wishes to be like, or even *be* Bergotte, and this is the source of his mimetic desire.

Compelling as it is, the very clarity of Girard's reading of Proust makes it subject to a Derridean critique of *parousia*. The image of triangular desire wants to apply a structured geometry, to locate and present desire in a defined set of vertices. But how can Girard's 'veritable artificial sun', this vertex, stay static: how can the object or mediator sign always as the same thing, and always retain the same meaning? We can usefully refer here to Derrida's description in *Signsponge* of the sun as

> a referent without possible substitute, without reproduction and without dissemination, without analog; as an absolute referent which is therefore outside of language, it seems not to let itself be suspended in its name, thereby escaping any placement in the text, any superimprinting remark, any placement in the abyss as well. (*SS* 140)

Because the sun is total, inimitable or non-iterable in its singularity, it exceeds any system – especially language. It cannot be 'suspended in its name' because it cannot be differen*ci*ated. It cannot belong to any system 'by virtue of its transcendental position (*epekeina tes ousias*) [. . .] One should not be able to put it into the abyss because it is the abyss' (*SS* 140). Girard's idea of an 'artificial sun' seems contentious then, but even if it can assume this *epekeina tēs ousias* and *become*, or rather *appropriate*, any system or model that it takes part in, it can only succeed in generating the abyss of desire. The model falls victim to the abyssal structure of iterability. Any vertex of the triangle is possibly, and becomes, all of the others, and as such, desire flows schizophrenically through its abyss, deferring without presence, tautologising any stricture.[10]

Deleuze and Guattari's critique of Freud's Oedipal triangle makes clear how their schizophrenic model of desire unpicks the Girardian structure of imitation. The Oedipal triangle, they write, 'implies in its essence a constituent prohibition, and that conditions the differentiation between persons: prohibition of incest with the mother, prohibition against taking the father's place' (*AO* 70). According to the logic of this imperative differen*ci*ation, Oedipal triangulation applies a 'strange sort of reasoning [which] leads one to conclude that since *it* is forbidden, *that very thing* was desired' (*AO* 70). The Oedipal model does not take account of the diversity of nonnumerical multiplicities which flow through and constitute subjectivity. Such a model cannot apply to all cases, nor to all (or any) of the differences that make every case different. Moreover, Deleuze and Guattari question the serial temporal sequencing of the Oedipal triangle. For them, there is nothing *prior* to the trace that gives difference: 'desire receives its first complete objects and is forbidden them at one and the same time' (*AO* 70). Because the 'schizophrenic process' of desire is always already inscribed, there can be no question of sequentiality in the model and the desire, as in Girard's account. Disseminating difference exists prior to 'modelled' desire, and it is this difference, and its schizophrenic interpretation, that *produces* desire – the 'soul' that Proust describes as sensing his narrator's desire, before that soul can be conscious of desire's cause.

The Oedipal triangle is thus not more stable than the Girardian triangle of mimetic desire. Deleuze and Guattari's critique of triangulation, of the difference-within-unity that appropriates the sense of form, allows us to see the analogy between desire and the trace[ ] of *restance*. As desire extends out into the external world, a triangulation could still apply, but its path from subject to object more likely resembles a thrown harpoon, one whose rope has split and frayed into illimitable points. This is because, as Per Bjørnar Grande notes, Proust is always interested in the way that the object of desire is dispersed in the 'time-span of a lifetime' – that is, in memory.[11] The 'mediation' which is this threadbare rope (the line that diverges from desiring-subject to desired-object) incorporates all of the necessary points in time *as* the pure *noēteon* of the desired object. Deleuze and Guattari cite Freud's insistent deployment of a 'common, transcendent, absent something' which operates as a '3+1', an extensive point to the triangle,[12] which transcends 'in order to designate "the" signifier that distributes the effects of meaning throughout the chain' (*AO* 73) – the divergent flow of desire. Deleuze and Guattari, however, problematise the singular 'the' in this excerpt: such a 'definitive' article overlooks the deferral, the opening out to the undetermined abyss of desire's sens*ing*. Desire, for them, is more than 'a despotic signifier from whose law the entire chain seems consequently to be suspended, each link triangulated. There we have a curious paralogism implying a transcendent use of the synthesis of the unconscious' (*AO* 73). The transcendent object is not simply the despotic signifier that determines the laws of the triangulation.[13] Rather, each vertex of such a triangle, in transcending these forms, dissolves into the multiple, possible flows of desire – all of which signify. It is transcendent because its imagined presence leads the subject immediately down the *propre* abyss of traces, that constitute 'its' form. Any vertex of a model for desire splits into its own vertices, of triangles in triangles – the points or objects that seek to *represent* desire are always-already overwhelmed by the deferring thread of desire's multiplicity.

The role of the synthesis, the constant making-virtual of consciousness, is to differen*ti*ate all the sensible data from its past[ ]. All the various signifiers exist as consciousness because they *have been*, they constitute the abyss of the *aiôn* and pull the subject towards explicating them. As such, the various vertices of the model flow towards the only form it can take, the constantly deferring *is* of the past[ ], the illimitable differen*t*iation of the *aiôn*. For Deleuze and Guattari, Freud's 'greatness lies in having determined the essence or nature of desire, no longer in relation to objects, aims, or even sources (territories), but as an abstract subjective essence' (*AO* 270). No longer must we affirm a role, or an object, for desire, but merely interpret it *as* subjectivity: the self's 'great decoded flows', 'the wide open spaces glimpsed for a moment', the 'drift of desire' (*AO* 270). In the instant of desiring, coming to the soul before its subject can be conscious of its cause, its line, or rather, its inaugurating bend away from the subject outwards (sometimes to an object, if the harpoon survives the journey through the abyss) splits across infinite varieties of pastness, of great decoded flows of subjectivity that are anchored across the great expanses of what *has been known*, of the times that *have been lost* – each only glimpsed for a moment.

Schizophrenic desire is desire as constantly and essentially productive, as producing, even in the generation of a lack, the movement towards the trace of this lack, the lack of the lack, the abyss of the *propre*, of the possibility of signing (for) the self. It instructs us that desire, even in lack, can only ever be productive, *producing* a creative, positive lack and producing *its* lack. In this respect, with Proust's novel as a mediator, Deleuze and Guattari's reading of desire can be compared to Derrida's logic of the abyss. In *The Post Card*, Derrida notes thus that the supplementary abyss of desire implodes any reasoning based on strictures, because 'if they necessarily produce dialectial *effects*, for example the entire dialectic said to be of the master and slave, they do not know negativity, lack, opposition; in this graphics desire is without "without," is a *without* without *without*' (*PC* 401). Desire, programming amongst *its* abyss, cannot know lack or supplementarity – it merely produces a dividual sense of what overflows, or a trace that desire is the movement towards, but which can only ever trace another trace to be once more desired. In Proust's attention to the forms that lead down this abyss of the trace (of its instituting repetition or its 'hollow'), we can note the strange, multiplying deferral of writing desire, writing '*without*s without *without*', just as his narrating ~~voice~~ defers the presentation of a confined self.

PLACING DESIRE – DESIRING PLACE

The particular, fluctuating narrative style and temporality of the *Recherche* imitates this superabundant, object-less conception of desire. In this way, following the traces of desire's movement also directs the traffic of Proust's narrative.[14] In the discussion that follows, I want to focus on what might be called an 'erotics of topography' in the novel. The recurrent trope of a desire motivated by the sense of place reveals that, paradoxically, even place – apparent presence – cannot be presented in totality. As we have seen, the expansive, metonymic Bois de Boulogne seemingly *produces* the narrator's desire by leading his perception towards the trace it cannot present. Desire supplements the presentation of these traces, and is 'directed' towards undefined, iterable, 'lovely strolling wom*en* [belles promeneus*es*]'. The flow of desire appropriates the possibility of lack. We can observe these flows emerging even, curiously, at the beginning of the novel, as the narrator chooses to portray for us a conversation between the Curé of Combray, his aunt and Françoise. After the Curé raises the topic of the state of the abbey, he notes that he has been denied the opportunity to restore the floor, because beneath it are preserved 'the tombstones of the Abbés de Combray and the Seigneurs de Guermantes, the old Comtes de Brabant [les tombes des abbés de Combray et des seigneurs de Guermantes, les anciens comtes de Brabant]' (S 105; 102). Immediately after introducing the subject of Roussainville, 'no more than a parish of farmers [ce n'est plus aujourd'hui qu'une paroisse de fermiers]', the Curé moves on to discussing its etymology, before deferring the conversation entirely: he is

> inclined to think the original name was Rouville, (*Radulfi villa*), analogous to Châteauroux (*Castrum Radulfi*), but we can talk about that some other time. (S 105–6)

> Je croirais volontiers que le nom primitif était Rouville (*Radulfi villa*) comme Châteauroux (*Castrum Radulfi*), mais je vous parlerai de cela une autre fois. (103)

These two ideas are then linked in the narrator's consciousness, associated, peculiarly, by their respective windows, mentioned by the Curé. What is interesting to note here is that the narrator himself is not present at the discussion he describes. Leading into his narration of this conversation, he notes (iteratively, of course) that his 'Aunt Léonie would gossip with Françoise, waiting until it was time for Eulalie [tante Léonie devisait avec Françoise en attendant l'heure d'Eulalie]' to visit, while he would 'read in the garden [je lisais au jardin]' (S 102; 99). He then weaves the specific visit of the Curé, in which he describes the etymology of Roussainville, amid this iterative 'scene' that he is absent from – because, one can only deduce, he is still, or again, reading in the garden. Thus, it is as if these links between Roussainville, Guermantes, and their histories are instituted into the novel, but have no origin (certainly not from the narrator's perspective): just as each narrator/'Marcel' defers its origin down the abyss of the iterative work of the text's *restance*, so does this link, the forging of this groove in the machine. The Curé's narrative occupies the anterior 'between' of narrators across the time of revelation that is the *Recherche*: it underlines the novel's interest in ever knowing the authenticity of a memory as it[']s *restance*, emerging *as* the text, without any explanation or origin.¹⁵

The subject of the Curé's philological speculations underlines this concern with absent origins: the 'primordial' trace of this conjunction between Guermantes and Roussainville, in the apparently 'forgotten' (to the narrator) scene, is narrated into the novel – and thus not forgotten. This formative incursion of the name Guermantes, before the narrative has encountered any actual objects of desire bearing the name, engineers itself – *rests* – across an interwoven, textual machine. 'Guermantes' is a name which designates no one, and barely any *thing* – certainly nothing defined, but merely the abstract, deferring sense of *noēteon*. In this sense, the name 'Roussainville' takes on the romance and wonder which 'Guermantes' steadily accrues across the immediately following pages. The concurrent iterability *and* intensity of these names weaves a network of sense into their 'form'. As in the episode of the Bois, Proustian desire seems to be essentially caught up in this network.

This scene stages the difficult, aporetic temporality of burgeoning desire. But, crucially, the narrator *reverses* this difficulty by directing his attention towards accounting for that trace, tracing the original *noēteon* of a desired Idea, before the ~~voice~~ could be aware of his desire. As the Idea of these correspondences weaves through the times he has lost – that he can no longer be liv*ing*, nor narrat*ing* – a desire to harmonise them plays across his new perceptions. He stands on the banks of the Vivonne in Combray, along the Guermantes way, and stops, his mind 'about to acquire some precious idea'.

> And it was with this, with its imaginary ground traversed by currents of seething water, that Guermantes, changing its appearance in my mind, was identified when I heard Doctor Percepied talk to us about the flowers and beautiful spring waters that could be seen in the park of their country house. (*S* 173)
>
> Et ce fut avec elle, avec son sol imaginaire traversé de cours d'eau bouillonnants, que Guermantes, changeant d'aspect dans ma pensée, s'identifia, quand j'eus entendu le docteur Percepied nous parler des fleurs et des belles eaux vives qu'il y avait dans le parc du château. (170)

In the shifting of meaning which the name assumes across its iteration, its phenomenal correspondences shift too, and further weave the memorial network, the differentiation, inherent within the Idea 'Guermantes'.[16]

Following the narrator's description, here we can note two significant points relevant to the argument above. Firstly, the emergence of desire: Proust's narrator is pulling us through, in a deferring, textual elaboration, the impressions that emerge as he delves further into the intensive qualities of that first impression. He has thus searched for, and formed into *re*iterating text, these evocative messages, these instants of memory, these flows of constituting intensity. This kind of scene seems inclined to explicate the infinite intensity of the trace; but the instant it is written, it iterates another infinity of signification. In the very next sentence, the poetic inferences are transported into a desired fantasy:

> I dreamed that Mme de Guermantes had summoned me there, smitten with a sudden fancy for me; all day long she would fish for trout with me. (S 173)
>
> Je rêvais que Mme de Guermantes m'y faisait venir, éprise pour moi d'un soudain caprice ; tout le jour elle y pêchait la truite avec moi. (170)

An object – Mme de Guermantes – emerges for this nascent desire, but this object is purely iterative, since no form has yet settled upon this name in the novel. This Mme de Guermantes could be anyone.

This is the second significant point, that here we can note the emergence of an object produced by, and producing, the narrator's 'desiring-machines'. For, as Deleuze and Guattari note, 'desiring-machines are precisely that: the microphysics of the unconscious, the elements of the microunconscious' (*AO* 183). The nature of this emergence (the fact that there is a developing sense of want, of abstract desire in the narration without a defined object) renders the model of a unified desiring subject problematic. As different decoded flows of desire interact, they produce the various forms of past-ness which arouse, or produce, desire itself, as a 'consummation or coherence of intensive qualities' (*AO* 84). It is this process that a subject senses *as* desire, the sense of its machines. The object is merely an always iterative production of this *restance*. Indeed, to the narrator at this stage, Mme de Guermantes is a 'real and presently existing [réel et actuellement existants]' (*S* 172; 169) person, but one whom he had never met, and at most could only picture as 'made of tapestry [je me les représentais tantôt en tapisserie]', or 'sometimes in changing colours [de nuances changements]' (*S* 172; 169), as Gilbert le Mauvais, the ancestor of Guermantes, appeared to him in the windows of the Combray church. The figure of Mme de Guermantes is aroused in his consciousness as a ready supplement, the romantic manifestation of a vessel for his restless sensuality. The character he desires is as abstract as an entirely imagined one, a desiring-production, for he has no Ideal perception of the 'real' Duchesse other than her revered name.

As has been mentioned above, the Curé's discussion of the ducal heritage of the name Guermantes and its abundant auxiliary content is followed by his mention of the village of Roussainville. Later in his recollections, the narrator describes the walks he used to take after hours spent reading 'that autumn' near that village, so rabidly enthusiastic that he could only interpret his inmost expressions 'by drawing them out [. . .] in an indistinct form that does not teach us to know them [en le faisant sortir de nous sous une forme indistincte qui ne nous apprend pas à le connaître]' (S 155; 153). This confused agglomeration of emotions, drawn from romantic pondering and inactivity, are a literary depiction of the multiple, schizophrenic flows of desire. '[T]he exhilaration' of 'being alone' is

> joined by another kind [of pleasure] that I was not able to separate distinctly from it, and that came from my desire to see a peasant-girl appear in front of me whom I could clasp in my arms. (S 156–7)

> Parfois à l'exaltation que me donnait la solitude, s'en ajoutait une autre que je ne savais pas en départager nettement, causée par le désir de voir surgir devant moi une paysanne, que je pourrais serrer dans mes bras. (154)

And here, the emergence of this utterly undefined, abstract object towards which his desire might flow is endowed with an *essential* uncertainty, similar to his imagined Mme de Guermantes. The object of desire has no quality other than that of belonging to the place in which his desire is stimulated: if

> this desire that a woman should appear added something more exhilarating to the charms of nature, the charms of nature, in return, broadened what would have been too narrow in the woman's charm. (S 157)

> si ce désir qu'une femme apparût ajoutait pour moi aux charmes de la nature quelque chose de plus exaltant, les charmes de la nature, en retour, élargissaient ce que celui de la femme aurait eu de trop restraint. (154)

As with the erotics of topography evoked by the Bois de Boulogne or the name of Guermantes,[17] here we have a dividual, differen*t*iated desiring machine, one that is too large for presentational logic. The narrator describes the feeling of object-oriented desire as being '[b]orn suddenly, and without [his] having had time to identify exactly what had caused it, from among very different thoughts [Né brusquement, et sans que j'eusse eu le temps de le rapporter exactement à sa cause, au milieu de pensées très différentes]' (S 157; 154), which he lists as a number of these materially separate, but poetically interlinked elements of the scene.

> Everything that was in my mind at that moment acquired an even greater value, the pink reflection of the tile roof, the wild grass, the village of Roussainville which I had been wanting to go for so long now, the trees of its woods, the steeple of its church. (*S* 157)

> Je faisais un mérite de plus à tout ce qui était à ce moment-là dans mon esprit, au reflet rose du toit de tuile, aux herbes folles, au village de Roussainville où je désirais depuis longtemps aller, aux arbres de son bois, au clocher de son église. (154)

It is necessary that the woman in some way *re*present the place that, like the Bois, can never *be present* in its entirety of differences. As such, he especially underlines the relationship between his sensuous perspective and the desire that emerges from it, stating his sense that, of all the features which this utterly abstract peasant-woman should possess, 'the beauty of the trees was also hers [la beauté des arbres, c'était encore la sienne]' (*S* 157; 154). Just as Derrida notes that 'the trace itself does not exist' (*OG* 182) because it *cannot* exist without being presented *as* some*thing* present (and as such lose its transversal, quality-less distinction *as* a trace), so the trace of this Ideal woman remains feature-less, disseminating her possible qualities across differences that exclude each other – she must *re*main as pure potentiality. And even the ambiguity of the narrator's 'ambiguous woman' cannot function as a defining quality, 'for the word "ambiguity" requires the logic of presence, even when it begins to disobey that logic' (*OG* 76). Her charm is traced only by desire for Roussainville, which conjures up the narrator's earliest conceptions of its uncertain presence, in the Curé's etymologies. The erotics of topography consists in the fact that the traces left by experience of a place can never be totalised, can never be presented atop each other, and cannot even be 'ambiguous'. The narrator's upsurge of desire can never take a determinate object. The *genius loci* that informs Proustian desire is a productive '*without* without *without*' (*PC* 401), because it cannot substitute the lack that the *singular* iteration of the place is for another without initiating further 'withouts', all of which it defers. As such, the narrator's desired woman is a pure trace: the narrator is compelled to imagine her, but only as she constitutes 'the presence-absence of the trace, which one should not even call its ambiguity but rather its play' (*OG* 76) – some kind of indiscernible 'flavour' of his abyssal desiring for place, and as such, her qualities must be virtually unintelligible: an extensive, deferring horizon of pure desire.

In the *restance* of his perspectives, Proust's narrator has come close to depicting the difficult temporal consistency of desire: either its constant unfolding or, precisely, its form-less, superabundant trace. He notes the overwhelmed source of this sensuality, and subsequently that the desire comes expressly from the links between these 'very different thoughts [pensées très différentes]' (*S* 157). This is the essential element of Proustian desire: it follows the trace, and as such, cannot present itself. As mentioned above, Proust's narrator's desire exists by creating an always inadequate object for itself. And the key link, the absolute opportunity that Proust devises to bridge the seemingly irreconcilable gap between *noēteon* and *noēton*, are the very fictional, proper names which allow him to iterate *and* intensify that essential quality that he desires. Just as writing desires to set a form to the trace, so does desire iterate as it becomes an object of writing. In saying that a girl must have the qualities of 'Roussainville' or 'Balbec', names that exist only in the *Recherche*, the reader must weave their own sense of these names' correspondences and intimations across the desire woven through, or as, the novel.[18] For the narrator,

> [to] meet a fisherwoman from Balbec or a countrywoman from Méséglise in Paris [. . .] would have subtracted from the pleasure which the woman would give [him] all those pleasures in which [his] imagination had enveloped her. (*S* 157–8)
>
> Connaître à Paris une pêcheuse de Balbec ou une paysanne de Méséglise, [. . .] ç'eût été retrancher au plaisir que la femme me donnerait tous ceux au milieu desquels l'avait enveloppée mon imagination. (155)

Proustian desire produces its abyssal '*without* without *without*' as the impossibility to *re*produce the initiating repetition of a sense of place. It is directed towards indeterminate women whose essence signals towards the trace of *genius loci*, but can never reproduce the specific iteration of that place. Years later, in a 'Gothic alley [ruelle gothique]' at Doncières, the narrator hopes to find a similarly undetermined woman, 'invested with mystery by the wintry night, the strange place, the darkness and the medieval ambience [à laquelle auraient prêté leur mystère l'hiver, le dépaysement, l'obscurité et le moyen âge]' (*GW* 94; 90). As with the Bois, it is not only that these topographies lend their 'ancient voluptuous charm [l'antique volupté]' (*GW* 94; 90) to a woman *from* there. Rather, the inability to appropriate the static ontology of its placeness, its presence in *parousia*, conjures the desire that is born 'suddenly, and without [his] having had time to identify exactly what had caused it' (*S* 157).

As such, in writing, enlisting the iteration of language, the narrator can suggest the vast, unique sense of these desired places. But there is always more, even temporally, which 'divides up' unceasingly, in its virtuality. And it is this that continues to motivate the narrator's experiences of desire, even after he has found particular women to become the actual, yet insufficient, objects for it. Indeed, the narrator notes definitively that the 'most exclusive love for any person is always love for something else [L'amour le plus exclusif pour une personne est toujours l'amour d'autre chose]' (*YG* 413; 397) – many things, it would seem, especially as this pertains to desire's wandering, essentially indeterminate search through flows and points of contact with the trace. Indeed, in this sense, the trace *is* desire, just as the *restance* of topography constitutes that unknown desire sensed by the narrator as a motivating horizon of what he cannot totally apprehend. It is only as these forms of desire incorporate their own absence, a *sumplokē* of their presence and absence, that the narrator senses, pursues, and inscribes desire. It is this weaving that adumbrates the trace.

> We need only to see in passing a single real feature of a woman, a glimpse of her at a distance or from behind, which can be enough for us to project beauty on her, and we imagine we have found it at last: the heart beats faster, we lengthen out stride and, on the condition that she disappears, we may be left with the certainty of having set eyes upon it – it is only if we succeed in catching up with her that we imagine our mistake. (*YG* 368)
>
> Qu'un seul trait réel – le peu qu'on distingue d'une femme vue de loin, ou de dos – nous permette de projeter la Beauté devant nous, nous nous figurons l'avoir reconnue, notre cœur bat, nous pressons le pas, et nous resterons toujours à demi persuadés que c'était elle, pourvu que la femme ait disparu : ce n'est que si nous pouvons la rattraper que nous comprenons notre erreur. (353–4)

Desire fluctuates across the hollow of a subjectivity it organises, yet defers:[19] this 'single real feature' is all that the narrator needs to notice the sense of desire already inscribed within his perception. But in turn, it immediately opens out towards the disseminating property of the trace and its ceaseless deferral – the desire feels manifest in the motion, the movement of becoming that is the lengthening of the stride, the projection of a beauty that can only be more extensive. But it is in the very uncertainty, the movement of desire as imagination and deferral, that this beauty becomes sensible – once a form can be attributed to it, once it is caught up to, it diminishes, in favour of the other possible deferrals that the movement of life in other directions offers.[20]

TRACING DESIRE

In this final section, I want to try to illustrate how this overwhelming, productive desire for the trace comes to take a prominent role in the development of the *Recherche*.[21] My first example is the famous *petite bande* at Balbec. The way that the narrator grapples with the immediate desire for this undetermined collectivity, before distinguishing any of its individuals, points towards an unintelligible desire for Balbec itself, as a multiplicity of place[ ]. To begin, notice how he first perceives the girls as a group, an amorphous, undefined body of desirable, feminine matter:

> a strange mass of moving colours, [. . .] five or six young girls, as different in their appearance and ways from all the other people one was used to seeing at Balbec. (YG 369)

> une tache singulière, [. . .] cinq ou six fillettes, aussi différentes, par l'aspect et par les façons, de toutes les personnes auxquelles on était accoutumé à Balbec. (354)

As described in the above section, the appearance of these girls is fortuitous, but probably inevitable; the narrator's sensuous desire for the trace of Balbec's *genius loci* translates itself into an appropriate medium. But in so far as this medium is directed towards the trace, it can only ever be an inadequate representation. As much as he refers to them inextricably, as their 'band', he notes that

> each of them was of a type quite different from the others, all of them were beautiful; but I had been looking at them for so few moments, and was so far from daring to stare at them, that I had not yet been able to individualize any of them. (YG 370)

> chacune fût un type absolument différent des autres, elles avaient toutes de la beauté ; mais à vrai dire, je les voyais depuis si peu d'instants et sans oser les regarder fixement que je n'avais encore individualisé aucune d'elles. (355–6)

The sense of his already-evoked desire wanders over their mass, but at the same time he cannot help sensing unintelligible differences between them, which he cannot quite pin down.

This experience suggests the difficulty of explicating schizophrenic desire, with its on-rush of various flows and intensities. In an always-multiplying bind, any attempt to discern this 'present' of perception moves further into its implex, or down the abyss. Before he gives a definitive account of the event, the narrator portrays the impressions coming towards him, seeking to depict the moment in its perceptual purity, breaking up the instant of perception into its micro-unconscious flows. He notes some of the more striking individual features: like one, whose

> straight nose and darker complexion marked her out amongst the rest, as a King of Arabian looks may stand out in a Renaissance painting of the Magi, they were knowable only as a pair of hard, stubborn, laughing eyes in one of the faces; as two cheeks of that pink touched by coppery tones

> suggesting geraniums in another; and none of even these features had I yet inseparably attached to any particular girl rather than to some other. (YG 370)

> nez droit, sa peau brune mettait en contraste au milieu des autres comme, dans quelque tableau de la Renaissance, un roi Mage de type arabe, elles ne m'étaient connues, l'une que par une paire d'yeux durs, butés et rieurs ; une autre que par des joues où le rose avait cette teinte cuivrée qui évoque l'idée de geranium ; et même ces traits je n'avais encore indissolublement attaché aucun d'entre eux à l'une des jeunes filles plutôt qu'à l'autre. (356)

The narrator attempts to record the initial impression, which contains not individuals but only the potential for later individuation: each 'feature' is both impossibly expressive and yet insufficient to individuate any girl rather than another.

> The fact that my view of them was devoid of demarcations, which I was soon to draw among them, sent a ripple of harmonious imprecision through their group, the uninterrupted flow of a shared, unstable and elusive beauty. (YG 371)

> Et cette absence, dans ma vision, des démarcations que j'établirais bientôt entre elles, propageait à travers leur groupe un flottement harmonieux, la translation continue d'une beauté fluide, collective et mobile. (356)

This 'ripple' is the instituting repetition of the trace. It is an 'uninterrupted flow' because, amid the multiplicity that informs his sense of the desire that runs in the background through all of his perceptions of this place, there runs this 'shared, unstable and elusive' trace. The narrator is caught between unity and multiplicity: language cannot doubly account for this nonnumerical multiplicity, cannot accurately describe girl and girls, without settling for either. And yet the narrator is attempting to do so, moulding the trace that is the (pre)instituting movement of his desire, if only he could grasp it. Rather than simply assume that the sense that motivates his writing is 'present' in his language for the reader, Proust works towards unbinding the discrete 'forms' that perception apparently presents.

The narrator describes how he saw

> their complex whole unfold before [him], wonderful because the most dissimilar aspects were mixed into it and all shades of colour were juxtaposed. (YG 370)

> l'ordre dans lequel se déroulait cet ensemble merveilleux parce qu'y voisinaient les aspects les plus différents, que toutes les gammes de couleurs y étaient rapprochées. (356)

And his mind, like the composer of a symphony, utilises all of these scales in order to create from his perceptions a work

> confused as a piece of music in which one cannot isolate and identify the phrases as they form, which once heard are as soon forgotten. (YG 370)

> qui était confus comme une musique où je n'aurais pas su isoler et reconnaître au moment de leur passage les phrases, distinguées mais oubliées aussitôt après. (356)

The dividual work of this perception, and its attempted transposition into literature, is plainly evident here. The narrator draws attention to the inconsistencies of 'logically present' distinctions in this excerpt – the way that the girls are a flowing, 'complex whole' of difference, which cannot be divided into its component parts in the instant of this perception without dispersing the sense of desire. The traces of this complex whole are later woven into the various differen*ci*ations of memory, but at this moment of inextricable sense, it is not coincidental that the narrator chooses to refer to it as 'confused as a piece of music'. As Bergson argued, the durational 'flow' of music is an example of how sense rushes over the distinct perceptions of consciousness. In the same way, we can witness the unique nature of Proust's narration in this passage, which seeks to describe the instantaneous sense of perception, in which all of its traces jostle atop one another, not yet bound by the presentational logic of chronology which comes only later to differenciate its perceptions.

Later, following the 'bold act' of one of the band jumping over an elderly banker, the narrator recalls that by this time, 'their charm was not blended into undifferentiated features [leurs traits charmants n'étaient plus indistincts et mêlés]' (YG 373; 358). The narrator, the writer, the reader, all trace the trace, attempting to capture and *re*count the essence of the flow amongst the girls' newly distinguished features, now that the narrator 'could separate these from one another and apportion them to individual girls [Je les avais répartis et agglomérés]' (YG 373). And still, somewhere *rest*ing in their now discrete perceptual remains – the fact that 'they were now separately identifiable' – is the original impression of their unity, which

> linked their separate and independent bodies into an invisible harmony, as though they shared the same warm shade, walked within a separate atmosphere, which made them an entity as alike in its parts as it was unlike the throng through which their closed little company wended its slow way. (YG 374)

> mettaient entre leurs corps indépendants et séparés, tandis qu'ils s'avançaient lentement, une liaison invisible, mais harmonieuse comme une même ombre chaude, une même atmosphère, faisant d'eux un tout aussi homogène en ses parties qu'il était différent de la foule au milieu de laquelle se déroulait lentement leur cortège. (359)

Here, the narrator draws attention, even after the seemingly discrete, memorial distinctions are able to 'represent' the girls, to the ineffable trace of this instituting desire that remains interwoven, as an 'invisible harmony', among each perception – just as the motivating trace of desire itself precedes its intelligible 'origination'. The micro-partition of differences-in-unity resembles the movement of his desiring self throughout the Bois, combining and differentiating in the same indissoluble becoming of desiring identity. As the graduation of each new perception intensifies meaning out of impression, so the 'invisible' sense of the perception remains.[22]

After he has met and become a familiar acquaintance of the painter Elstir, the narrator misses a chance to be formally introduced by him to the girls of the *petite bande*. He takes solace, however, in the fact that he now possesses an opportunity to be introduced to them later on. As he entertains this idea, the narrator considers what his perception of the *petite bande* consists of, at that precise moment in time – and its relationship with a specific, and now temporally distinct, desire.

> They were no longer surrounded by the great turbid swirl which kept us apart, which was nothing but the translation of the desire – perpetually ablaze, mobile, urgent, constantly fuelled by worry – ignited in me by their inaccessibility, their possible disappearance from my life for ever. This desire for them could now be turned down, kept in reserve, alongside so many others the fulfilment of which, once I knew this was a possibility, I postponed. (*YG* 443)

> Autour d'elles ne flottait plus comme ce grand remous qui nous séparait et qui n'était que la traduction du désir en perpétuelle activité, mobile, urgent, alimenté d'inquiétudes, qu'éveillaient en moi leur inaccessibilité, leur fuite peut-être pour toujours. Mon désir d'elles, je pouvais maintenant le mettre au repos, le garder en réserve, à côté de tant d'autres dont, une fois que je la savais possible, j'ajournais la réalisation. (427–8)

Here, the narrator points directly to the necessary movement of desire, the deferral that stimulates its becoming. But at the same time, he acknowledges that desire, while operating above his perceptions and informing their productions, is in turn always becoming *restance*; his sense of it can still be left, deferring, 'perpetually ablaze', moving away from itself and him, yet 'postponed'. It is still not, and never will be, 'presented', or knowable as a representational image of thought in its fullness, but here at least he can come to terms with its lability. While this desire had been a pleasure to him, 'it was a pleasure which had *remained* hidden [ce plaisir m'était *resté* caché]' (*YG* 443; 428, my emphases), that is, traced, never fully presentable. He then compares it to a guest who enters a party inconspicuously, only alerting us to their presence after the other guests have left. But the guest is always there; the perception may not present them, but they remain, are *rest*ing in some corner of the room, interacting with the other party-goers. And so it goes for the sense of desire or affect more generally; they interact with other 'forgotten' senses and memories. The narrator always seeks to reveal these, noting in this instance that the guest is 'patient, they do not weary, and when the last visitor has gone, there they are looking at us [ils sont patients, ils ne se lassent pas et dès que tout le monde est parti nous les trouvons en face de nous]' (YG 443; 428). Not without, however, having taken some interesting detail from another member of the party, and sharing it with us in the course of the coming conversation: the horizon of *noēteon* that produces its always deferring sense.

This is the relationship that desire has with the horizons of perception that motivate its machine, which derive from its various flows: the guest mingles warmly at the party, leaving traces in the form of conversations with other guests. The narrator quickly returns from the metaphor to note its relevance to the larger project of the novel, how sometimes

> we feel that we cannot find the strength in our weary mind to entertain these memories, these impressions for which our feeble self is the only habitable place, the sole medium of their realization. (YG 444)
>
> il nous semble que nous n'aurons plus dans notre pensée défaillante assez de force pour retenir ces souvenirs, ces impressions pour qui notre moi fragile est le seul lieu habitable, l'unique mode de realization. (428)

As all of these memories and impressions intersect in the chiasmata of Being, as they work through the hollow of sense, the feeling that they are forgotten is, in this passage, replaced by belief in their unconscious interaction. It is only because Being *has been* among the *same* being, from its 'sole medium of their realization', that these memories and impressions give their trace to the sense of every ensuing impression and memory. And because they do, the totality of Being works as this kind of fractal appropriation of an abyss. As the signature disseminates the singular, totalisable self, it traces across the deferring abyss of that self – desired, sensed, but never fully intelligible. Just like Proust's narrator, the self that can sense such *restance* inscribes itself as both immanent part *and* transcendent whole prior to the imagination of any other self.

The narrator's developing awareness of desire becomes a fractal *re*production of varied intensities, those that it cannot *re*present in totalised intelligibility. It is within desire that he feels, at this still early stage of his reflective development, the romance of longing within time 'forgotten out' of intelligibility. As the narrator notes,

> we do not change; we bring to the feeling we associate with a person the many dormant elements that person awakens in us but which are foreign to the person in question. (*GW* 117)
>
> on ne change pas, on fait entrer dans le sentiment qu'on rapporte à un être bien des éléments assoupis qu'il réveille mais qui lui sont étrangers. (112)

While his desire still reaches towards and retains the inferred qualities of the *noēteon* in the sensible, he has noted the *restance* which is the unintelligible content of such desire, and patiently waits for the party to subside in order to enjoy the guest's company. Bound within the chain of supplements that is writing, his narration, like desire itself, notes and becomes the abyss that it 'is' appropriating.[23] He cannot fully account for the trace that generates his desire in the trace that is writing or naming, and so is forever bound to a reflection of a reflection, that does not capture the essence of the *noēteon* itself. Proustian desire is always the desire to write the trace, and as such, it can only ever defer 'itself': it *is* a deferral, *as* a deferral. This is the novel's *restance*: the attempt to account for desire amid the iterative supplement of literary ~~voice~~ is the same horizon that is, yet never is – a *sumplokē*, as literary inscription itself.

One final example will help to illustrate this paradoxical, yet generating, law of desire. Fatigued and withdrawn from society, in the final episode of the novel the narrator returns to Paris to attend a musical matinée provided by the Princesse de Guermantes. Present among the attendees are many who played important roles in his youthful ascent into society, but the narrator at first does not recognise them. As he considers asking Gilberte to introduce him to certain young women, he notes that, regarding the desired women from his past, 'even earlier than this attraction to each of them was [his] sense of the mystery surrounding them [J'aurais dû pourtant penser qu'antérieur à chacune était mon sentiment du mystère où elles baignaient]' (*FT* 297; 294). Thus, he realises that, if he were directly introduced to them, these women would lose their appeal (they would be without the necessary timbre of desirability: a carefully furnished 'mystery' of unintelligible, yet *rest*ing horizons of place). He then describes the appeal of the desired women of his past: while desire may have begun as a 'mystery', as 'the unknown, and the almost unknowable [l'inconnu, et presque l'inconnaissable]' (*FT* 298; 294–5) that he wished to colour with his own memories and perceptions (such as his desire for the Duchesse being inhabited, in some way, by his desire to have her go 'trout-fishing' with him), it 'had become the known, familiar, indifferent or painful, yet it always retained something of the charm it had once possessed [était devenu le commun, le familier, indifférent ou douloureux, mais retenant de ce qu'il avait été un certain charme]' (*FT* 298; 295). A dividual multiplicity, this desire disseminates as it retains/remains that 'charm'. If these new women could not be perceived with these kinds of traces, then the narrator's desire for them would become impossible, for desire to him is borne from the schizophrenic flow of the *re*peatable, iterative sense of place that can never be captured, or presented.

Continuing to recount *how* he had desired in the past – *re*iterating – the narrator makes this even more plain. He notes that

> there was not one of [his] years which might not have had as its frontispiece, or intercalated between its days, the image of a woman [he] had desired; an image made even more arbitrary by the fact that sometimes [he] had never seen the woman. (*FT* 298).

> il n'était pas une de mes années qui n'ait eu à son frontispice, ou intercalée dans ses jours, l'image d'une femme que j'y avais désirée ; image souvent d'autant plus arbitraire que parfois je n'avais pas vu cette femme. (295)

This image of interleaving is like the *sumplokē* of the text: desire is not traceable to any particular day, but is rather interleaved between them, a kind of rhythm or punctuation. Desire programs the 'images' of desired, fictional, iterable 'women', who exist to him each only as

> an ideal body, its height dominating a landscape in the part of the country where, as [he] had read in the *Annuaire des châteaux*, her family estates were to be found.[24] (*FT* 298)

> un corps idéal dominant de toute sa hauteur un paysage de la province où j'avais lu, dans l'*Annuaire des Châteaux*, que se trouvaient les propriétés de sa famille. (205)

He desires them because they can never be present; he can never present them because he desires them. As for 'women whom [he] had known [les femmes que j'avais connues]', assuming the desiring that his memory has accrued, 'the landscape was at least twofold [ce paysage était au moins double]'. He asserts that this is because

> [e]ach woman arose, at a different point in [his] life, [...] seen from the viewpoint of memory, surrounded by the places where [he] had known her and of which she reminded [him], remaining attached to them. (*FT* 298)

> Chacune s'élevait, à un point différent de ma vie, [...] vue du côté du souvenir entourée des sites où je l'avais connue et qu'elle me rappelait, y restant attaché. (295)

Leafing through the *Annuaire des châteaux*, the narrator can always turn to another page and defer the brimming desire he was just contemplating, resting it in the party of his other memories, dividually rendering it ever more intense. Indeed, the scene of his reading the *Annuaire* is one that only rests in the novel, interacting with and developing the sense of other scenes, but is never present in itself.

Writing, then, becomes the necessary vehicle, the supplement, for this desire. Literature cannot present its origin; neither can the desire portrayed by Proust in his novel. This kind of desiring retro-jects the expansion of the associations that he imagined for the 'ideal body' as the women the narrator has known throughout his life. And the retro-jection is figured as a kind of 'second person, born not of desire but of memory [cette seconde personne, celle née non du désir, mais du souvenir]', a personality which 'was not for any of these women a single figure [n'était, pour chacune de ces femmes, unique]': they were all 'steeped in dreams of a different colour [baignant dans des rêves d'une autre couleur]' (*FT* 299; 295–6). They are always repeated, the same but in a different way, like the iterative *re*mark that intensifies language, literature, and the dividual function of multiplicity, like how 'a Milky Way of nebulae was the result of the disintegration of one single star [qu'une voie lactée de nébuleuses était due à la segmentation d'une seule et même étoile]' (*FT* 299; 296). As such, Gilberte, with all of her possible desired selves from the narrator's past, perceived in simultaneity through the *aiôn*, becomes 'no longer anything to [him] but Mme de Saint-Loup [n'était plus pour moi que Mme de Saint-Loup]' (*FT* 299; 296), a nebulous, yet 'single star': the bracketed *noēteon* traced throughout her apparent, deferring presence.

Desire is instinctively made up of a drawing towards primordial time, the *aiôn*, an atemporal fullness of any object's trace[ ]. But in order to perceive that object in a temporal and conceptual form, its infinity must be constricted, it must be bracketed into a *re*peatable form. The narrator, the author, the reader, are confronted with the same *re*iterating language, ideas, forms, that seem to signify so many variously woven traces that mark and *re*mark concepts both intelligible and unintelligible. Therefore, as he perceives Gilberte before him, gatekeeper to (or signatory for) the desirable possibilities of other unknowable girls, noting that '[a]ll the memories which composed the original Mlle Swann had in effect been subtracted from the Gilberte of today [Tous les souvenirs qui composaient la première mademoiselle Swann étaient, en effet, retranchés de la Gilberte actuelle]' (*FT* 300; 296), he is conscious of the tyranny of iteration, that he cannot be immediately conscious of all the traces which constitute his complex, 'coloured' perceptions of Gilberte. He cannot make present 'the part played in [his] love for her, which she had also forgotten about, by [his] admiration for Bergotte, for Bergotte once again simply the author of his books, without [his] remembering (save in rare and entirely distinct moments of recollection) [au rôle qu'avait eu jadis dans mon amour, oublié lui aussi par elle, mon admiration pour Bergotte, pour Bergotte redevenu pour moi simplement l'auteur de ses livres, sans que je me rappelasse (que dans des souvenirs rares et entièrement séparés)]' (*FT* 299–300; 296) other constituent horizons of that 'forgotten' part. And yet, these traces seem, by the logic of *parousia*, still present to him, because otherwise they could not be woven into his narrative – he could not tell us of that trace of Bergotte he has forgotten, that we can always *re*read, retrace and retrace differently. As he perceives this 'subtracted' version of Gilberte, 'kept at a distance by the powers of attraction of another universe [retenus bien loin par les forces d'attraction d'un autre univers]', his narration weaves through the deferral of these nascent impressions on the horizon of sensibility, ever tracing the trace, further down the abyss, but never totally explicating it. All of her iterating versions circulate before him, 'grouped around a phrase of Bergotte's with which they fused into a unity, and steeped in the scent of Hawthorn [autour d'une phrase de Bergotte avec laquelle ils faisaient corps et baignés d'un parfum d'aubépine]' (*FT* 300; 296), extending off through these memories to the eternity of forgotten, but extant, differen*t*iation. As though literature could write it all! As the 'fragmentary Gilberte of today [La fragmentaire Gilberte d'aujourd'hui]' listens and *re*presents infinite versions of herself to him, she too 'began to think about it, [and] her face took on a more serious expression [en se mettant à y réfléchir, elle prit un air sérieux]' (*FT* 300; 297): willing her senses to wind her, too, through eternal time.

NOTES

1. See, for example: Leo Bersani, *Marcel Proust: The Fictions of Life and Art* (New York: Oxford University Press, 1965); Stephen Gilbert Brown, *The Gardens of Desire*; Emma Wilson, *Sexuality and the Reading Encounter: Identity and Desire in Proust, Duras, Tournier and Cixous* (Oxford: Oxford University Press, 1996); Margaret Topping, 'Errant Eyes: Digression, Metaphor and Desire in Marcel Proust's *In Search of Lost Time*', in *Digressions in European Literature: From Cervantes to Sebald*, ed. Alexis Grohmann and Caragh Wells (New York: Palgrave Macmillan, 2011), 106–17; and Volker Roloff, 'Desire, Imaginary, and Love: Erotic Readings of the *Recherche*', trans. Jane Kuntz, in *Proust in Perspective: Visions and Revisions*, ed. Armine Kotin Mortimer and Katherine Kolb (Urbana and Chicago: University of Illinois Press, 2002), 157–71.
2. An approach that follows Deleuze's formula, according to Simon, 'of two terms: woman/landscape, which characterises Proustian desire'. Simon, *Trafics de Proust*, 150.

3. On this point, Phillip Lacoue-Labarthe argues that, because 'desire's obsession is originality, desire wants its origin negated and its essence forgotten'. Phillip Lacoue-Labarthe, *Typography: Mimesis, Philosophy, Politics*, ed. Christopher Fynsk (London and Cambridge, MA: Harvard University Press, 1989), 102.
4. Patton argues that Deleuze and Guattari's reliance on 'schizophrenic delirium lies in the suggestion that the experience of intensity is the real motor of the process of desire as production', because for them both 'art and desire in its schizo form have an affinity with those states that carry the potential for change or metamorphosis'. Paul Patton, *Political Deleuze* (London and New York: Routledge, 2000), 72–3.
5. In *Understanding Deleuze* (Sydney: Allen & Unwin, 2002), Claire Colebrook notes that for Deleuze and Guattari, 'desire is not a relation between terms – the desire of the subject and the absent object, which they lack; desire is production. All life is desire, a flow of positive difference and becoming', because their philosophy 'frees desire from representation' (99).
6. See Dosse, *Intersecting Lives*, 217.
7. As Deleuze notes of Foucault in an interview: 'The last time we saw each other, Michel kindly and affectionately told me something like the following: I can't stand the word desire; even if you use it differently, I can't stop myself from thinking or feeling that desire = lack, or that desire is repressed' (*TR* 130).
8. René Girard, *Deceit, Desire and the Novel: Self and Other in Literary Structure*, trans. Yvonne Freccero (Baltimore: Johns Hopkins University Press, 1965), 18.
9. Girard, *Deceit, Desire and the Novel*, 30.
10. While following Girard's model, Per Bjørnar Grande opens the possibility for a more inclusive account of the flows of desire. He attests that '[w]hen the subject's desire becomes more and more based on the desires of the mediator's desire, desire is in a process of becoming metaphysical, which means that desire gradually loses its original direction.' Per Bjørnar Grande, 'Proustian Desire', *Contagion: Journal of Violence, Mimesis, and Culture* 18 (2011): 40. Desire's 'becoming metaphysical' is its becoming schizophrenic, inverting the model's vertices down the abyss.
11. Grande, 'Proustian Desire', 40.
12. Deleuze and Guattari assert that this 'absent' signifier is present throughout many of Freud's models: 'everywhere we encounter the analytic process that consists in extrapolating a transcendent and common something, but that is a common-universal for the sole purpose of introducing lack into desire, in situating and specifying persons and an ego under one aspect or another of its absence, and imposing an exclusive direction on the disjunction of the sexes. Such is the case in Freud: for Oedipus, for castration, for the second phase of the fantasy "A Child is Being Beaten," or again for the famous latency period where the analytical mystification culminates' (*AO* 72–3).

13. Colebrook contrasts Deleuze and Guattari's concept of desire to that of psychoanalysis, which structures desire on a 'negative difference'. In psychoanalytic theory, we 'desire presence, to have what *is*, but our desire must be articulated through a system that *is not*'. Colebrook, *Understanding Deleuze*, 17.
14. Bersani points out the link between desire and the development of the narrative. 'The desires of ["]Marcel["] – sexual, worldly, aesthetic – define his self; they impart their design on the world and give his narrative its unique form.' Leo Bersani, 'Déguisements du moi et art fragmentaire', in *Recherche de Proust*, 17.
15. Bowie argues that Proustian 'desire – agile, Protean, acquisitive and experimental as it may be – has in each local instance its inescapable prehistory, its determining pattern of choices already made and its moorings within a sensate organism'. Malcolm Bowie, *Freud, Proust, and Lacan: Theory as Fiction* (Cambridge and New York: Cambridge University Press, 1987), 95.
16. As a popular reading of Proust goes, and Landy best describes, Proust's narrator's 'fantasy is that everything belonging to a given site shares a common essence, that there is so to speak a *Raumgeist* as well as a *Zeitgeist*, that there is some property held in common among all neighboring elements, that a town such as Balbec magically invests its buildings, streets, seas, and trees – even its name – with a single unique nature.' Landy, *Philosophy as Fiction*, 74.
17. An idea that so much of this chapter has been devoted to because, even metaphorically, it elucidates the problem of *parousia* appropriating a total essence, just as a horizon cannot be presently totalised (even the word that comes to 'represent' it reduces its flowing, manifold 'thought' as difference and traces).
18. As Barthes notes, the entire *Recherche* 'emerges from a few names'. Roland Barthes, *New Critical Essays*, trans. Richard Howard (New York: Hill & Wang, 1980), 62.
19. For Bersani, 'psychological continuity thrives on the frustration of desire; desire, duplicated and sublimated in ideas and mental faculties, organizes a self'. Leo Bersani, *A Future for Astyanax: Character and Desire in Literature* (New York: Columbia University Press, 1984), 272.
20. In a compelling phenomenological argument that I could not do justice to here, Renaud Barbaras aligns desire with motility, that 'movement, which is appropriation of external matter, is exclusively in the service of need. Perception and desire then take on sense from this movement of satisfaction', or closer to my reading here, to the movement of the abyssal production of deferring (motile) satisfaction. Renaud Barbaras, 'Life, Movement, and Desire', trans. Jen McWeeny, *Research in Phenomenology* 38, no. 1 (2008): 9. See also Renaud Barbaras, *Desire and Distance: Introduction to a Phenomenology of Perception*, trans. Paul B. MIlan (Stanford: Stanford University Press, 2006). Also see Barbaras, 'The Phenomenology of Life:

Desire as the Being of the Subject', trans. Darian Meacham, in *The Oxford Handbook of Contemporary Phenomenology*, ed. Dan Zahavi (Oxford: Oxford University Press, 2012), 94–112, where he argues that desire 'never meets its object except in the mode of the object's own absence' (94), and that '[e]verything occurs as if desire had no object, not in the sense of not desiring anything but rather because it is oriented towards that which transcends all objects' (100).

21. We should link this reading to Bersani's observation that 'literature is not merely instructive *about* desire; in a sense, desire *is* a phenomenon of the literary imagination'. Bersani, *A Future for Astyanax*, 10.

22. Patrick ffrench points out that the social differences between the characters involved constitute another complex trace in this passage. The narrator 'imagines that the distinctiveness of the girls' movement is determined by reasons having to do with the evolutionary stage of the class to which they belong'. Patrick ffrench, 'Proust and the Analysis of Gesture', in *Proust and the Visual*, ed. Nathalie Aubert (Cardiff: University of Wales Press, 2013), 62.

23. This becomes the abyssal 'trace' of the Derrida's 'arche-writing'. As Hägglund argues, 'the minimal condition for life itself is an "arche-writing." Such writing testifies that nothing can be given in itself but is always already passing away. [. . .] If writing is originary, then it is because there is no life without the movement of survival which can persist only by leaving destructible traces for an unpredictable time to come'. Hägglund, *Radical Atheism*, 49. In terms of my argument here, this is the abyssal, dividual hollow of the *aiôn*.

24. As Landy reminds us, the narrator's 'is fundamentally a spatial imagination [. . .] clustering objects and individuals according to their geographical locality'. Landy, *Philosophy as Fiction*, 75.

4. Love: Differentiating Groups, Faciality and the Black Hole/ White Wall System

In this chapter, I want to consider what the narrator comes to call 'love' in the *Recherche*.[1] This reading will treat love as an extension of the *restance*, the remains of *noēteon* or the trace that, I argued in the previous chapter, constitute desire. I have suggested that the general structure of Proustian textuality enacts a deferral of *parousia*, which we can describe using a philosophical vocabulary developed by Deleuze and Derrida. In this chapter, I examine how the theme of love can be considered through this lens. Drawing, in particular, on Deleuze's *Proust and Signs* and *A Thousand Plateaus*, I examine how the narrator's love for Albertine seems to be generated by his very inability to assign a stable identity to her. I trace this pattern, first, in his first encounters with the *petite bande* in *À l'ombre des jeunes filles en fleurs*, and then, in different forms, in the later course of his relationship with Albertine. An important figure in this chapter is the beloved's shifting, unfixable face – a trope that I explain in terms of Deleuze and Guattari's '*black hole/ white wall system*' and Derrida's remarks in *Writing and Difference* on the face of the Other.

If the previous chapter argued that desire is aroused as a superabundance of sense over a static presentation, triggering an abyssal desire for the further becoming of desire, then what is love for Proust? While love in Proust's novel is often discussed in terms of his narrator's 'neediness, his hunger for possession and completeness',[2] I would like to suggest that the *sense* of love, as textually depicted in the *Recherche*, precedes its own origin, and thus bears witness to the deferring (present-absent) trace. With respect to Swann's obsessive love for Odette de Crécy, Descombes posits that the 'true formula of Swann's love is: a taste for certain particular sensations that Swann feels only in the presence of Odette'.[3] In many respects, this formula is an accurate reading of how love operates in the *Recherche*, but it is the very constitution of these 'particular sensations' that brings the formula into question: if they are forged 'only' in Odette's presence, then why are they made up, not only of Odette's varying, ungraspable presence, but also her absences? Swann's love, like the narrator's for Albertine, is a constant negotiation between the impossibly united differences that Odette contains and the always-insufficient 'totality' that her apparent, actual 'presence' implies. When Compagnon notes that the 'high point in the subjective exercise called love necessarily travesties the other',[4] he is identifying the persistent, irrevocable movement *away* from an intelligible totality of the beloved.[5] The aporia of Proustian love exemplifies the more general, immutable deferral of sense that I have traced in the *Recherche*. The questions in this paragraph are thus revealed to be their own answer: Proustian love is distinguished from desire because it reaches towards the ideal of a static, knowable beloved: but, as with desire, love can never fully contain the other's iterability.

In a suggestive essay in the collection *Between Deleuze and Derrida* (2003), John Protevi has examined the theme of 'Love' as one that crosses between Deleuze's and Derrida's oeuvres. For Deleuze, he argues, 'the sense of the *expérience* of love is the English "experiment": that which one does in order to provoke a novel occurrence, to elicit a new event, to produce a new body'.[6] In what follows, I want to suggest that this movement of love as *expérience* can be read as the *dividual becoming* of the beloved, and the constant *re*-interpretation of that process. Protevi concludes that,

> [s]ince it's impossible to experience in the living present the love of the other, because it's precisely the other that rends the living present, then the self-presence of the living present itself must be a fiction, it must have always already been rent asunder by an originary alterity.[7]

This rending-asunder of the 'living present' is the original alterity of the trace, which undermines the primacy of originality in favour of repetitive alterity. If love can be reimagined in terms of the trace, then its fictive properties are those of a virtual movement outside of immanent and transcendental distinctions – it works to inscribe an illimitable *noēteon*. As Compagnon notes, Proust teaches us that we 'hypothesize the existence of laws – an ideal book, an ideal woman – but they are never the ones we love. And we love the others precisely because that is not what they are.'[8] Writing and rewriting these laws is the irrepressible, present-absent movement of loving: its motor is the virtual overwriting of its fictions. In Proust, one loves the thing that is not what it is. Although in many ways this chapter continues the argument about desire presented above, it also addresses the important distinction that Proust makes between desire and love: it draws us closer to an imagined possibility of present plenitude (it is *necessitated* by that imagination), only to underline the impossibility of any such presentation.

ALBERTINES

To begin, I want to return to the narrator's attempt to differenciate the various girls of the *petite bande*. In this episode, we are told that he

> noticed the emergence of a pale oval, of two green eyes, or black ones, [he] had no idea whether they were those whose charm had struck [him] a moment before, in [his] inability to single out and recognize one or other of these girls and allot them to her. (*YG* 370–1)
>
> je voyais émerger un ovale blanc, des yeux noirs, des yeux verts, je ne savais pas si c'était les mêmes qui m'avaient déjà apporté du charme tout à l'heure, je ne pouvais pas les rapporter à telle jeune fille que j'eusse séparée des autres et reconnue. (356)

As the narrator finds himself initiated into the *petite bande*, as he begins to conceive of its members as distinct, objective entities, still linked to the original 'charm' and fluidity of the feminine form which was his first positing of their group, he finds aroused in himself amorous perceptions of their individual, distinctive features. In *A Thousand Plateaus*, Deleuze and Guattari note that, from the differenciations of the *petite bande*, eventually,

> Albertine is slowly extracted from a group of girls, with its own number, code, hierarchy; and not only is this group or restricted mass suffused by an unconscious, but Albertine has her own multiplicities that the narrator, once he has isolated her, discovers on her body and in her lies. (*TP* 36)

Her differentiation is *constituted by* the 'unconscious' flows of desiring; the slow extraction is a flow itself, as duration is constituted by the virtual coexistence of instants. The original emergence of 'Albertine' is swallowed among the multiplication of these codes. This unintelligible mass of feminine beauty is like an instantaneous, pure *noēteon*, lacking any distinct forms. As the narrator's desire passes over this conglomerate, the multiplicities inherent in his desiring machines go to work in determining, 'slowly', their associations with the codes that determine this 'Albertine'.

Let us take a moment to examine this 'slow extraction' more closely – for this is the necessary hinge which translates amorphous desire into love. It occurs across the horizon, the smooth space which produces the narrator's understanding of the *petite bande*. On his walks through the Balbec region or on his afternoons spent on Balbec-Plage, the narrator notices a member of the *petite bande*, a young golfer, frequently walking to, he assumes, her friend's house. Having kept watch for her and her friends for iteratively countless afternoons, the narrator finally discovers the girl's name, and begins to attach an identity to the transient 'golfer [joueuse de golf]', so fluid before this point that she could have dissolved back into the 'group' of the 'shared, unstable and elusive' *bande*. Indeed, acknowledging that it 'was almost certain that Albertine and the girl going to her friend's house were one and the same [qu'Albertine et cette jeune fille entrant chez son amie fussent une seule et même personne, c'était pratiquement une certitude]' (*YG* 425; 409), he seems to point towards the instability and virtuality of this ontological, identity-assigning operation:

> [A]lthough the innumerable images that the dark haired golfing-girl showed me at later times, however dissimilar they are, can be superimposed on one another, because I know she was the model of them all, and though, if I wind in the clew of my memories of her, I can follow the same identity from one to the other, find my way through the labyrinth and come back always to the same person, on the other hand if I try to find my way back to the girl I passed when I was with my grandmother, I lose my way. (*YG* 425)

> tandis que les innombrables images que m'a présentées dans la suite la brune joueuse de golf, si différentes qu'elles soient les unes des autres, se superposent (parce que je sais qu'elles lui appartiennent toutes), et que si je remonte le fil de mes souvenirs, je peux, sous le couvert de cette identité et comme dans un chemin de communication intérieure, repasser par toutes ces images sans sortir d'une même personne, en revanche, si je veux remonter jusqu'à la jeune fille que je croisai le jour où j'étais avec ma grand'mère, il me faut ressortir à l'air libre. (409)

This passage recalls the quality of desire that we considered in the previous chapter: the narrator seeks to trace the trace, in perception, in memory, in writing, but can only ever defer it. This 'clew' of memories is wound back and disseminated by the 'innumerable images' of this idea, which emerges from the group, the *petite bande*, into her own group, the 'innumerable images' of herself – Albertine or the 'golfing-girl'. As Deleuze notes, there 'are so many Albertines that we should give a distinct name to each, and yet there is something like the same theme here, the same quality under various aspects' (*PS* 68). This 'same theme' seems to shadow and connect all of the names 'Albertine' or 'dark haired golfing-girl' or 'girl I passed with my grandmother', or any other 'distinct name' that should be given to another – but more strangely, its 'various aspects' also prevent each name from being identical to the others. Just as, in the Bois or Roussainville, the narrator found his desire to be 'born suddenly' (*S* 157) from a kind of difference in unity, so the identity of these various, iterating names for the many Albertines offers differing/deferring 'innumerable images', that then take on a form and a name.[9]

As Deleuze notes in *Proust and Signs*, 'each love contributes its difference, which was already included in the preceding love, and all the differences are contained in the primordial image that we unceasingly reproduce at different levels' (*PS* 68). As these images are dividual productions (the possibility of love for *an* or *the* Albertine), they emerge out of the group[ ] in pure multiplicity – similar difference. As Deleuze notes, 'in order to become a term in the series of loves, Albertine must be isolated from the group in which she first appears' (*PS* 77). This differen*c*iation as distinction is the key to the emergence of love, but it is aporetic, because it is a deferral, a halting just before the moment of separation. Like the iterability of language, which defines *and* disseminates, so love must remain determining *and* obscuring. More accurately, then, Deleuze and Guattari ask:

> What does it mean to love somebody? It is always to seize that person in a mass, extract him or her from a group, however small, in which he or she participates, [...] then to find that person's own packs, the multiplicities he or she encloses within himself or herself which may be of an entirely different nature. To join them to mine, to make them penetrate mine, and for me to penetrate the other persons. Heavenly nuptials, multiplicities of multiplicities. (*TP* 35)

It is 'always to seize that person' amid a tide of desiring flows that define and also generalise them. For Deleuze here, love is not the absolute individuation of romantic culture, but the constant emergence and submergence of the beloved in their own 'packs', differen*t*iated from themselves.[10] Apropos of the memory of Albertine, the narrator notes that his

> love kept some 'slack' between it and the image of Albertine, enabling it, like a badly adjusted beam of light, to settle briefly on others before returning to focus on her. (*YG* 425)
>
> mon amour garda parfois entre lui et l'image d'Albertine certain « jeu » qui lui permettait, comme un éclairage mal adapté, de se poser sur d'autres avant de revenir s'appliquer à ells. (410)

This 'slack' (or 'play [« jeu »]') is a kind of flowing mobility, affecting all of Albertine's 'packs' or 'groups', both those that she emerges from and those she herself generates. We might call these *noēteons* '*petite bande* with its green and brown eyes', as well as 'Albertine' and 'the dark haired golfing-girl'. And in entertaining this 'play' that is 'like a badly adjusted beam of light', this flickering of reductive certainty between the Idea strictly of Albertine and the groups which Albertine's body emerges from and plunges back into, the concept 'Albertine' derives even greater complexity. After all, a play around an image is a play of being and not being: a *sumplokē* of presence and absence, like the work of literature itself.

The image of love that we find in in Proust's novel again problematises stable ontologies based on *parousia*, because the beloved is constantly emerg*ing* from a distinct coding or grouping that problematises her unifiable, static presence. Later in the novel, the narrator describes love as a

> synthesis become visible but no more rational, which the man who gathers the precious residue on the face of the woman he loves tries in his turn, in order to understand what is going on behind it, to analyse and break down into its intellectual components. (*PF* 321)

> synthèse devenue visible mais non plus rationnelle, et que celui qui en recueille le précieux résidu sur le visage de l'être aimé essaye à son tour, pour comprendre ce qui se passe en celui-ci, de ramener par l'analyse à ses éléments intellectuels. (*P* 334)

This synthesis is not *rational* in the sense of a chronological or even logical hierarchy, but is, rather, a fluctuation of intensities aroused from the *aiôn* of the beloved, emerging from the flows of pastness inherent to desire. Again, the narrating ~~voice~~ seeks to transform *noēteon* into a present perception, only to discover the irrational flows of multiplicity that constitute it. Conducting this 'analysis', he is 'sure it must be Albertine' whom he finds, but

> all the other images remain separate from this one, because [he] cannot give it in retrospect an identity it did not have for [him] at the moment when it impinged on [his] sight. (*YG* 425)

> Je suis persuadé que c'est Albertine que je retrouve, [. . .] mais toutes ces images restent séparées de cette autre parce que je ne peux pas lui conférer rétrospectivement une identité qu'elle n'avait pas pour moi au moment où elle a frappé mes yeux. (409–10)

Albertine's pure immanence, and its multiplicities, challenge her transcendental 'identity'. Perennially altered by the images of the ensuing 'Albertines', of the dark-haired young golfer, and all of those identities which the *petite bande*, Balbec, the weather, the narrator's myriad moods and countenances bestow upon her, that original image of 'that particular girl with full cheeks [cette jeune fille aux grosses joues]' whom he first noticed on the front, the narrator notes, he 'was never to see again [au sens strict du mot revoir, je ne l'ai jamais revue]' (*YG* 425; 410).

Albertine's being splinters into new multiplicities, which activate the equivalent multiplicity of the novel's many narrators. The reduction the lover seeks to make – reducing their beloved to 'intellectual components' – is a task with no end, for the immanent beloved can always offer a countenance, a look, a behaviour, express a desire, which contradicts or unsettles that reduction, or which challenges the striation of that 'analysis'. So, while loving is to 'seize a person in a mass', while it seems to be seizing them *from* the mass (the unknown, yet particular girl with the full cheeks the narrator has never seen again), the seiz*ing* is always an implex: the beloved is 'being seized' in *and* from the mass, retaining and shedding its characteristics by turns. The indeterminate 'play', the known, and once-known concepts intermingle in this image of thought, to the point that the narrator notes it

> enabled [him], for a split second, to make reality vanish, not just external reality, [. . .] but also the inner, purely subjective reality. (*YG* 425–6)

> Ce qui me permettait, l'éclair d'un instant, de faire évanouir la réalité, non pas seulement la réalité extérieure [. . .] mais même la réalité intérieure et purement subjective. (410)

Intelligibly vanished, but always in the act of return*ing* as the sense of *noēteon*.

The narrator describes a particular moment in which he is first trying to 'focus on the memory' he had 'taken away [je pus voir le souvenir que je rapportais]' of one girl who,

> by the magician's sleight of hand, had been substituted for the girl [he] had had watched so often along the esplanade, and who had nothing in common with her. (*YG* 453)

> grâce à l'habileté du prestidigitateur, sans avoir rien de celle que j'avais suivie si longtemps au bord de la mer, lui avait été substituée. (437–8)

He is confronted with two Albertines: 'the unremarkable and touching Albertine [la médiocre et touchante Albertine]' from his conversation that afternoon, and the previously seen and imagined other, 'mysterious Albertine, against the backdrop of the sea [la mystérieuse Albertine en face de la mer]': both 'memories, pictures [des souvenirs, c'est-à-dire des tableaux]' (*YG* 453), though conflicting, produce this *sumplokē* of the same, yet different, person. Trying to comprehend a multiplicity of differing Albertines, the narrator notes that,

> since memory immediately begins to take snap-shots which are quite independent of one another, abolishing all links and sequence among the scenes they show, in the collection of them which it displays, the latest does not necessarily obliterate the earlier ones. (*YG* 453)

> puis comme la mémoire commence tout de suite à prendre des clichés indépendants les uns des autres, supprime tout lien, tout progrès, entre les scènes qui y sont figurées, dans la collection de ceux qu'elle expose, le dernier ne détruit pas forcément les précédents. (438)

In viewing differing photographs of the same person, the narrator notes that the accumulated snapshots of memory set up a disquieting *restance*, or remains, which informs the sense of the most recent photograph, or memory. Similarly, across Proust's literary *restance*, there is no ~~voice~~ that determines *a* distinct Albertine: as *resemblance*, the literary does not 'present' any discrete, totalised being. The 'present' photograph of Albertine is a pure, flowing multiplicity – a trace, unnameable or, rather, unintelligible – yet ostensibly compliant to this unifying name. But as Deleuze notes, each varying Albertine seemingly deserves a distinct name. By engaging directly with these phenomenal and iterative problems, Proust's woven text mobilises the aporetic *restance* of literary presentation, tossing us, him and his narrator[ ] down the traced, presence-less abyss.

GROUPING LOVE, LOVING GROUPS

Therefore, as Proust describes love, the subject is confronted with a constant tension between a seemingly static, present-able beloved, the myriad degrees of absence they indicate/implicate, and the weaving between these two poles that their 'form' evokes. Love is more than an attempt to unify desiring-multiplicity; indeed, as we can witness throughout the generation of the *Recherche*, the *restance* of love – its constancy throughout every perception made by the characters experiencing it – is obdurate and unremitting: it ends by seemingly absorbing every perception it encounters. The narrator describes a 'type of mental obsessiveness which, under the aggravation of love, becomes the exclusive rehearsal of the memory of a certain person [cette sorte de manie mentale qui, dans l'amour, favorise la renaissance exclusive de l'image d'une certaine personne]' (YG 403; 387). Absence, just like apparent presence, cannot be ontologically totalised, because it recurrently evokes these images. Like the problem of literary inscription itself, love is directed towards the iterations of itself that surpass its 'present' appearance. As Slavoj Žižek argues, 'the excess of the beloved, what in the beloved eludes my grasp, is the very place of the inscription of my own desire into the beloved object – transcendence is the form of immanence'.[11] In Proust's novel, this 'exclusive rehearsal of memory' distinguishes love (always emerging from the mass or pack, from the flows of desire) as atemporal, and, for that reason, renders it incapable of being confined to immanent or transcendental categories. The incessant flow of this recurrence rejects logical stability: rather, each of the variant Albertine[ ], as we have noted, exceed an originating form, and as such they overflow from their imagined source before it can be presented.

Because love rejects this kind of organised logic, it cannot be reasoned with. We can love what we do not desire, sometimes in defiance of our wellbeing.[12] It will be helpful here to borrow an insight from Max Scheler's discussion of love in *The Nature of Sympathy* (1923). Challenging the assumption of intentionality, Scheler's phenomenological interpretation of affect offers us an understanding of love removed from presentational reasoning. In this reading, the priority of love depends precisely on its mediating indeterminacy – its being present when it is not present, absolutely unintelligible yet tracing its impressions onto perception. Love never reveals its origin, though its seeming *cause* – the beloved – is immanent, right there before the lover ('the latest [version] does not necessarily obliterate the earlier ones' (*YG* 453)). Scheler argues that love and hate

> are entirely *primitive* and *immediate* modes of emotional response to the value-content itself; so much so that, phenomenologically speaking, they do not even disclose a process of apprehending value, (e.g. feeling, preference etc.) let alone the making of a value-judgment.[13]

The 'primitive and immediate' complexion of love and hate abolish the intellectual distance required for a determination of value. Scheler cites Franz Brentano's description of love and hatred as 'acts of an elementary kind', pointing out that Brentano 'actually regards them as prior even to judgment itself'.[14] Hence, Scheler argues that love *precedes* the reasons that a lover might give to account for its emergence, noting 'the extraordinary perplexity which can be seen to ensue when people are asked to give "reasons" for their love or hatred. It is then that one sees how these "reasons" are invariably looked for after the event'. Love is not itself a value judgement, but rather, 'necessarily fastens upon the individual core of things, the *core of value* [...] which can never be wholly resolved into values of susceptible judgment'.[15] Like the trace, that is, love emanates from an unpresentable, originary repetition: it is conditioned by nothing but itself.

For Scheler, love reaches towards a '*core of value*'. In the vocabulary that I proposed in Chapter 2, the lover's attempt to give reasons for loving is tantamount to transposing love into the realm of durational chronology and signification. This strikes us, Scheler writes, as 'a kind of offence and transgression, a profane intrusion upon love

[...] that we should apply conceptual categories of valuation to the values of objects we love'.[16] In the temporal and sense-ual terms of the *Recherche*, the mass of love cannot be reduced to any one of its parts – to any particular perception, when its nature is to spread out across all of the varying adumbrations of the beloved, across different times. Love for Proust is the kind of machine that Deleuze and Guattari call an *agencement* (assemblage), irreducible to its parts, yet tracing them into perception – unintelligibly.[17] The narrator perceives some sense of the complex *agencement* that constitutes these affects. As opposed to ontology, which rounds off the complexity of all of these (to use the narrator's metaphor) 'photographs' to an intelligible essence, *agencement* is the complex network of the unnameable traces that make up love.

In *Le Côté de Guermantes*, alone in his family home in Paris, the despondent narrator is suddenly cheered by a visit from Albertine. As Françoise ushers her into his bedroom, the narrator describes how 'the plenitude of her body [la plénitude de son corps]' seemed to contain 'the days spent in that Balbec to which I have never since returned [les jours passés dans ce Balbec où je n'étais jamais retourné]' (*GW* 349; 340). The passage dwells upon the way in which a whole web or labyrinth of past experiences seems to radiate outwards from her person.

> On each of Albertine's smiling, questioning, hesitant features I could spell out the questions: 'And what about Madame de Villeparisis? And the dancing-master? And the confectioner?' When she sat down, her back seemed to be saying: 'There are no cliffs here, I know, but you don't mind if I sit beside you, as I used to in Balbec, do you?' She was like an enchantress representing a mirror of time. (*GW* 349)
>
> Sur chaque trait rieur, interrogatif et gêné du visage d'Albertine, je pouvais épeler ces questions : « Et Madame de Villeparisis ? Et le maître de danse ? Et le pâtissier ? » Quand elle s'assit, son dos eut l'air de dire : « Dame, il n'y a pas de falaise ici, vous permettez que je m'asseye tout de même près de vous, comme j'aurais fait à Balbec ? » Elle semblait une magicienne me présentant un miroir du Temps. (340)

Albertine produces, or reiterates, so much of what might be reductively termed 'Balbec', but also the *noēteon* that escapes definition and language, something we could come close to describing as 'concept-time-passing-in-Balbec', or 'concept-first-amorousness-in-Balbec-at-sunset'. As Husserl argues, '[a]*ll components of the Thing-Idea are themselves Ideas, Each implying the "and so forth" of "endless" possibilities*'.[18] The attempt to define such a production of Ideas underscores the fundamental discrepancy between impression and signification: each perception of Albertine initiates a trace that could never be described, or presented, in its fullness. Thus, each varied *noēteon* is constituted by its irreducible *this-ness*, or, what Deleuze and Guattari (after Duns Scotus) refer to as a 'haecceity', from the Latin *hic*, or 'here'.

In using *re*markable language to attempt to articulate the distinct, diverse intensities which make up the Idea Albertine, and which provide the 'invariable reappearance' of the 'images' from the past offered by Albertine's various 'features', we fall into the same trap as we would if we described them as an image: a 'concept-anything-Balbec' is precisely a haecceity. And indeed, for the narrator, it *must* be a haecceity, because this is what brings time as sensible, but not always intelligible, in the 'mirror of time' which reflects it. The haecceity's very this-ness is its expansion *as* all of its possibly determinable points, everything that contributes to rendering it possible as differen*c*iation. This goes for all spheres of interpretation: temporality, phenomenality, density, malleability – any distinction that can give form or type. So, for argument's sake, in the temporal sphere, Albertine might secrete an image from the narrator's memory of 'first-Monday-at-Balbec-,noon', and also, 'first-Monday-at-Balbec-,13h'. They differ on a temporal axis, but incorporated within their Ideal complexity are the differen*c*iating features of these haecceities. As Deleuze and Guattari write in *A Thousand Plateaus*: 'A shorter day and a longer day are not, strictly speaking, extensions but degrees proper to extension, just as there are degrees proper to heat, color, etc.' (*TP* 253). Differen*c*iating schemata produce haecceities across sensible axes of 'contrariety'.

Across various points of intensity, these haecceities are each 'a perfect individuality lacking nothing' (*TP* 261), which become substantial as the multiplicity of impressions in the lover's subjective *agencement*. Each Idea is made up of various judgements: each of these judgements necessarily has its own perfect individuality, which is a haecceity, like the combinative, *virtual* Idea itself. Each plurality produced by consciousness is both singular *and* plural in virtual coexistence, and as such transcends and incorporates, as well as divides up and renders sensible, its haecceities.

In this light, Deleuze and Guattari answer their question from Proust's narrator's perspective:

> What is a girl, what is a group of girls? Proust at least has shown us that their individuation, collective or singular, proceeds not by subjectivity but by haecceity, pure haecceity. 'Fugitive beings.' They are pure relations of speeds and slownesses, and nothing else. (*TP* 271)

The 'speeds' of the interminable individuation of various, multiple haecceities that constitute a beloved, interweave across the multiplicities and planes that constitute the lover's many selves. It is for this reason that the programming, the syncing of these two machines is such a profoundly complex task – that of love. Albertine is always a fugitive.[19] Her 'presence' is always implying past Albertines that have escaped forever. Each of her 'lies', Deleuze and Guattari point out,

> is nearly devoid of content; it tends on the contrary to merge with the emission of a particle issuing from the eyes of the beloved, a particle that stands only for itself and travels too fast through the narrator's auditory or visual field. (*TP* 271)

The 'particle', the lie, moves too fast in the moment, but once it becomes part of the narrator's Idea of Albertine (and its *aiôn*) it is caught in the gears of his loving-machine. The haecceity of each of the beloved's aspects, each momentary emission, becomes embroiled with other haecceities in her Idea, further complexifying the machine.

As with a *noēteon*, a haecceity's rich, 'perfect individuality' can come about only through its complexity. This may be due to the intricate positioning of its event across the chronological structure of the subject's duration, but it also has to do with the complexity of multiplicities which *give* haecceity. Two blue spheres might be thought to be identical; only upon a closer inspection could we determine that one is Earth, rendered unique and thus accruing its this-ness from the absolutely necessitous compilation of every infinitesimal detail on its surface. All of its intensities extend topologically, intensely, as its own complex image of thought. The 'plane of consistency or of composition of haecceities [. . .] knows only speeds and affects' – intensities – which is not the 'altogether different plane of forms, substances and subjects. And it is not even the same time, the same temporality. *Aeon*: the indefinite time of the event' (*TP* 262). The sensible dimension of the *aiôn* incorporates, produces, *intensifies* a haecceity. The degrees of speed collapse into planes of intensities: the 'fastest can even connect its intensity to the slowest, which, as an intensity, does not come after the fastest but is simultaneously at work on a different stratum or plane' (*TP* 174). This is a nonnumerical multiplicity, the dividual incorporation of speeds. The unique rhythm of the *aiôn* is not chronological: it encompasses 'a simultaneous too-late and too-early, something that is both going to happen and has just happened' (*TP* 262).

The trace leads one into *restance*, or the abyss of multiplicity. During the scene in *Le Côté de Guermantes* when the narrator speaks with Albertine in his room in Paris, he is considering his 'optimistic assumption about the likelihood of her obliging' his desires.

> I should probably have replied that this assumption was provoked (*as the forgotten outlines of Albertine's voice retraced for me the contour of her*

personality) by the emergence of certain words which had not previously formed part of her personality, at least not in the sense she now gave them. (*GW* 353, my emphasis)

j'aurais peut-être répondu que cette hypothèse était due (*tandis que les traits oubliés de la voix d'Albertine redessinaient pour moi le contour de sa personnalité*) à l'apparition de certains mots qui ne faisaient pas partie de son vocabulaire, au moins dans l'acception qu'elle leur donnait maintenant. (344, my emphasis)

Within his attempts to 'analyse and break down' Albertine into 'her intellectual components' (*PF* 321), he encounters not only the 'emergence' of the trace, but also seemingly 'forgotten outlines'. As traces, though, they are not strictly forgotten, because they are now, in part, remembered. They constantly infer themselves as the sense of the narrator's perceptions of Albertine, but they also remain 'unremembered', neither present nor absent, but *implied* by the *sumplokē* of the text. Every adumbration of the beloved not only traces the intelligible data she secretes, but also the 'forgotten outlines' which contribute to the constant fashioning, by the lover, of the beloved's 'personality'.[20] The narrator thus must come to terms with the illimitable multiplicities, the speeds and planes by which these 'components' – the haecceities from various speeds, as intensities, of pastness – constitute the Idea of the beloved's 'personality': her codes, her complex machine, her *noēteon*.

ALBERTINE'S FACE AND THE 'BLACK HOLE/WHITE WALL SYSTEM'

Love integrates the horizons of sensibility, the full *noēteon* of the beloved, the beloved's 'own packs, the multiplicities he or she encloses within himself or herself'. In *A Thousand Plateaus*, Deleuze and Guattari introduce the curious idea of a '*black hole/white wall system*' to describe a certain tension between signification and subjectification, legibility and obscurity, surface and depth, in the flux of the identification. They write: '[s]ignifiance is never without a white wall upon which it inscribes its signs and redundancies. Subjectification is never without a black hole in which it lodges its consciousness, passion and redundancies' (*TP* 167). The 'abstract machine' of love operates in the space in which these two axes meet, or mutate into each other. Or, as Deleuze and Guattari put it, the 'very special mechanism' which is 'situated at their intersection' is, '[o]ddly enough', a 'face: the *white wall/black hole* system. A broad face with white cheeks, a chalk face with eyes cut in for a black hole' (*TP* 167). The *face* is the figure that Deleuze and Guattari propose for this intersection of irreconcilable spatial metaphors: the white surface that signifies the legibility of the symbolic order, and the depth or hollow of subjectivity, the part of the subject that cannot be reduced to the system of signs.

For Deleuze and Guattari, it is not so much faces themselves which generate this system, but rather the apparatus of *faciality* [*visagéité*], the manner in which faces 'define zones of frequency or probability' and set a determination or a 'field' (*TP* 168) within the black hole/white wall system. The form of faciality sets an instituting repetition, a trace, in the respective void/infinity of absolute subjectification/signification; it is purely dividual, the lower limit of one in the other, the smallest white wall in a black hole and, contiguously, vice versa. It is 'not exactly' that the face 'constitutes the wall of the signifier or the hole of subjectivity. The face, at least the concrete face, vaguely begins to take shape *on* the white wall. It vaguely begins to appear *in* the black hole' (*TP* 168). Vaguely: the emergent horizon of the sensible is the 'atmosphere' of perception, 'constantly enshrouded by those mists that we call the sensible world or history'.[21] Mists, torpors, whirlwinds, pink hazes, flows: these are fitting metaphors for the intensities that fluctuate across sensibility.

> Sometimes faces appear on the wall, with their holes; sometimes they appear in the hole, with their linearized, rolled-up wall. [. . .] Thus the black hole/white wall system is, to begin with, not a face but the abstract machine that produces faces according to the changeable combinations of its cogwheels. (*TP* 168)

In love, these 'cogwheels' are the multiplicities, the forgotten outlines, the speeds and codes of the beloved that the lover seeks to join to and penetrate. The black hole swallows the lover's temporalities, the 'particles' the beloved emits. This abstract machine is thus *dividual*, dissolving the possibility of a distinction between immanence and transcendence.

Derrida, too, contemplates the signifying infinity of the other's face, an infinity that always transcends its ideation. In *Writing and Difference*, he argues that the 'expression of this infinity is the *face*', and describes how the 'absolute overflowing of ontology – as the totality and unity of the same: Being – by the other occurs as infinity because no totality can constrain it' (*WD* 98). The infinity Derrida refers to is the *epekeina tēs ousias* that renders such an infinitude a trace – it can be thought, but only in the terms which cannot give it, or present it – 'infinity irreducible to the *representation* of infinity' (*WD* 98). Thus, representation, or the signification that Deleuze and Guattari imagine as the white wall, cannot account for the infinitude aroused by the trace, but any conception of this kind of signification is necessarily a trace itself. As Derrida notes, the possible presence of spoken language – its 'forgotten outlines' – once disseminated as iterable performance or writing, becomes 'a signification which I do not possess because it is a signification. Theft is always the theft or speech or text, of a trace' (*WD* 175). The iterable possibility of infinity (the abyss of subjectification) is infinite, and infinitely irreducible to its signification. The possibility of inscribing infinity is writing, the abyssal chain of supplements, the 'overflowing of ontology'.

Albertine's own face presents an illustrative example of this irreducibility. Upon first attempting to individuate Albertine, the narrator tries 'to remember the little beauty spot on her cheek, just below the eye [ce petit grain de beauté sur la joue au-dessous de l'œil]'. He remembers seeing Albertine previously from Elstir's window, and that he 'had seen' this beauty spot 'on her chin [j'avais vu ce grain de beauté sur le menton]' (*YG* 453; 438). Then, in order to effectively contract the real concept of Albertine's facial mole, he notes that his 'misguided memory moved it about her face, sometimes putting it in one place, at other times in another [ma mémoire errante le promenait ensuite sur la figure d'Albertine et le plaçait tantôt ici tantôt là]' (*YG* 453–4; 438). In an attempt to validate its true position, he 'took advantage of this brief immobility to make a thorough check of the place where the beauty spot was to be found [Je profitai de cette immobilité pour regarder et savoir définitivement où était situé le grain de beauté]' (*YG* 455; 440).

As each of these various Albertines are perceived with their shifting moles, each signifies as a kind of verifying watermark of every separately valid perception of the beloved. These may hover over perceptions and impart no sense of certainty or error, or chronology, for each implies all the others. The black hole of the narrator's subjectivity creates an infinitely various range of spaces and temporalities for the white wall of signification – the haecceities of Albertine-with-mole-where? It is across all the planes of consistency where these *could intersect* that the faciality of these haecceities emerges. 'Faciality is always a multiplicity' (*TP* 182), and, as such, its overflowing origin, the intersection of the black hole/white wall axes as a *system* is always multiple: the compilation of virtual haecceities in an Ideal *noēteon*. All of these definitively true *and* false moled-Albertines populate the black hole/white wall of her faciality, and the narrator's love. The narrator draws an analogy between this problem of Albertine's mole and his efforts to identify motifs from the Vinteuil sonata in the expanded septet. In its musical transience, its present-less movement across durational time, the ~~voice~~ notes that his 'memory kept moving [it] from the *andante* to the finale [ma mémoire faisait errer de l'andante au finale]'. Only later, 'with the score in hand [ayant la partition en main]', is he finally 'able to find it and localize it where it belonged, in the *scherzo* [je pus la trouver et l'immobiliser dans mon souvenir à sa place, dans le scherzo]' (*YG* 455; 440). But the *scherzo*, the sonata, the phrase, are merely simulacra of that impossible to pinpoint implex of their perform*ing* and remember*ing restance*. And as, in his intensify*ing* narrative, the narrator focuses on the *sense* of the reduction that positions impressions in their most accurate order, a definitive perception of Albertine is arrived at: the mole comes 'to rest for ever on her upper lip, just under her nose [s'arrêta à jamais sur la lèvre supérieure au-dessous du nez]' (*YG* 455; 440).

So what to do with all of these other real Albertines, truthfully perceived in a past that surely is as real as the past now committed to memory of the apparently real Albertine with the mole just below her nose? Because their mole is in the wrong place, does this render the entire version, too, inaccurate as memory? Surely not: the other Albertines with their other moles will continue to populate the black hole/white wall system of the narrator's love for Albertine, its faciality retaining and promoting a trace across the length of the horizons of each perception of her.[22] Therefore, the mole does not come 'to rest for ever on her upper lip': its inscription is as iterable as the language that describes it. Later in the novel, the narrator speaks of the 'effigies, stored intact in the memory [effigies gardées intactes dans la mémoire]', and how it is that

> when we return to them, [they] astonish us by their lack of resemblance to the being we know now; we understand then how they are daily, painstakingly remodelled by habit. (*PF* 57–8)

> quand on les retrouve, on s'étonne de leur dissemblance d'avec l'être qu'on connaît ; on comprend quel travail de modelage accomplit quotidiennement l'habitude. (*P* 60)

It is this 'remodelling' that is performed, not daily, but *instant*aneously, by virtual contraction, as the work of love.

Deleuze and Guattari argue that Proust's portrayal of love in the *Recherche* depicts the black hole/white wall system distinctly. Specifically, they evoke '[t]he face of Odette with her broad white or yellow cheeks, and her eyes as black holes. But this face continually refers back to other things, also arrayed on the wall' (*TP* 185). It is the faciality of this intersection between the infinitely signifying iterations of the beloved, and the Proustian lover's interpretation of his own dividual subjectivity, that defines the narrator's interest in love. Deleuze and Guattari may be correct in noting that the French novel 'is too concerned with measuring the wall, or even building it, with plumbing the depths of black holes and composing faces. [. . .] It stuffs its characters down the hole and bounces them off the wall' (TP 186). However, Proust's conception of love utilises the faciality at the intersection of the wall in the hole, the hole in the wall, and plunges down the abyss that is language, literature, le propre, and ontology itself. The Recherche may be interested in building the wall or stuffing itself down the hole, but Proust's interest in the aporia of iteration shows that loving constantly walls up the hole: at every possible conception, the wall has already paved itself across the hole, and the hole has already bored itself through the wall.

SHATTERING THE FACE

Thus, in attempting to love, in individuating Albertine from the 'pack' of desire to her own packs and multiplicities, the narrator recognises that Albertine is similar to a person who one has not seen for some years; a wall emerging through the hole. And yet: 'with Albertine, there was something more [avec Albertine il n'y avait que cela]' (GW 349; 340). In the past, the narrator was

> always surprised when [he] caught sight of her; she changed so much from day to day. But now she was hardly recognizable. No longer bathed in a pink haze, her features now stood out like those of a statue. (GW 350)
>
> j'étais toujours surpris en l'apercevant tant elle était journalière. Mais maintenant on avait peine à la reconnaître. Dégagés de la vapeur rose qui les baignait, ses traits avaient sailli comme une statue. (340–1)

In noting that 'she was hardly recognizable', the narrator is still seeking to locate the various speeds of Albertine's own being, to individuate her and program his desire into her various production-haecceities. That is, not only does she revive the intellectual elements in the narrator's memory of those pure individualities (specific moments which did occur, singularly, at Balbec), but also the new forms of their syntheses, as additional degrees of sense. When Albertine is imagined as asking 'you don't mind if I sit beside you, as I *used to* in Balbec, do you?' (GW 349, my emphasis), she is not only recalling to the narrator each haecceity of the event(s), the actual times that she did, physically, seat herself beside him at Balbec, but also the false, the virtual, the iterative productions which, in the act of virtual contraction, memory and narrative, are constantly produced by the numerous narrators who remember Albertine. This textual, iterative 'used to' conjures the time[ ] she used to sit near him at Balbec: the synthetic, woven, real and false *sumplokē*, just like the Balbec morning[ ] considered in Chapter 1. All of these various productions, intertwined through the *restance* of the text (being either the narrator's remembering in time, or the reader's reading in it) are haecceities themselves: specific and unique instants, tears in the fabric of duration, *noēteon*. Vying with these is the heavy weight seized effortlessly by the virtual.

This 'seizing' occurs on myriad levels. Interestingly, the narrator later reaches a point in which he notes that Albertine 'had another face, or rather she had a real face at last [Elle avait un autre visage, ou plutôt elle avait enfin un visage]' (*GW* 350; 341). Her individuation is apparently complete. But this does not arrest the labour of production that occurs across the various planes of loving. The narrator notes that she indeed has 'a real face at last', a (re)memorable entity by which to observe the flows of his impressions, or rather, a plane of consistency on which they can populate, forget themselves, and virtualise. But even as this face emerges, as it becomes known, Albertine still fluctuates between the narrator's various versions of her, what Deleuze and Guattari call the 'series of views that are like different personalities' (*AO* 69). Just as there sensibly exists in the Ideal recognition of 'Albertine' haecceities of the unknown golfer and a chin-moled-Albertine, each perception emerges 'with Albertine's face jumping from one plane to another' (*AO* 69). Albertine may have now come to take 'form', but it is iterable, one of 'the "boxes," the "vessels" [that] all have their positive determinations, and enter into aberrant communication following a transversal that runs through the whole work' (*AO* 69). Albertine, sitting next to the narrator on his bed in 'total' presence, still *re*marks, *re*iterates, various, disseminating selves.[23] But just as when Balbec or the Méséglise way return, they bear no resemblance to their original haecceity or this-ness, so this vessel 'Albertine', always emerg*ing* from the vapour like a statue, still produces impressions which divide at the same time as they reinforce their signification. Albertine as the narrator reads her (as the fictive, readable person that can be imagined, and the iterable word) is doubly iterative – her fictive construction constantly challenges the stability of her form.

As Albertine's face jumps across various planes, often in direct contradiction to what she signifies, 'within the magnified proximity' by which perception is endowed by this 'vessel' of signification, 'everything [still] falls apart like a face drawn in sand, Albertine's face shatters into multiple partial objects' (*AO* 69). And it is this constant shattering, the integration and weaving through of multiple planes of consistency in the apparatus of faciality, the sensibility of the multiple in the real, that defines Proustian love. For his narrator,

> [the] human face is truly like that of a god in some Oriental theogony, a whole cluster of faces side by side, but on different planes and never all visible at once. (*YG* 493)

> Le visage humain est vraiment comme celui du Dieu d'une théogonie orientale, toute une grappe de visages juxtaposés dans des plans différents et qu'on ne voit pas à la fois. (477–8)

The face itself is a primary cultural signifier, but its content, what its faciality signifies, is intermittent. As Derrida notes, just as 'the face of Yahweh is the *total* person and the *total* presence', the 'face of God which commands while hiding itself is at once more and less a face than all faces' (*WD* 108). The presence of the beloved iterates – presents – more versions of itself than it could ever hide, and yet hides this '*total*' person and presence across the 'different planes' of consistency that her faciality arouses, and shatters, in the same movement.

The narrator is constantly describing his paving and digging across the various planes of the beloved's white wall/black hole system. But he is distinctly aware of their systematisation: the graft, the disparate elements that constitute the *sumplokē* of his love, that are seemingly 'present'. Much later in the novel, he makes a captive of Albertine by settling her in his apartments and attempting to know all her wishes and movements, pushing his love, its black hole/white wall system, to its limits. The narrator is tortured by doubt as to Albertine's '*mauvais genre*': her moral constitution, her tastes and desires. In coming to terms with the impossibility of ever knowing her completely, the narrator returns to considering the 'innumerable images', the faciality, of the beloved.

> Each time, a girl is so unlike what she was the time before (shattering as soon as we see her the memory we had kept of her and the desire we had planned to experience) that the stable identity we ascribe to her is purely fictitious, a convenience of language. (*PF* 55)

> À chaque fois, une jeune fille ressemble si peu à ce qu'elle était la fois précédente (mettant en pièces dès que nous l'apercevons le souvenir que nous avions gardé et le désir que nous nous proposions), que la stabilité de nature que nous lui prêtons n'est que fictive et pour la commodité du langage. (*P* 57)

The narrator has almost entirely come to terms with the fact that the Idea of Albertine is constantly in flux, shattered in the uncertainty of the present. Indeed, 'a convenience of language' is *the* convenience of writing, of signification itself, that cannot incorporate the haecceities, or the fullness of multiplicity, which it professes to represent. For the narrator, in Albertine's full white wall of signifying possibility, the 'steel had turned to cotton wool [L'acier était devenu coton]', blurring the media that inscribe her memory so that 'there would be no question of trying to break her resistance as she had already completely changed consistency [nous n'aurions plus rien à essayer de briser, puisque d'elle-même elle perdait toute consistence]' (*PF* 56; *P* 58). This 'formal' inconsistency is the essence of love, which is determined, the narrator says, as much by the intermittent absence of the beloved as by her presence:

> we need hardly repeat that love is often only the association between the image of a girl (of whom otherwise we would very quickly have tired) and the increased heart rate inseparable from a long, futile wait when the young lady in question has 'stood us up.' (*PF* 56)
>
> nous en avons parlé trop souvent pour le redire, bien souvent un amour n'est que l'association d'une image de jeune fille (qui sans cela nous eût été vite insupportable) avec les battements de cœur inséparables d'une attente interminable, vaine, et d'un « lapin » que la demoiselle nous a posé. (*P* 59)

The repetition of this attendant heart-rate is the rhythm of love's deferring-machine, an inconsistency inscribed through all the levels of its plane of immanence.

The iteration of a beloved person, with all its myriad and contradictory knowledge and times, disperses love's *agencement* within the narrator's black hole. This is why the white wall of the beloved's constant signification within and across the lover's black hole poses questions about the chronological experience of loving. In the same section of *La Prisonnière*, the narrator notes the impossible desire to totalise *agencement*, and posits a kind of inscription as a possible solution.

> And, in themselves, what were Albertine and Andrée? To know the answer, we should have to be able to arrest your movement, stop our lives being one long wait for you, who when you arrive are always different; to fix your image we should have to stop loving you, no longer experience your endlessly postponed and always disconcerting arrival, O young girls, O successive flashes in the whirlwind where we tremble to see you reappear, barely recognizing you in the dizzying velocity of light. (*PF* 54–5)
>
> Et, en elles-mêmes, qu'étaient Albertine et Andrée ? Pour le savoir, il faudrait vous immobiliser, ne plus vivre dans cette attente perpétuelle de vous où vous passez toujours autres ; il faudrait ne plus vous aimer, pour vous fixer, ne plus connaître votre interminable et toujours déconcertante arrivée, ô jeunes filles, ô rayon successif dans le tourbillon où nous palpitons de vous voir reparaître en ne vous reconnaissant qu'à peine, dans la vitesse vertigineuse de la lumière. (*P* 57)

Love can only be postponed; love can only be come to terms with, or known, once one is out of it, supplementing ontology with aporia. As a lover, the narrator desires to present a static presence of his beloved to himself. But the beloveds themselves iterate endlessly, like the names that apparently designate, or preserve them. In his emerging hypothesis, finding its bearing in the frustrated desire to love in uncertainty, the narrator 'bounces himself', to use Deleuze and Guattari's image, off the wall of the 'endless postponement': the beloveds' 'successive flashes in the whirlwind' of duration. And yet, the desire to impose some kind of determination upon the limitlessly signifying wall is his hope to stuff himself down the black hole of his own ipseity, 'the dizzying velocity of light' – the ultimate light of or within a black hole (or the white wall within it) – at which he 'trembles'. However, the desire to immobilise, to totalise these speeds or particles that the beloveds emit is unattainable; love deterritorialises both the lover and the beloved across varied planes of consistency, the planes of the white wall/black hole system. As the forms of these two verbs splice, and open out so that the wall is tunnelled through as much as the hole is paved, (constantly by the Proustian narrators' every inscribed facialisation of temporal data, as on the face of the clock), we can see the absent origin that faciality arouses shattering, 'like a face drawn in the sand' (*AO* 69), into the intensities that de-temporalise and de-spatialise within the *aiôn*.

Thus, across the 'always different' arrivals of his beloved, the narrator can only settle on her interminable iteration. But iteration itself iterates: there cannot be stability even in instability. Derrida argues that no 'process or project of idealization is possible without iterability, and yet iterability "itself" cannot be idealized' (*LI* 71). As such, the narrator must continue to remodel his beloved, appreciating the overflowing infinity of his task, while never being able to 'know' or appropriate it. This renders Albertine

> a strongly modelled figure with mysterious shadows. Its three-dimensional character was due to the superposition, not only of the successive images that Albertine had been for me, but also of admirable traits of intelligence and feeling, and grave faults of character, all unsuspected by me, which Albertine, in a kind of germination, a multiplication of herself, a sombre-hued flowering of flesh, had added to a nature once almost characterless, but now difficult to know in depth. (*PF* 59)

> se modelait avec de mystérieuses ombres et un puissant relief. Il était dû, d'ailleurs, à la superposition non seulement des images successives qu'Albertine avait été pour moi, mais encore des grandes qualités d'intelligence et de cœur, des défauts de caractère, les uns et les autres insoupçonnées de moi, qu'Albertine, en une germination, une multiplication d'elle-même, une efflorescence charnue aux sombres couleurs, avait ajoutés à une nature jadis à peu près nulle, maintenant difficile à approfondir. (*P* 61)

Malcolm Bowie refers to this section in explicating his idea of Proustian 'superimposition'.[24] As he suggests, this kind of 'strongly modelled figure with mysterious shadows' is a complex integration of forms which defers the totality of the beloved. Albertine is '*difficile à approfondir*' – she will never be totalised, never be reduced to ontology, yet she can be referred to by a total, ontological epithet: Albertine. This iterably textual Albertine illustrates for the narrator the abyss of infinity – its formless, conceptual transversality. A black hole that signifies endlessly, a white wall paved with subjectification: there is no way to measure her ontology, because all that one could ever forget is inscribed upon her face, is swallowed in her eyes.

STRAIGHTENING THE LINE

The difficulty of totalising the beloved, of rendering their differen*t*iation absolutely present, is insurmountable, but this same difficulty is the generator of love itself. The narrator notes that whenever Albertine 'moved her head she created a new woman, often undreamed of by [Chaque fois qu'elle déplaçait sa tête, elle créait une femme nouvelle, souvent insoupçonnée de moi]' him (*PF* 61; *P* 64). Throughout the fusion of times and perceptions, any Albertine invites perceptions contemporaneous not only with past Albertines, but forgotten correlations with other women: such is the infinitely productive quality of the instantaneous, intense *noēteon*. The narrator feels that he 'possessed not one, but innumerable young girls [Il me semblait posséder non pas une, mais d'innombrables jeunes filles]' (*PF* 61–2; *P* 64), all emerging from the one woman who

> should be attached, like Rosita and Doodica, to another woman whose different beauty makes us deduce the existence of another character, and that to see the one we should have to look at her in profile, the other full face. (*PF* 62)

> Mais combien il est plus étrange qu'une femme soit accolée, comme Rosita et Doodica, à une autre femme dont la beauté différente fait induire un autre caractère, et que pour voir l'une il faille se placer de profil, pour l'autre de face. (*P* 65)

Awash among the flows of the *aiôn* and the tides of the Lethe, perceptions emerge as pure intensities whose differen*t*iations course across varied planes of (in)consistency, each distilling their qualities into the others. This is perhaps why the narrator uses the metaphor of Rosita and Doodica, a curious example of a pair of conjoined twins exhibited in Paris by Barnum's circus. This image of separate but connected beings, exhibiting a family resemblance to one another, seems an apt figure for Albertine's multiplicity.²⁵ In the same, often-quoted scene,²⁶ the narrator describes how he feels able to 'arrest the movement [immobilizer]' (*PF* 54; *P* 57) of his beloved – whose 'speeds', and 'nothing else', are what constitutes her individuation, according to Deleuze and Guattari (*TP* 271) – while she is sleeping. Even here, however, he discovers that the intensities of differen*t*iation flow, as in a black hole/ white wall system, as differen*c*e-*in*,-and-*as*,-unity. In her sleep, he notes that he 'already knew several Albertines in one; now I felt I was seeing many more at rest beside me [Moi qui connaissais plusieurs Albertine en une seule, il me semblait en voir bien d'autres encore reposer auprès de moi]' (*PF* 61; *P* 64) – exploding out of the abyss of her stasis, interweaving with the traces of his imagination. This perception does not banish the sensible infinity unperceivable in *chronos*, but traces its infinity as *aiôn*. The trace of faciality arouses the possibility of recognition, the origin of subjectification *in* signification and vice versa, the traced same-yet-other 'faces' in the perception of the face.

This understanding reaches its culmination when the narrator reflects upon the novel he must write, and determines that the 'writer's task and duty are those of a translator [Le devoir et la tâche d'un écrivain sont ceux d'un traducteur]' (*FT* 199; 197). In interpreting the memories which constitute the lived life, the writer must contemplate not experience itself, but the trace that these experiences leave. In this process, a whole chain of temporally distinct experiences, of mental states, must be made cohesive: they must be straightened out into the form that the novel takes – which can never account for the trace itself. In the final volume, the narrator reflects on how difficult it is to remember a love affair accurately, because the original 'impressions' are supplanted by the lover's distorting interpretations of them, the 'passionate dialogue with ourselves' which is what we really remember when we remember being in love. The narrator speaks of how the writer's task of translating (especially where the obfuscations of vanity are at play) should be focused on

> realigning interior indirect speech (which as it goes on moves further and further away from the original, central impression) until it coincides with the straight line which ought to have run directly from the impression. (*FT* 199)
>
> le redressement de l'oblique discours intérieur (qui va s'éloignant de plus en plus de l'impression première et cérébrale) jusqu'à ce qu'il se confonde avec la droite qui aurait dû partir de l'impression. (197)

However, whenever 'love is involved', this process

> becomes painful. All our pretence of indifference, all our indignation against those lies which are so natural, so like the ones we tell ourselves, in a word

all those things we have not only, whenever we felt wretched or betrayed, said endlessly to our loved one, but even said over and over again to ourselves while we were waiting to see her, sometimes speaking aloud, breaking the silence of our bedroom with comments such as: 'No, really, that sort of behaviour is intolerable,' and; 'I consented to see you one last time, but I won't pretend it isn't painful,' to bring all that back to the truth of experience when it has moved so far away from it means putting an end to all that we value most, to everything that, when we have been alone with our over-excited plans for letters and approaches, has constituted our passionate dialogue with ourselves. (*FT* 199)

devient douloureux. Toutes nos feintes indifférences, toute notre indignation contre ses mensonges si naturels, si semblables à ceux que nous pratiquons nous-mêmes, en un mot tout ce que nous n'avons cessé, chaque fois que nous étions malheureux ou trahis, non seulement de dire à l'être aimé, mais même, en attendant de le voir, de nous dire sans fin à nous-mêmes, quelquefois à haute voix, dans le silence de notre chambre troublé par quelques : « non, vraiment, de tels procédés sont intolérables » et « j'ai voulu te recevoir une dernière fois et ne nierai pas que cela me fasse de la peine », ramener tout cela à la vérité ressentie dont cela s'était tant écarté, c'est abolir tout ce à quoi nous tenions le plus, ce qui, seul à seul avec nous-mêmes, dans des projets fiévreux de lettres et de démarches, fut notre entretien passionné avec nous-mêmes. (197)

The narrator's imagery here is suggestive. The passage draws attention to the necessarily curved line[ ] that makes up subjectivity, diverging away from every 'impression', even amid the briefest implex of sense. Writing the novel, creating the work of art, are attempts to straighten out the errant line of our own self-awareness over time, to attempt to recover our 'impressions'. Within any *noēteon* there is always contradictory impression-data: as with Albertine's mole, the narrator notes that it is the writer's task to 'realign' these inconsistencies. But in the case of love, this becomes impossible. For Bersani,

> [to] write about love should [. . .] be to write about a process of painful self-discovery. Or, more precisely, it is in the reflection on a failure of self-possession that the self is discovered; the detailed memory of that failure outlines an individuality that could never be satisfactorily reflected in the woman's eyes.[27]

Love, throughout times and memories, reveals to the collative author the fluctuations of intensity that mark different experiences, the *restance* of intensities intelligible only as unpresentable traces.

To the narrator, explicitly,

> [w]e imagine that love has for its object a being which can lie down before us, enclosed in a body. Alas! It is the extension of that body to every point in space and time which that being has occupied and will occupy. (*PF* 88)

Nous nous imaginons qu'il a pour objet un être qui peut être couché devant nous, enfermé dans un corps. Hélas ! il est l'extension de cet être à tous les points de l'espace et du temps que cet être a occupés et occupera. (*P* 91–2)

In attempting to make sense of this universe of 'points' on the graph of loving, while we 'cannot touch all these points' (*PF* 88), the act of loving involves a ceaseless attempt to trace a line through them, a line that can never materialise. This is the futile, yet inescapable, process of attempting to know, to individuate some*one*, and thus to be in love. In paying attention to what is sensible, straightening out the depth of forgotten pasts in iterative perceptions, Proust's novel structures love around a nucleus which integrates the literary act across the intensities, the unbounded planes of sensibility that constitute the textual consistency of his narrating ~~voice~~. In so far as loving is the attempt to interpret and compile these forgotten perceptions which are its sensible composition, Proust's narrator provides emphatic evidence for one of the novel's most critical hypotheses. 'Love is space and time made apprehensible to the heart [L'amour c'est l'espace et le temps rendus *sensibles* au cœur]' (*PF* 356; *P* 371, my emphasis), he argues, where this sensibility is the crossing of the 'mysterious furrow' of pre-figurality (or faciality), where writing can be sensed, but its 'meaning' remains deferred. The elusive inscription of the *Recherche* (sensible, but never entirely apprehensible across its enormous length) attests to the narrator's claim here: it is the depth[ ] that the heart can sense – rendering love sensible long before the intellect can distinguish its causes – that re-iterates its writer's labour.

NOTES

1. Proust's idea of love has attracted considerable critical attention. See, for example, Julius Rivers, *Proust and the Art of Love* (New York: Columbia University Press, 1983); William C. Carter's excellent, semi-biographical *Proust in Love* (New Haven: Yale University Press, 2006); Robbie Kubala, 'Love and Transience in Proust', *Philosophy* 91, no. 4 (2016): 541–57; Alison Finch 'Love, Sexuality and Friendship', in *The Cambridge Companion to Proust*, ed. Richard Bales (Cambridge: Cambridge University Press, 2001), 168–12; and Martha Nussbaum, 'The Ascent of Love: Plato, Spinoza, Proust', *New Literary History* 25, no. 4 (1994): 925–49.
2. Martha Nussbaum, *Love's Knowledge: Essays on Philosophy and Literature* (Oxford and New York: Oxford University Press, 1990), 287.
3. Descombes, *Proust*, 213.
4. Compagnon, *Proust between Two Centuries*, 70.
5. Deleuze and Guattari trace this Proustian logic in their interpretation of

love as 'a war machine endowed with strange and somewhat terrifying powers. Sexuality is the production of a thousand sexes, which are so many uncontrollable becomings' (*TP* 278).
6. John Protevi, 'Love', in *Between Deleuze and Derrida*, 183.
7. Protevi, 'Love', 186.
8. Compagnon, *Proust between Two Centuries*, 272.
9. In a complex reading of denomination in the work of Walter Benjamin, Alexander García Düttmann posits that since the name 'allows the nameless to appear, the name cannot be a name without being what it is not, what does not appear without it. The name must erase itself. That is why denomination is always over-naming. What is over-naming if it is not the erasing of the name? To name is to experience what is nameless.' Alexander García Düttmann, *The Gift of Language: Memory and Promise in Adorno, Benjamin, Heidegger, and Rosenzweig*, trans. Arline Lyons (London: Athlone Press, 2000), 37.
10. Frida Beckman usefully summarises this idea in Deleuze and Guattari's philosophy: 'Held together and fuelled by desire, such packs are fluent and irreducible to the One. This is also how we must understand making love. [...] These packs are the multiplicities enclosed within that person. Love is joining these multiplicities together.' Frida Beckman, *Between Desire and Pleasure: A Deleuzian Theory of Sexuality* (Edinburgh: Edinburgh University Press, 2013), 125.
11. Slavoj Žižek, *The Parallax View* (Cambridge, MA: The MIT Press, 2006), 356.
12. As Jose Ortega y Gasset argues, 'in some manner or form we also want what we love; but on the other hand, we obviously want many things that we do not love, things which leave us indifferent on a sentimental plane. Desiring a good wine is not loving it, and the drug addict desires drugs at the same time as he hates them for their harmful effect.' José Ortega y Gasset, *On Love: Aspects of a Single Theme*, trans. Toby Talbot (London: Cape, 1967), 11.
13. Max Scheler, *The Nature of Sympathy*, trans. Peter Heath (London: Routledge & Kegan Paul, 1979), 149.
14. Scheler, *The Nature of Sympathy*, 148.
15. Scheler, *The Nature of Sympathy*, 149.
16. Scheler, *The Nature of Sympathy*, 149.
17. In an interview, Deleuze highlights that if there is any 'unity' to *A Thousand Plateaus*, it is 'the idea of an assemblage [*agencement*] (which replaces the idea of desiring machines). [...] In assemblages you find states of things, bodies, various combinations of bodies, hodgepodges; but you also find utterances, modes of expressions, and whole regimes of signs. [...] An assemblage is carried along by its abstract lines, when it is able to have or trace abstract lines' (*TR* 177–8).
18. Husserl, *Ideas*, 415.
19. The constituting elusiveness of Albertine's character is of major critical

interest in the *Recherche*. Bowie refers to her as 'stratified, intermittent, brought before the mind's eye in her discontinuous incarnations [...] an immensely powerful algorithm'. Bowie, 'Reading Proust between the Lines', *The Strange M. Proust*, 129. Or, as he puts it elsewhere: 'Albertine is endlessly cancelled and reborn.' Bowie, 'Proust and the Art of Brevity', in *The Cambridge Companion to Proust*, 228.

20. In light of the implicating sense of literary 'forgotten outlines' that Proust highlights to describe his narrator's love, Hannah Freed-Thall details the complexity of Proustian nuance, which among the mediating machinery of literary *restance*, illuminates writing's attempt to encompass haecceities. She notes that 'Proust's sentences tend to slow down, spill out, and multiply possibilities in order to render the nuances of the in-between. As we meander through the *Recherche*, we often find ourselves drifting this way and that though sentences that distend, puff out, engorge into one shape, then another. We float in the interstice of the hypothetical.' Hannah Freed-Thall, *Spoiled Distinctions: Aesthetics and the Ordinary in French Modernism* (New York: Oxford University Press, 2015), 69–70.
21. Merleau-Ponty, *The Visible and the Invisible*, 84.
22. For Samuel Beckett, the mole episode establishes 'the *pictorial* multiplicity of Albertine that will duly evolve into a *plastic* and moral multiplicity, [...] a multiplicity in depth, a turmoil of objective and immanent contradictions over which the subject has no control.' Beckett, *Proust* (New York: Grove Press, 1931), 32. Garin Dowd notes that 'Beckett here is alert to aspects of Proustian individuation which Deleuze would later schematize in terms of the "white wall, black hole" model of identification.' Dowd, 'Apprenticeship, Philosophy, and the "Secret Pressures of the Work of Art" in Deleuze, Beckett, Proust and Ruiz; or Remaking the *Recherche*', in *Beckett's Proust/Deleuze's Proust*, ed. Mary Bryden and Margaret Topping (Basingstoke: Palgrave Macmillan, 2009), 95.
23. The calibrating movement of identity in Deleuze's conceptuion of love is identifed by Jerry Aline Flieger, who refers to how 'Deleuze is strikingly original in arguing that "becoming", in love or other transgressive processes, is not a question between individual subjects, but of multiple assemblages [or *agencements*].' Flieger, 'Becoming-Woman: Deleuze, Schreber and Molecular Identification', in *Deleuze and Feminist Theory*, ed. Claire Colebrook and Ian Buchanan (Edinburgh: Edinburgh University Press, 2000), 43.
24. Bowie, 'Reading Proust between the Lines', in *The Strange M. Proust*, 128.
25. As Michael Murphy notes in *Proust and America* (Liverpool: Liverpool University Press, 2007), the image of 'conjoined' women invites another possible interpretation: 'Albertine's duplicity about her lesbian relationships' (46). But it seems important that the 'other woman' is a duplicate Albertine, just as 'the letters someone writes to us could be so similar to each other, could create an image so distinct from the person we know, that they constitute a second personality [On comprend, à la rigueur, que

les lettres que vous écrit quel'qun soient à peu près semblables entre ells et dessinent une image assez différente de la personne qu'on connait pour qu'elles constituent une deuxième personnalité]' (*PF* 62; *P* 64–5). If this image expresses the narrator's paranoia regarding Albertine's lesbianism, lesbianism also figures the narrator's sense of Albertine's own multiplicity.

26. Landy, for instance, argues that what the narrator desires here is 'not the truth, but a convincing lie', 'a mere dream of knowledge, protecting him from its real-life counterpart' across the novel more broadly. It is because of this wilful ignorance that the narrator 'may not always look at [Albertine's] face during his jealous interrogations, when it might have something to reveal, but he is careful to scrutinize it when it can show nothing', as when she is asleep. Landy, *Philosophy as Fiction*, 96–7. Elizabeth Landerson cites the scene as (however ironically) the narrator's 'perfect moment' with Albertine: 'it is the only time he does not need her permission, and he is able to "possess" her in the absence of any trace of her subjectivity.' Elizabeth Landerson, *Proust's Lesbianism* (Ithaca, NY, and London: Cornell University Press, 1999), 76–7.

27. Bersani, *Marcel Proust*, 104.

5. Jealousy: Absolute Knowledge as a Dream (of) Writing

Proust's narrator notes that 'love is nothing but the ripple effect of those disturbances which, in the wake of an emotion, stir up the soul [L'amour n'est peut-être que la propagation de ces remous qui, à la suite d'une émotion, émeuvent l'âme]' (*PF* 13; *P* 14). Proustian jealousy, which is a key philosophical concept in the *Recherche*,[1] desires to stimulate these ripples, but the soul is stirred in such a way that the ripples overflow. Jealousy thus translates love's production of iterations into an compulsive will to present them. It upturns love's initial pleasure before the infinity it generates into a futile will for an endlessly deferring knowledge. In what follows, I want to suggest that jealousy, as an epistemological process – an obsessive desire to know – seeks to present the trace, although it can only ever succeed in deferring it. This obsessive search for knowledge, directed towards a beloved who can never be totalised, thus resembles the aporetic desire of metaphysics to structure epistemology on presentational logic. Jealousy in the *Recherche* constructs narratives of its own, which further disseminate the trace[ ] that its strongest, jealous desire is to make present. In this sense, it is like the *Recherche* itself – endlessly delaying, elaborating and adding one more detail to its narrative[ ]. As Bersani notes, in the narrator's love for Albertine he 'not only suffers from his jealousy; he also discovers jealousy as a rich source of novelistic invention'.[2] Proust depicts the supplementarity of jealousy and its fictions deferring down an un-presentable abyss of reference, which always points towards another possible element of the narrative to be known. In this regard, the aporetic contemporaneity of jealousy's signature, written over both the jealous lover's knowledge, and the multiplicity of possible 'signs' the beloved emits, weaves its dissemination into the virtual *restance* of the literary simulacrum, a real resemblance of the real.

SEEING JEALOUSY

As we have seen, Proust's narrator notes that the lover's role is to interpret the 'synthesis become visible but no more rational' of the beloved's face, to 'analyse and break [it] down into its intellectual components' (*PF* 321). This is the task of loving for Proust's characters: to attempt to totalise the beloved across their iterative, supplementary becoming. This task has an ontological dimension (because the totalised essence of the beloved person is so unstable, forever deferring its qualities) but is also epistemological, involving the interpretation of signs, a search for knowledge of the beloved. Jealous love, in particular, creates a condition of perpetual epistemological uncertainty about the reality of the beloved's desires. In this model, love becomes what Maurice Merleau-Ponty calls 'the feeling of being shut out of the life of the beloved, and of wanting to force one's way in and take complete possession of it'.[3] Merleau-Ponty takes Swann's love for Odette as an example, noting that, 'Swann's love does not cause him to *feel* jealousy', but rather, it '*is* jealousy already'. Swann's pleasure in looking at Odette 'bore its degeneration within itself, since it was the pleasure of being the only one'[4] to take his unique pleasure in looking at her. As Swann's certainty regarding Odette and her signs disintegrates, it becomes impossible for him to determine the concept 'Odette' in any given moment. As Merleau-Ponty explains, 'Swann's love for Odette *causes* the jealousy which, in turn, *modifies* his love, since Swann, always anxious to win her from any possible rival, has no time to contemplate Odette.'[5]

Love '*causes* the jealousy' depicted in the *Recherche* because it seeks to determine the necessarily inconsistent signs emitted by the beloved. This can often develop into apathy, because, as noted in the previous chapter, Proust portrays love as utterly unstable, as most fully present in its absence. The narrator's love wanes whenever he feels close to 'knowing' the beloved, but, at the same time, completely present, available knowledge is impossible. Once you 'establish your life with this woman [Vivez tout à fait avec la femme]', the narrator notes in *Le Côté de Guermantes*, 'you will cease to see anything of what made you love her [vous ne verrez plus rien de ce qui vous l'a fait aimer]' (*GW* 350; 341). Even in this state of familiarity, however, uncertainty can return:

> If, after a long period of living together, I was to end up seeing Albertine as no more than an ordinary woman, an intrigue between her and someone she had loved at Balbec would possibly have been enough to reincorporate within her the amalgamation of sea-shore and breaking waves. (*GW* 350-1)

> Si après un long temps de vie commune je devais finir par ne plus voir en Albertine qu'une femme ordinaire, quelque intrigue d'elle avec un être

qu'elle eût aimé à Balbec eût peut-être suffi pour réincorporer en elle et amalgamer la plage et le déferlement du flot. (341)

For the narrator, this kind of 'intrigue' reanimates forgotten impressions of Albertine, just as a chance perception of Odette resembling Botticelli's Zipporah has for Swann the potential to regenerate his past hopes or disappointments. Once the beloved has become familiar, these 'secondary associations no longer captivate the eye [ces mélanges secondaires ne ravissant plus nos yeux]', are no longer present as perceptions, but they can still make themselves felt: 'it is to the heart that they speak in their deadly way [c'est à notre cœur qu'ils sont sensibles et funestes]' (*GW* 351; 341–2). Love, we recall, is 'space and time made apprehensible to the heart' (*PF* 356): so the heart can receive the promptings of jealousy, in a temporality different from the chronology of ordinary perception. Peter Brooks points out that '[s]ight is the sense that represents the whole epistemological project; it is conceived to be the most objective and objectivizing of the senses, that which best allows an inspection of reality that produces truth.'[6] It is the role of the eyes to detect the data of knowledge, to undertake the epistemological project. But the passage above suggests that these 'secondary associations', the forgotten impressions hidden within the beloved, no longer appeal to the 'epistemological project', represented by the sense of sight. Rather, it is to the heart that they 'speak in their deadly way'. It is the 'heart' that gives access to what I have called the *noēteon*: the heart senses the forgotten networks sought for by jealousy, which the eyes cannot see. The eyes, which denote the 'whole epistemological project', search incessantly for knowledge of the beloved, but cannot epistemologically 'see' her totality.

I would like to pursue this link between jealousy and the supplementary chain of writing and *parousia*, of the *present*ation that the 'eyes' of jealousy desire. For Derrida, jealousy always desires a possible 'absolute knowledge', or *savoir absolu*, which Derrida abbreviates in *Glas* to '*Sa*'.

> In *Sa*, jealousy has no place any more. Jealousy always comes from the night of the unconscious, the unknown, the other. Pure sight relieves all jealousy. Not seeing what one sees, seeing what one cannot see and who cannot present himself, that is the jealous operation. Jealousy always has to do with some trace, never with perception. Seen since *Sa*, thought of the trace will then be a jealous (finite, filial, servile, ignorant, lying, poetic) thought. (*G* 215)

Jealousy draws in and consumes the aporias of the trace and its apparent, dialectical opposite: *parousia*. In this reading, jealousy seeks epistemological development or depth, precisely to present or to see 'what one cannot see'. *Sa* should present the trace if jealousy is to be satiated – if knowledge is to be absolute. However, because the trace can never be presented, *Sa* is always jealous *of* the trace that withholds its absolute fulfilment.⁷ Thus, jealousy is only ever concerned with a disseminating trace, rather than an impossible *Sa*, in which the trace is always lacking. The circularity that seems to appropriate these terms would do so only if it could present the trace: because it cannot, we can *see* here a strange appropriation, an abyss. Jealousy, which always has to do with the trace, mimes Derrida's criticism of *parousia*: it is concerned *absolutely* with seeing – *present*ing – the trace, as the search for *Sa*.

And yet, like infinity, we can name *Sa*, and therefore think we can apprehend it. But in being written or named (an imagined totalisation), *Sa* iterates, and thus frays out from itself a multiplicity of traces. In jealousy, the eyes go about compiling these data which no longer captivate them, accruing impressions which may be translated as sense by the heart. In turn, the heart applies the forgotten, barely sensible data within the Ideal expanse of the beloved and integrates it, contests it, in the direction of what this *Sa* seeks to appropriate. In the passage above, the narrator describes sensing the trace which rekindles jealousy, deferring the *agencement* he senses as both the content and form of his narration. The narrator is sometimes explicit about the kind of *agencement* that jealousy performs: the beloved's traces, or 'dissociated elements[,] can be reunited by jealousy [éléments désunis, la jalousie peut à nouveau les rejoindre]' (GW 350; 341). The chance appearance of the beloved, connected to an 'intrigue' from her past, can reincorporate forgotten perceptions: it is jealousy that retraces the connecting links of deferring, affective *agencement*, and senses them across a varied plane, in a renewing light.

Here, however, the narrator admits that he is 'anticipating the course of events [j'anticipe les années]' (GW 351; 342). The jealousies and intrigues to which he refers remain relatively innocent at this stage in the novel. In a prolepsis, the narrator confesses his regret at ever leaving this innocent condition:

> [he] did not have the sense simply to keep [his] collection of women as someone might keep a collection of antique opera-glasses, never so complete, behind the glass of their cabinet, that there is not always room for another pair, rarer still. (GW 351)

> Et je dois seulement ici regretter de n'être pas resté assez sage pour avoir eu simplement ma collection de femmes comme on a des lorgnettes anciennes, jamais assez nombreuses derrière une vitrine où toujours une place vide attend une lorgnette nouvelle et plus rare. (342)

But this candid description of his forthcoming jealous despair overlooks perhaps its key feature: it cannot hope to simply 'present' what motivates it in such a readily available form. The fatal potential of uncertainties regarding the beloved takes on 'so dangerous a guise' that one cannot 'regard the renewal of the miracle as a thing to be desired [On ne peut sous une forme si dangereuse trouver souhaitable le renouvellement du miracle]' (GW 351; 342) – one cannot want jealousy to revive the trace. And yet, these many, doubting perspectives of his singular beloved are *themselves* Ideas, and, as such, possessions, which match the 'antique opera-glasses': the lover's intellect is constantly deferring in search of another, 'rarer still'. In that sense, the 'infinity' that constitutes all of the possible signs emitted by the beloved is like this 'cabinet', in which there is 'always room for another'. And it is the transformation of his love into jealousy (which 'reunites' its 'dissociated elements') that activates the compulsion towards *Sa*. *Sa, savoir absolu*, is what his wish for the 'cabinet' of superficial encounters with women might in his fancy pretend to, but could never provide. Because Proustian love '*is* jealousy already', is always searching for knowledge of the beloved, the 'cabinet' is never full – as the narrator's image suggests.

The narrator's regret therefore generates two possibilities, both of which are destined to end up with a cabinet of 'antique opera-glasses' or *souvenirs*: either one full of superficial memories attributable to many women, or a codex of adumbrations relative to one. These are the immanent, Ideal versions of the beloved, which transcend the various knowledge*s* that constitute them. This affinity between eros and knowledge is what Brooks calls 'the metaphysical Don Juan tradition: the idea that the need to seduce and to know large numbers of women, and to move on constantly from one to another, is connected with a continually unsatisfied quest for knowledge'.[8] Brooks's interpretation, in light of the narrator's regret, underscores the special interdependence between transversal Proustian *agencement* and epistemology. In 'knowing' the *noēteon* that constitutes the beloved, there is always more to know. The narrator determines that, even in his hypothetical wish for a redemptive life of loving others, his knowing or desire to know must take on some outlet: better it be, for the safety of his heart, a superficial approach to love, than the depths of infinite love and jealousy for a single person. But in both instances, the *restance* that is the 'unsatisfied quest for knowledge' remains.

The narrator describes jealousy's power to 'reunite' the forgotten traces[9] of loving *agencement*. Jealousy, he says, belongs 'to that family of unhealthy doubts far more easily removed by the vigour of an affirmation than by its plausibility [la jalousie appartenant à cette famille de doutes maladifs que lève bien plus l'énergie d'une affirmation que sa vraisemblance]' (*SG* 233; 227). Jealous love thus

> makes us at once more mistrustful and more credulous, makes us quicker to suspect the one we love than we would have another woman, and be readier to lend credence to her denials. (*SG* 233)

> C'est d'ailleurs le propre de l'amour de nous rendre à la fois plus défiants et plus crédules, de nous faire soupçonner, plus vite que nous n'aurions fait une autre, celle que nous aimons, et d'ajouter foi plus aisément à ses dénégations. (227)

For the narrator, if we are not in love with someone, we do not care about their desires or virtuousness, but by the very fact of our loving, we are necessarily tied up in the need to know something of them. He notes that,

> just as it is first created by desire, love is later kept alive only by painful anxiety. [...] Love, in painful anxiety as in happy desire, is the need for complete possession. It is born, it lives only for so long as there is something left to conquer. We love only that which we do not wholly possess. (*PF* 94)

> ainsi qu'au début il est formé par le désir, l'amour n'est entretenu plus tard que par l'anxiété douloureuse. [...] L'amour, dans l'anxiété douloureuse comme dans le désir heureux, est l'exigence d'un tout. Il ne naît, il ne subsiste que si une partie reste à conquérir. On n'aime que ce qu'on ne possède pas tout entier. (*P* 98)

This statement bears upon the absence inherent in the present, the inference of the sensible which we are steeped in, but appear never to 'possess'. It is the deferring appropriation of love, the inability to have or present it entirely, that stimulates jealousy. As an implex, an always superfluous, deferring ontology, jealousy thus seems to combine Derrida's rethinking of *parousia* with Deleuze's deterritorialization of static ontology. In seeking such a stratified 'whole', jealousy runs after lov*ing*'s past epistemological fringe: the margins of *noēteon* sensible to the heart.

There are many examples of this kind of revivifying, superabundant jealousy throughout the novel. In *La Prisonnière*, for instance, the narrator describes a memory which he '[s]ometimes [Parfois]' noticed 'during those hours when [he] felt the greatest indifference to [dans les heures où elle m'était le plus indifférente]' Albertine. It returns him to a time before he knew her, and a female companion with whom he was 'now almost sure that she had had relations [avec qui j'étais presque certain maintenant qu'elle avait eu des relations]': in the memory, Albertine is 'laughing loudly while giving [him] an insolent look [elle éclatait de rire en me regardant d'une façon insolente]' (*PF* 156; *P* 163).

Remembering this 'affront' revives within the narrator all of the original perceptions that had accompanied the first desired Albertine. And this version, in which 'Albertine, surrounded by her friends, was the most beautiful of all [Albertine, au milieu de ses amies, était la plus belle]', being unapproachable in the company of the other girls, arouses a jealousy,

> a hatred mixed with admiration for the beautiful, worshipped young girl, with her marvellous hair, whose sudden laugh on the beach was an affront. (*PF* 156)

> une haine mêlée d'admiration pour la belle jeune fille adulée, à la chevelure merveilleuse, et dont l'éclat de rire sur la plage était un affront. (*P* 163)

This jealously traced Albertine forces him to perceive her across multiple versions. While '[s]hame, jealousy, the memory of initial desire and its dazzling setting had given Albertine back her former beauty, her value', in his perception of her

> there alternated, with the slight weight of boredom [he] felt when [he] was with her, a trembling desire, full of splendid images and regret for the past. (*PF* 157)

> La honte, la jalousie, le ressouvenir des désirs premiers et du cadre éclatant avaient redonné à Albertine sa beauté, sa valeur d'autrefois. Et ainsi alternait, avec l'ennui un peu lourd que j'avais auprès d'elle, un désir frémissant, plein d'orages magnifiques et de regrets. (*P* 163)

In seeking to present all of these traces of Albertine, jealousy has compressed these 'splendid images' of lost times into a flux of traces:

> Albertine, now removed from that setting, possessed and retaining little value, and now placed in it once more, escaping from [him] into a past [he] could not know. (*PF* 157)

> Albertine, tantôt sortie de ce milieu, possédée et sans grande valeur, tantôt replongée en lui, m'échappant dans un passé que je ne pourrais connaître. (*P* 163)

In reflecting these differing lights shed upon and altering the *Sa* of 'Albertine' – what Proustian jealousy see(k)s – his 'possession' of her is rendered ever more unstable. His emergent jealousy throws the narrator under the surface of that 'amphibious love [d'amour amphibie]' (*PF* 157; *P* 163) that necessarily draws its water from Lethe: a body of perceptions either unknown at the time, or instantly forgotten, rendering each Albertine cyclically anew, forever seeking the possessive *Sa* of her fictions.

SEING JEALOUSY

In this way, Proustian jealousy, and the present-absent trace bound and sought by it, relates to possession, to *le propre*. I'd like to consider this relation more closely for a moment. In a historical analysis of jealousy in nineteenth-century France, Masha Belenky points out that 'nineteenth-century conceptions of jealousy are intricately connected to gendered notions of property and ownership'.[10] Belenky argues that jealousy became a 'man's prerogative and even duty' as a result of changes set out in the Napoleonic Code, which accorded any child born within a marriage a claim on the husband's property, irrespective of biological paternity. Under these conditions, a husband was popularly expected to be suspicious of his wife and jealous of her interactions with other men, since failing do to so results, not only in the shame of cuckoldry, but also the subversion of property. In this post-revolutionary moment,

> [a] husband's jealousy thus served a well-defined public function. [. . .] Failing to be jealous amounted to a betrayal of his role as upholder of bourgeois social values and was thus considered an assault on those very values. Cast as a tool of husbandly control, jealousy was construed as a shield that protected the wife's virtue, safeguarded the integrity of the husband's property, and thus contributed to social health.[11]

Jealousy, viewed from this perspective, was an ingrained social imperative. The 'anxiety of dispossession' of Belenky's study expresses a view of jealousy's ideological function. But Proust's use of jealousy to investigate the very epistemological bases for this 'possession' calls the concept of possession as subjective appropriation into question. Would the possibility of *Sa* underwrite total epistemological possession of the beloved? At the breakdown of total presence, or the immanent–transcendent distinction, the *sumplokē* that 'possesses' real and not real, what is imagined, fictive, ironising or certain weaves through the possibility of such possession. This challenges a consistent version, not only of the one whom *Sa* seeks to possess, but also the one who imagines its possession. For example, Proust's narrator finds that he could not fully 'experience a rare pleasure' in going out driving with a woman, when he did not know, or desire to know, enough about her. With Albertine, he notes that he now 'felt this pleasure, because our knowledge is not of those things outside ourselves that we wish to observe, but of our involuntary sensations [Je ne l'éprouvais que maintenant parce que la connaissance est non des choses extérieures qu'on veut observer, mais des sensations involontaires]' (*PF* 149; *P* 155–6) – the traces that emerge, unwilled, from a seemingly infinite Albertine and which make

Jealousy

the narrator question how many other sensations are awaiting him, 'outside' himself. These 'involuntary sensations' may be examples of 'involuntary memory', but more importantly for my purpose here, they are rapidly and constantly generated by the engine of the beloved's present-absent *sumplokē*. In the Deleuzian terms that I introduced above, when driving with a woman he did not care about, the white wall she presents was not paved with his black hole. His sensuous cogwheels were not set in motion:

> even though a woman was in the same carriage with me; she was not *really* beside me, so long as she was not recreated for me there from moment to moment by need of her such that I had for Albertine, so long as the constant caress of my gaze did not renew in her complexion those colours that constantly need to be retouched, and my senses, ever-wakeful even when satisfied, lend taste and consistency to those colours; and so long as jealousy, joined with the senses and the imagination that exalts them, did not keep this woman suspended next to us by a balanced attraction as powerful as the law of gravity. (PF 149)

> parce qu'autrefois une femme avait beau être dans la même voiture que moi, elle n'était pas *en réalité* à côté de moi tant que ne l'y recréait pas à tout instant un besoin d'elle comme j'en avais un d'Albertine, tant que la caresse constante de mon regard ne lui rendait pas sans cesse ces teintes qui demandent à être perpétuellement rafraîchies, tant que les sens, même apaisés mais qui se souviennent, ne mettaient pas sous ces couleurs la saveur et la consistance, tant qu'unie aux sens et à l'imagination qui les exalte, la jalousie ne maintenait pas cette femme en équilibre auprès de moi par une attraction compensée aussi puissante que la loi de la gravitation. (P 156)

These 'colours' or traces *possess* the jealous *Sa* (*savoir absolu*) of possession. The possession, or *le propre* sought by jealousy, is a flux, a system of substitutions 'suspended' in equilibrium by jealousy. The *aiôn*, which traces the full sense of the beloved's incessant signifying, challenges the rigid, separated consistencies between jealousy's subject and object as each possesses the other – the movement of jealousy's possessive apostrophe. Weaving the presents of his narrative down the abyss of signification and appropriation in writing (which is never present), and by his narrating (which never presents himself), and by our reading (which we can never present), Proust incorporates jealousy as a motif which further underscores the *sumplokē* of presence-absence, of fluctuating *restance*. By pointing out the relationship between the 'things outside ourselves', the 'colours that constantly need to be retouched' and the 'consistency' of those colours that are 'suspended' by jealousy, the narrator underlines the relationship between seemingly disparate selves that make up subjectivity – always gesturing towards an 'outside' belonging to one of our forgotten selves.

Derrida's reading of jealousy in *Glas* is pertinent here, because it traces the temporal affinity between the impossibility of present plenitude and jealousy's desire to appropriate the trace of knowledge.

> Jealousy is always excessive because it is busy with a past that will never have been present and so can never be presented nor allow any hope for presentation, the presently presenting. One is never jealous in front of a present scene – even the worst imaginable – nor a future one, at least insofar as it would be big with a possible theater. Zeal is only unchained at the whip of the absolute past. (G 134)

The *Sa* sought by Proustian jealousy – incorporating the unpresentable trace that *parousia* is jealous of – is always deferred. One is never jealous of a 'present scene', even if such a scene were present-able, because it is always busy with the trace. Jealousy seeks the trace that would complete that particular *Sa* it is jealous of: the beloved, and all of her traces, her significations already resting in her *restance* – the literary act of reading her. Just as Deleuze and Guattari argue that Proustian jealousy is the teleological generation of love, and, particularly, of interpreting love's signs – 'jealousy being the meaning of signs – affect as semiology' (WP 175) – Derrida describes the possessive jealousy of *Sa*, which futilely seeks to appropriate, or sign for, the present, localised jealous object. This impossibly ever-present signature, for Derrida, is a *seing*:

> So one is only jealous of a *seing* or, what comes down here to the same, of an *already*.
>
> This is why metaphysics, which is jealous, will never be able to account, in its language, the language of presence, for jealousy. (G 134)

What Derrida refers to here as the '*seing*' is an archaic term used to describe an inscribed signature, one that, as Ian Magedera notes, 'is linked with singularity' but 'also promotes a resistance to singularity' because there is always 'a parallel between undecidability of reference and the illegibility of "seing"'.[12]

This *seing*, whose alarm signifies throughout *Glas*, is the signature as a sign, the apparent ideographic singularity of the sign which the *jaloux* see(k)s to understand, but which remains undecidable. It appropriates the sign*ed* of the sign, that past of its absent origin that jealousy obsesses over, but cannot present. The *seing* can never fully signify *which* sign, which version of the signatory signs it. Because the *seing* is always *already* (as, for Merleau-Ponty, Proustian love is jealousy already), the *jaloux* can only disseminate the beloved's *seing* as imagined, signed, *by* the *jaloux* himself. The possible signs (and signatories) of jealousy, its *seing*, descend into the same abyss of language and property – iteration. As Derrida writes in *Monolingualism of the Other*, because 'there is no natural property of language, language gives rise only to appropriative madness, to jealousy without appropriation. Language speaks this jealousy; it is nothing but jealousy unleashed.'[13] Language attempts to fix the *noēteon* into a property that it will consume entirely, where it will know *Sa*. Because its inscription cannot not disseminate other Ideas, other knowledges – thus deferring the possibility of *Sa* – language is always jealous of itself. And, as we have seen, jealousy too is self-generating, because it runs itself down the abyss, disseminating and seeking its signs *already*: a multiplicity that cannot present its diversity aside from a *seing*, a trace, that is always undecidable because it can never present a singular, totalised form.

The *seing* can never be accounted for in language, or by a metaphysical structure that seeks to present it. The proper language that dictates the signature and *seing* is an aporetic naming, a simultaneous drive towards distinction *and* dissemination. For Derrida, *le propre* itself, defining and disseminating down the abyss, is 'the most driven drive' because it is the movement towards distinction (life and being) and dissemination (death and nothingness) *as* 'itself'. Nothing absolves this drive: it is the *sumplokē* that gives presence-absence and the possibility of perception and forgetting. The proper seeks to name and define; in doing so, 'a division must be maintained. This forbids the drive of the proper from being designated by a pleonastic expression defining a simple relation to itself of the inside' (*PC* 356). *Le propre* seeks to diffen*t*iate *and* differen*c*iate, and, in doing so, defers a distinction or dissemination of either down the abyss – the event of either is the trace, of which metaphysics is always-already jealous. Therefore, the *seing* (whose undecidability stimulates the multiple versions of the beloved that necessarily, and primordially in love, generate jealousy) can never be appropriated by the subject, inside or outside an abyss that is always-already its own.[14]

JEALOUS WRITING

What can jealousy tell us about the Proustian text, as a deferral of traces? At one point in the novel the narrator, in Paris and holding Albertine 'captive', reflects upon his second visit to Balbec, and realises 'how much more Albertine belonged to [him] now! [Combien je possédais plus Albertine aujourd'hui !]' (*PF* 72; *P* 75). But it also becomes painfully clear to him that such 'total' possession can lead only to further uncertainties. He learns that 'everything can be transposed', because the 'magical memories that [he] had not chosen, which, the moment before they appeared, were invisible [nouveaux souvenirs enchantés, que je ne choisissais pas, qui, l'instant d'avant, m'étaient invisibles]' (*PF* 73; *P* 75) can emerge from anywhere or nowhere, at any moment. Contemplating these memories, he remembers that it was from Aimé that he had learned of Albertine's being at Balbec, and with that memory, he in turn remembers that Aimé had mentioned to him that he thought Albertine looked 'not quite the thing [Il m'avait dit qu'il l'avait rencontrée, qu'il lui avait trouvé mauvais genre]' (*PF* 73; *P* 76) – that she had a 'mauvais genre'. Now, accumulating all of the signs and traces that he has since generated from Albertine, it dawns upon the narrator that 'perhaps [Aimé] meant a lesbian look [peut-être avait-il voulu dire genre gomorrhéen]' (*PF* 73; *P* 76). Instantly, '[b]orn of a new suspicion, the fit of jealousy [Né d'un soupçon nouveau, l'accès de jalousie]' (*PF* 74; *P* 76), a jealous desire for *Sa* takes over the narrator's perception(s) of Albertine and seeks to compose a definitive narrative. Once she assumes this guise, 'the future seemed appalling [l'avenir m'apparaissait atroce]', and '[t]his sadness left [him] only if a new jealous suspicion plunged [him] into further inquiries [Ces tristesses ne me quittaient que si un nouveau soupçon jaloux me jetait dans d'autres recherches]' (*PF* 74; *P* 77). The narrator cannot stop tracing the possible traces that the *Sa* of jealousy seeks to present. Jealousy here gives rise to another *sumplokē*, a weaving of being and resemblance: the fiction woven by jealousy that is by turns *more and less* fictive than the fiction of the *Recherche*, because it explodes into new truths, and new possibilities, each time it is reimagined. These interweave and impress upon forgotten traces from our own pasts. Fictions always multiply:

> How many people, towns, pathways jealousy makes us desperate to know! It is a thirst for knowledge thanks to which we come to have, on a series of isolated points, all possible information except the information we really want. We never know when a suspicion will arise, for suddenly we remember a phrase that was unclear, an alibi which must have been given for a purpose. It is not that we have seen the person again, but there is a jealousy after the event, which arises only after we have left the person in question, a 'staircase jealousy' like staircase wit. (*PF* 75)

> Combien de personnes, de villes, de chemins, la jalousie nous rend ainsi avide de connaître ? Elle est une soif de savoir grâce à laquelle, sur des points isolés les uns des autres, nous finissons par avoir successivement toutes les notions possibles, sauf celle que nous voudrions. On ne sait jamais si un soupçon ne naîtra pas, car, tout à coup, on se rappelle une phrase qui n'était pas claire, un alibi qui n'avait pas été donné sans intention. Pourtant, on n'a pas revu la personne, mais il y a une jalousie après coup, qui ne naît qu'après l'avoir quittée, une jalousie de l'escalier. (*P* 77–8)

In acquiring 'all' possible information, the narrator notes the iterative potential of jealousy's *Sa*. Any jealous vision can be woven into the literary trace of the *Recherche*, just as real as its previous realities. As such, the lover's jealousy not only finds signs hidden in details innocuous to anyone else, but also seeks to interpret and interlink *imagined* signs. And the weaving of these together, the unearthing and fastening of minute details onto one another is the creation of jealous narratives: the staircase is never traversed. As Jonathan Walsh argues, '[i]f the desire to know and to ascertain knowledge is one of the motivating factors behind jealous-envy, then narrative is particularly well suited to representing the jealous pursuit of signs'.[15] Indeed, but it is also the narratives that jealousy *itself writes* that animate its signs: the sensuous signs of the trace that jealous *Sa* pursues, and weaves into a *sumplokē* that is neither real nor resemblance.

This 'thirst for knowledge' is insatiable, and it drives the emergence and self-perpetuation of jealousy. In asking how far the signifying *seing*, or white wall, of his jealousy extends into the black hole of his subjectification (the trace of his various pasts), the narrator unveils a catalogue of sensuous signifying moments. He begins by considering 'the habit [he] had developed of keeping certain desires secret within [l'habitude que j'avais prise de garder au fond de moi certains désirs]' himself, and goes on to list many of these in rapid succession, from his sensual desire for a 'young girl of good society [désir d'une jeune fille du monde]', or 'the desire for pretty lady's-maids, and particularly Mme Putbus's [désir de belles femmes de chambre, et particuliérement celle de Mme Putbus]', to evocations of scene and place, like

> the desire to go to the country in spring and see the hawthorns again, the desire for storms, for Venice, to set to work, to live like other people. (*PF* 75)
>
> désir d'aller à la campagne au début du printemps, revoir des aubépines, des pommiers en fleurs, des tempêtes, désir de Venise, désir de me mettre au travail, désir de mener la vie de tout le monde. (*P* 78)

This might remind us of a critic who compresses significant episodes from the novel in an effort to make a theoretical point, but here the narrator is going about that work for himself, in order to reveal something far richer. '[P]erhaps', he thinks,

> the habit of keeping all these desires alive in me without satisfying them, simply promising myself that I would not forget to realize them one day, perhaps this habit, formed over so many years, of perpetual postponement, of what M. de Charlus damned under the name of procrastination, had become so general in me that it had invaded even my jealous suspicions and led me, while making a mental note that one day I would certainly demand an explanation from Albertine about the young girl (or young girls, for this part of the story was confused, half erased, in other words unreadable in

my memory) in whose company Aimé had met her, to delay this demand. (PF 75)

> peut-être l'habitude de conserver en moi, sans assouvissement, tous ces désirs, en me contentant de la promesse faite à moi-même de ne pas oublier de les satisfaire un jour, peut-être cette habitude vieille de tant d'années, de l'ajournement perpétuel, de ce que M. de Charlus flétrissait sous le nom de procrastination, était-elle devenue si générale en moi qu'elle s'emparait aussi de mes soupçons jaloux et, tout en me faisant prendre mentalement note que je ne manquerais pas un jour d'avoir une explication avec Albertine au sujet de la jeune fille (peut-être des jeunes filles, cette partie du récit était confuse, effacée, autant dire infranchissable, dans ma mémoire), avec laquelle – ou lesquelles – Aimé l'avait rencontrée, me faisait retarder cette explication. (P 78)

To 'procrastinate', to 'keep' and to 'delay' these sensuous moments, is to defer their trace, in the dispersive becoming of literature. The narrator's jealousy defers its details as it advances them, inscribing possibly heretofore unknown multiplicities (young girl or young girls: young girl[ ]), imitating the 'digressive' quality of the *Recherche* itself. The narratives that jealousy seeks to write in order to know, to pull itself further into this *sumplokē*, add further details to be deferred: a 'delay' of the present traces that motivate all of these interweaving narratives, even in each reading of them. The sense of the trace that motivates jealousy is the pulling of a textual thread, winding out of an infinitely larger narrative.

As Bersani explains, 'an emotion such as jealousy creates a situation in which the imagination, desperately and gratuitously rich, cannot settle for any one story'.[16] The Proustian imagination works itself through various epistemological planes in jealousy. In reimagining *parousia*, 'Proust insists on the paradoxical nature of jealousy':[17] the jealous narrator seeks the truth, but in his attentiveness, his 'urgent, obsessive need to know', he submits to losing himself 'in the confusing variety of solutions' which he 'inevitably imagines'.[18] The 'thirst for knowledge [soif de savoir]' (PF 75; P 78) seeks its narrative, but the magnetism of its intense attention will always attract more truths than the definitive unity it desires, each more real than the last. Jealousy's desire to seize upon the most minute details of the beloved applies the 'synthesis' – 'visible but no more rational' – sought by the heart to interpret the intensity of forgotten impressions, without linking them to a rational schema. Jealousy,

> whose eyes are bandaged, is not only powerless to see anything in the surrounding darkness; it is one of those tortures where a task has constantly to be begun again, like that of the Danaids or Ixion. (PF 135)

qui a un bandeau sur les yeux, n'est pas seulement impuissante à rien découvrir dans les ténèbres qui l'enveloppent, elle est encore un de ces supplices où la tâche est à recommencer sans cesse, comme celle des Danaïdes, comme celle d'Ixion. (P 141)

When the narrator speaks of the 'revolving fire of jealousy [les feux tournants de la jalousie]' (PF 91; P 95), he coins a metaphor which aptly identifies the nature of jealousy's trace. Jealousy oscillates and indicates, sporadically shadowing and illuminating spaces of emphasis across the white wall of the beloved's signification. And because the latency of this illumination is a trace, the interaction between illumined and shadowed perspectives of the jealous-object abyssally mingles shadow and illumination. Jealousy's illumining fire projects a flickering chiaroscuro, the kind in which Deleuze notes that 'white is darkened and black is toned down',[19] a melding of sensible-forgetting across the perceived beloved's plane of immanence. Illumined in a black hole, the forgotten, infinite adumbrations of the beloved merely serve to scratch at shadows across her white-wall.

In Swann's experience of love, and particularly that of loving the infinitely signifying Odette-white-wall,

> things had regained for him a little of the delightful interest they had once for him, but only insofar as they were illuminated by the memory of Odette. (S 276)

> les choses avaient repris pour lui un peu de l'intérêt délicieux qu'il leur trouvait autrefois, mais seulement là où elles étaient éclairées par le souvenir d'Odette. (269)

Thus, the enlightening experience of trying to know, of attempting to make sense of his beloved throughout each of her appearances, recalls for Swann the excitement he once felt when pursuing academic knowledge:

> the curiosity that he now felt awakening in him concerning the smallest occupations of this woman, was the same curiosity he had once had about History. (S 276)

> cette curiosité qu'il sentait s'éveiller en lui à l'égard des moindres occupations d'une femme, c'était celle qu'il avait eue autrefois pour l'Histoire. (269–70)

This new form of knowledge, however,

> taking its light only from her, [is] a completely individual truth whose sole object, of an infinite value and almost disinterested in its beauty, was Odette's actions, her relationships, her plans, her past. (S 276)

> ne recevant sa lumière que d'elle, vérité tout individuelle qui avait pour objet unique, d'un prix infini et presque d'une beauté désintéressée, les actions d'Odette, ses relations, ses projets, son passé. (269)

Just as history is a grappling with the shadows of forgetting, with striating knowledge and narrative in order to rescue the past from total darkness, so do love and jealousy instigate a pursuit of the trace of the past.

> [O]ur jealousy, digging in the past for clues, finds nothing; always turned towards the past, it is like a historian trying to write a history for which there are no documents. (*PF* 131)

> notre jalousie fouillant le passé pour en tirer des indications, n'y trouve rien ; toujours rétrospective, elle est comme un historien qui aurait à faire une histoire pour laquelle il n'est aucun document. (*P* 137)

While it is the impulse of the *jaloux* to seek out these documents, jealousy is constantly wri*ting* its 'history', throughout the search.

JEALOUS DREAM-WRITING

Jealousy 'thrashes about in the void [La jalousie se débat dans le vide]' (*PF* 131; *P* 137); the narrator notes that it leaves us victim to gaps of certainty and memory, but desiring to make sense of its events all the same, as we 'do not know, we shall never know, we struggle to put together the debris of a dream [Nous ne le savons pas, nous ne le saurons jamais ; nous acharnons à chercher les débris inconsistants d'un rêve]' (*PF* 131; *P* 137). It is in this dreamlike state that jealousy, constantly generating conflicting narratives of the beloved's whereabouts, expressions and desires, relentlessly turns the Proustian lover about, like Ixion. The 'life' of the jealous lover is a

> life of inattention to what we do not know is important to us, attention to what we think important but is perhaps not, a life made nightmarish by beings who have no real connection with us, filled with forgetfulness, gaps, vain anxieties: a life most like a dream. (*PF* 132)

> notre vie distraite devant ce que nous ignorons être important pour nous, attentive à ce qui ne l'est peut-être pas, encauchemardée par des êtres qui sont sans rapports réels avec nous, pleine d'oublis, de lacunes, d'anxiétés vaines, notre vie pareille à un songe. (*P* 138)

The narrator likens jealousy's impossible, multiplying and dividual narratives to those we seek to piece together after a dream. Unlike waking life, the sense of a dream is plural, superimposed; it is the unencumbered multiplicity of *aiôn*. Jealousy, in its hyper-sensitivity, takes its sense from the same kind of overlaid multiplicity. All of the 'forgetfulness, gaps, vain anxieties' are the traces which jealous narratives follow to forge their separately valid hypotheses, all freed in the same moment from the injury of doubt, as the time[ ] and space[ ] 'rendered sensible to the heart': synthesising known, forgotten and possible signifiers as forms of knowledge, but never as stable, concrete essences.

The aporia of jealousy is that this 'struggling' to piece together gaps and anxieties is an essential condition of its narratives, even as it seems to confuse them. Like the unremitting flow of the Danaïdes' labour, or Ixion's dreamlike, incessant spinning on a feathered wheel, the stories that jealousy writes flow and turn throughout the *jaloux*'s every possible imagining. 'Jealousy', as Belenky puts it, 'plays the role of a fiction-maker';[20] in Bowie's formulation, 'it is an experience of manifold potentiality; it is a stimulus to the making of fictions; it is a comprehensive way of inhabiting space and time':[21] a space and time the *jaloux* is steeped in, but which is un-presentable both in perception and literature. Proust's jealous lovers produce manifold, contradictory potential versions of the same beloved person, from the various narratives that their jealousy writes. In these narratives the spheres of invention and memory intersect, in a schizophrenic deferral *and* appropriation. In this way, jealous thinking resembles the effect of a dream: the jealous consciousness weaves its narratives across Carbone's simultaneous 'I did not know' and 'I have always known it', never certain which (in)attention the *aiôn* will suddenly reveal to be what it already knew. Jealousy for the narrator creates possible versions (chaste, deceptive, docile, preparing an assignation with another man in the restaurant) of the beloved that connect with other possible versions from the past, seeking confirmation or disavowal, but always inviting further elaboration.

It is no wonder that this narrator, who has 'always been so interested in the dreams we have while we are asleep [je m'étais toujours tant intéressé aux rêves que l'on a pendant le sommeil]' (*FT* 220; 218), should describe jealousy as being like a dream. If the narratives of jealousy trace the *noēteon* sensed by the heart, then the hieroglyphic, rebus forms that dream-content assume are an apt comparison. In *The Interpretation of Dreams* (1899), Freud describes the condensed complexity of dream-content by comparing it to 'the "determinatives" used in hieroglyphic script, which are not meant to be pronounced but serve merely to elucidate other signs'.[22] Dream-writing is like the intensive script of a hieroglyph. As Derrida notes in *Glas*,

> The hieroglyph was uprooted from painting, does not show some thing. In expressing a thought the hieroglyph announces language, but its mute writing does not yet reach language. The hieroglyph lacks a self that stands there as such, carrying outside what it is inside, expressing an 'inner signification.' (G 252–3)

In the *aiôn* of the dream, the differen*t*iation of intensities is communicated as a rebus or hieroglyphic. Just as in his dream Swann is both himself and the young man in the fez, so these various temporal and formal differen*c*iations are irrelevant to the structure of the dream.

In 'Freud and the Scene of Writing', Derrida uses Freud's model of dream interpretation to argue that the 'border between the non-phonetic space of writing (even "phonetic" writing) and the space of the stage (*scène*) of dreams is uncertain' (WD 217). We can define the

> fundamental property of writing, in a difficult sense of the word, as *spacing*: diastem and time becoming space; an unfolding as well, on an original site, of meanings which irreversible, linear consecution, moving from present point to present point, could only tend to repress, and (to a certain extent) could only fail to repress. (WD 217)

Writing is the present-less metaphysics of 'diastem' and 'time becoming space', but only as a deferral along a 'linear consecution'. In this analysis, dream-content is expressed as '*Bilderschrift*: not an inscribed image but a figurative script, an image inviting not a simple conscious, present perception of the thing itself – assuming it exists – but a reading' (WD 218). *Bilderschrift*, image-writing, is a figure for the *restance* of language, its openness to ever-renewable 'reading[s]'. In this respect, it operates in the time of the *aiôn*: the time that makes origins and temporal sequence problematic. In *Bilderschrift*, as in jealousy, '[e]very sign – verbal or otherwise – may be used at different levels, in configurations and functions which are never prescribed by its "essence," but emerge from a play of differences' (WD 220). So, too, the narratives of jealousy leave all possibilities open: they cannot cancel out any sensation, any jealous 'clue', even those the jealous lover knows to be wildly spurious. Eschewing the differen*c*iation of chronological time, these subjunctive narratives reach towards the differen*t*iation of the *aiôn* – the 'different levels' of signification operative simultaneously, as intensities.

The radical opening out of dream *Bilderschrift* can be illustrated by J. Hillis Miller's analysis of the lie told to the *jaloux*. In the shifting epistemology of Proustian jealousy, any truth can become a lie: any seemingly innocuous passing perception can turn out to be a fallacy of staggering magnitude. As the *jaloux* seeks the truth among the infinite fictions he writes, we can see how, in Miller's words, '[e]ach perfect lie functions rather as an art of invention in the sense of discovery, it opens a window on a new and unknown world that was always latently there, though our sleeping senses were not awake to it.'[23] This is the 'latent world' that I have described as the *noēteon*, sensible, but not intelligible. Sleeping senses like a dream; it *senses*, but does not open the 'eyes'. For the jealous consciousness, the lie becomes an interplay between temporal possibilities: it 'opens the window' to 'all those different and incommensurate universes'[24] that the perfect lie invents/discovers. These windows open and close throughout the narration of the *Recherche*. As the lie opens out onto the *aiôn*, it reinscribes the traces that motivate it into the trace of literature.

The lie, and the equally possible jealous narratives that crowd around and inform it, evoke a kind of writing that inscribes and effaces itself in the same *seing* – the same signature. This, as Derrida continues in 'Freud and the Scene of Writing', is the very work of traces: 'they are constituted by the double force of repetition and erasure, legibility and illegibility'. As '[a] two-handed machine, a multiplicity of agencies or origins' (*WD* 226), the trace is the root of language and fiction, of their *re*producibility and iteration. Dreams, for Derrida, *pre*figure this multiplicity of origins and agencies, because, he says, quoting Freud, they 'follow old facilitations' – the priority of an imagined originary signification, *before* iteration and *re*producibility. Because dream-signification is steeped in the *aiôn*, alien to the linear, sequential time of waking life, each dream is an originary signification, with no need of *re*production. The sense of a dream is primary: jealousy's narratives are a *Bilderschrift* because they seek the traces of a life unable to be *known*, in the sense of Derrida's *Sa*, *savoir absolu*, but primordial, sensible and traced by the lie.

The lie is a privileged interpretive figure for the *jaloux*: the perfect counterpart to the jealous imagination's hermeneutics of suspicion. Not only does its deceptive drive offer possibilities for jealous interpretation, but so does the truth of its deception, or the truth of its truths: finally, the ability to even note the trace of a lie (irrespective of its truths) within the lover's rolling quotidian discourses becomes radically important. The narrator notes that

> among the multitude of gestures, remarks, minor incidents that fill a conversation, it is inevitable that we should come close, without detecting anything in them to attract our attention, to those that hide a truth our suspicions are blindly seeking, and that we should stop, on the other hand, at those behind which there is nothing. (*S* 282)

> dans la multitude des gestes, des propos, des petits incidents qui remplissent une conversation, il est inévitable que nous passions, sans y rien remarquer qui éveille notre attention, près de ceux qui cachent une vérité que nos soupçons cherchent au hasard, et que nous arrêtions au contraire à ceux sous lesquels il n'y a rien. (275)

Each of these 'minor incidents' make up only one conversation! The lover's task, then, is to blindly search throughout the mass of signs that are sensed by their heart, written into a *Bilderschrift* that cannot be unpacked in *re*iterative signification – the perception of the beloved as well as the apparent textual production of her. Lies iterated, imagined, told, and all of the *re*-s of these qualities, are woven into the narrative, and yet they only ever attempt to 'stage' the beloved's multiplicity that the narrator is trying to, yet can never fully, explicate. The text, the *Recherche* itself, then, is only a trace of this total *Bilderschrift* that it resembles, yet never was.

During the course of his obsessive scouring of Odette's behaviour, Swann is struck by her excessive display of emotion when parting from him at the Verdurins'. This is strange, the narrator tells us, because Swann believed that Odette cared for him very little at this time, so that his leaving could not have meant very much to her: 'it was a thing unimportant enough so that the pained air she continued to have ended by surprising him [C'était pourtant une chose assez peu importante pour que l'air douloureux qu'elle continuait d'avoir finît par l'étonner]' (S 283; 276). Suddenly, retrospectively, Odette's behaviour, innocent at the time, takes on the appearance of a lie. Her expression of regret triggers a play of resemblance, first because her face at this moment reminds Swann 'even more than usual' of certain women in Botticelli's paintings. Then, in the midst of *this* echo of past time, and its other Odettes, Swann becomes aware that Odette's expression also resembles another of his memories of her. 'He had once before seen such a sadness in her, but he no longer knew when [Il lui avait déjà vu une fois une telle tristesse, mais ne savait plus quand']: among the infinite versions of Odette that Swann possesses, this one is at first only sensed by his heart, as *noēteon*. Then, 'suddenly [tout d'un coup]', the forgotten perception returns.

> [H]e remembered: it was when Odette had lied in talking to Mme Verdurin the day after that dinner to which she had not come on the pretext that she was ill and in reality in order to stay with Swann. (S 283)[25]

> il se rappela : c'était quand Odette avait menti en parlant à Mme Verdurin le lendemain de ce dîner où elle n'était pas venue sous prétexte qu'elle était malade et en réalité pour rester avec Swann. (276)

How many more clues, how many more lies, lie waiting in Swann's memory to be unmasked? How many more correspondences will spring up between two different, *resemblantes* Odettes from the past? The lie that resuscitates this forgotten past is part of a larger tapestry, like the one that Proust 'writes', the one the ~~voice~~ 'narrates', the one the 'reader' reads – and the one that Swann, in this lengthy episode, seeks to unravel. But the book is never total. This *Bilderschrift* will never be unravelled, un-texted: explicating the narratives that the lie conjures and extends only serves to weave it tighter into the textual *sumplokē*. Swann senses that

> it was not merely the truth about the incident in the afternoon that she was endeavouring to hide from him, but something more immediate, that had perhaps not yet transpired and was quite imminent, something that might enlighten him about this truth. (S 283)

> ce n'était pas seulement la vérité sur l'incident de l'après-midi qu'elle s'efforçait de lui cacher, mais quelque chose de plus actuel, peut-être de non encore survenu et de tout prochain, et qui pourrait l'éclairer sur cette vérité. (276)

Even if he could predict, see or come to know the truth of a lie, it would spread its influence into the future and the past. No wonder the narrator describes Swann's jealousy as being

> like an octopus that casts a first, then a second, then a third mooring, [which] attached itself solidly first to that time, five o'clock in the afternoon, then to another, then to yet another. (S 286)

> comme une pieuvre qui jette une première, puis une seconde, puis une troisième amarre, s'attacha solidement à ce moment de cinq heures du soir, puis à un autre, puis à un autre encore. (279)

Jealousy has the ability to wrap a person, a place, an object, or a fiction in its tentacles and return them completely altered, but it can also cast its moorings through *sensed* time, disfiguring and reiterating the character of other epochs.

In *Proust and Signs*, Deleuze posits that, 'because the concealed things unceasingly grow larger like a black snowball, the liar is always betrayed' (PS 78–9). The possibilty of the lie's exposure is an essential part of its structure: the octopus-lie spreads itself across an unlimited series of moments, only to meet one revelatory instant that demolishes it all. In attempting to verify the truth of the lie, and the truth of its truths, the liar creates added fictions or lies: he 'traces asymptotes, imagining he is making his secret insignificant by means of diminutive allusions', and it is the role of the *jaloux* to follow, rewrit*ing* the traces. The lie seeks a *Sa*, but also to be the total book that could anticipate any *Sa*. Like jealousy, it tends to expand and ramify through time: '[s]ince what the liar denies increases, he increasingly avows as well' (PS 79). Thus, for Deleuze, the atemporal, tentacular 'phantasy' of the *jaloux* is mirrored in the exploding structure of the lie.

> In the liar himself, the perfect lie would suppose a prodigious memory oriented toward the future, capable of leaving traces in the future, as much as the truth would. And above all, the lie would require being 'total'. These conditions are not of this world. (PS 79)

'The lie would require being "total"': it would require a *Sa*, jealous of the trace that it can never present. The metaphysics of the lie is like a schizophrenic machine, based on nonnumerical multiplicity – the complete tally of its possible, cancelling truths, this future-oriented 'prodigious memory', is required at its origin. The lie, in 'supposing' this 'prodigious memory' before it is uttered, is a *Bilderschrift* – 'an image inviting not a simple conscious, present perception of the thing itself [. . .] but a reading' (*WD* 218), which is only ever provisional.

In a conversation with Charlus at the Verdurins', the Baron reveals to the narrator that Mlle Vinteuil and her friend, the object of his jealousy, were to attend a rehearsal that Albertine had expressed a desire to attend. The narrator notes the 'dreadful pain that [he] felt on juxtaposing (as one does an effect, originally unexplained, and its finally discovered cause) Albertine's recent desire to come to the Verdurins' and the expected presence [l'affreuse douleur que j'avais à rapprocher subitement (comme de l'effet, seul connu d'abord, sa cause enfin découverte) de l'envie d'Albertine de venir tantôt, la présence annoncée]' (*PF* 204; *P* 212), previously unknown to him, of the other girls. He has already devised many equally possible versions of Albertine, and, upon confronting this fresh unexpected possibility, he asks himself whether there can be any end to this train of unforeseen eventualities. For

> many further doubts had found their way into [his] mind; one thinks that each one must be the last, that one can bear no more, and still one finds room for the newcomer, and once it has established itself in our inner life it finds itself competing with so many desires to believe, so many pretexts to forget, that quite soon they settle down together and in the end we hardly pay attention to it any more. (*PF* 204)

> Beaucoup d'autres y avaient déjà pénétré ; à chaque nouveau doute on croit que la mesure est comble, qu'on ne pourra pas le supporter, puis on lui trouve tout de même de la place, et une fois qu'il est introduit dans notre milieu vital, il y entre en concurrence avec tant de désirs de croire, avec tant de raisons d'oublier, qu'assez vite on s'en accommode, on finit par ne plus s'occuper de lui. (*P* 212)

The dividual multiplicity of sense never imposes finite limits. In extending out towards the trace, it incorporates each 'newcomer' into the Idea's constantly expanding differen*t*iation. The 'competition' among the imagined, jealous narratives is collapsed into a superabundant, productive *restance*. Each new doubt

> survives only as a half-deadened pain, a mere threat of future suffering, and being the other face of desire, a thing of the same order, it lodges at the centre of our thoughts and irradiates them, as if from an immense distance,

with subtle hints of sadness, just as desire does with pleasures of unrecognizable origin. (*PF* 204–5)[26]

> Il reste seulement comme une douleur à demi guérie, une simple menace de souffrir et qui, envers du désir, de même ordre que lui, et comme lui devenu centre de nos pensées, irradie en elles, à des distances infinies, de subtiles tristesses, comme le désir des plaisirs d'une origine méconnaissable. (*P* 212)

Jealousy is inscribed as the 'other face' of desire: both alike are prey to *restance*, to a restless multiplication of traces. Earlier, when the narrator compared desire to the suffering that jealousy brings, he noted that love, which acts as the nexus between them, 'is the insistence of a whole'. In the same way, jealousy's wheel, radiating along an 'infinite circumference', insists upon and seeks its own whole, the depths of the sphere's *area* (or the place on the globe that Ixion, or the *jaloux*, occupies) – the black (w)hole of subjectification, the self and everything it has ever forgotten. Just as desire radiates 'pleasures of unrecognizable origin', jealousy radiates along the 'infinite circumference' through the channels of forgotten perceptions – the wheel's spokes, the radii. Through jealousy, this radiation is 'rendered sensible to the heart': sensible, but not intelligible. In seeking love's, or *Sa*'s, jealous 'insistence upon the whole', this circumferential radiation leads to an expression of their superimposition, of their unity: an unbounded time of cohesion, the *aiôn* as circumferences-becoming-depths. The weave of jealousy's infinite circumference is a ball of yarn, fraying into itself.

CONCLUSION: SIGNING JEALOUSY

This fraying is the *sumplokē* of jealous textuality: in a structure of supplements, its trace[ ] will never be presented. In this way, Proustian jealousy sheds light on the abyssal appropriation of fiction. The illimitable narratives that jealousy writes resemble the 'ripple effect' of fictions, the way that they must go on being written, go on appropriating. Consider one final example of jealousy in the novel, taken from *Sodome et Gomorrhe*, at a moment when Swann, the jealous protagonist of much of the first volume, is old enough to look back on his jealousy with equanimity. At a party being held by the Princesse de Guermantes, the narrator seeks to find out the details of a conversation between Swann and the Prince de Guermantes. In response to his inquiry, Swann wonders:

> how can what the Prince said to me be of any interest to anyone? People are very inquisitive. I've never been inquisitive myself, except when I've been in love and when I was jealous. And for all that taught me! (*SG* 106–7)

> comment cela peut-il intéresser les gens, ce que le Prince m'a dit ? Les gens sont bien curieux. Moi, je n'ai jamais été curieux, sauf quand j'ai été amoureux et quand j'ai été jaloux. Et pour ce que cela m'a appris ! (101)

Upon being told that the narrator has never been jealous, Swann replies that a little jealousy is 'not altogether unpleasant, [pas tout à fait désagréable]' because it cultivates an interest in the lives of others, and 'because it gives you quite a good sense of the sweetness of possession [parce que cela fait assez bien sentir la douceur de posséder]' (*SG* 107; 101). This is the 'pleasure' that Swann attributes to jealousy: and yet, he confesses that he has 'seldom experienced [je les ai peu connues]' it (*SG* 107). Because jealousy is the search for a whole, radiating across the infinite circumference of jealous *Sa*, Swann indeed cannot fully possess its pleasures without them passing on, deferring their traces elsewhere. But he adds that

> [e]ven when you no longer care about things, it still means something that you did so once, because it was always for reasons that escaped other people. (*SG* 107)
>
> Même quand on ne tient plus aux choses, il n'est pas absolument indifférent d'y avoir tenu, parce que c'était toujours pour des raisons qui échappaient aux autres. (101)

Oddly – but not surprisingly for a Proustian character – Swann derives satisfaction from the trace of jealousy: from the knowledge that he *has been* jealous.

The value of the memory of jealousy, Swann asserts, lies in individuation: only he could have developed, and cherished, the unique memories and narrative scenes of his love and his jealousy. The 'reasons' the *jaloux* has for acting as he does always 'escaped other people'. The singular collection of memories that jealousy has crafted for Swann remains his alone – and yet, as his jealous *seing* disseminates down the abyss, the *propre* of his distinction[ ] (of what constitutes and separates 'himself', his 'total' consciousness) disseminates also. With respect to both jealousy and love, he tells the narrator that we

> feel that the memory of those feelings is only in us; it's into ourselves we must return in order to look at it. (*SG* 107)
>
> Le souvenir de ces sentiments-là, nous sentons qu'il n'est qu'en nous ; c'est en nous qu'il faut rentrer pour le regarder. (101)

As he signs and erases his signature in the same stroke, Swann goes further into 'himself', further into the abyss of the dividual *aiôn*. Swann wants to say that he has 'loved life and [has] loved the arts [j'ai beaucoup aimé la vie et que j'ai beaucoup aimé les arts]' (*SG* 107; 101):

perhaps too much of each to allow him to be truly great at either. But what does that matter to this Swann, in his last days? Like the narrator's '*vitrine*' of 'antique opera-glasses', Swann both possesses and disseminates 'these old feelings that [he has] had, so personal [ces anciens sentiments si personnels à moi, que j'ai eus]' which are, to him, 'very precious [très précieux]' (*SG* 107; 101–2).

> I open up my heart to myself like a sort of showcase, and I look one by one at so many loves that other people won't have known. (*SG* 107)

> Je m'ouvre à moi-même mon cœur comme une espèce de *vitrine*, je regarde un à un tant d'amours que les autres n'auront pas connus. (102, my emphasis)

Swann is 'now even more attached [maintenant plus attaché]' to this 'collection' of memories and sentiments than he is to 'other people, [. . .] a little like Mazarin with his books [qu'aux autres [. . .] un peu comme Mazarin pour ses livres]' (*SG* 107; 102). Swann's 'collection' of jealous fictions could entertain him longer than the largest libraries of the world. And why not? Even in this moment of reserved sentimentality and reflection, these libraries continue to write themselves.

NOTES

1. In addition to the critics I engage with below, important studies of the theme of jealousy in the *Recherche* include 'Proust, Jealousy, Knowledge' and 'Freud and Proust' in Bowie's *Freud, Proust and Lacan*; 'The Anguish and Inspiration of Jealousy' in Bersani's *Marcel Proust*; Philippe Chardin, 'De l'amour-jalousie chez Proust', *L'Amour dans la haine, ou, La Jalousie dans la littérature moderne: Dostoïevski, James, Svevo, Proust, Musil* (Geneva: Droz, 1990); and the recent edited collection *Cent ans de jalousie proustienne*, ed. Erika Fülöp and Philippe Chardin (Paris: Classiques Garnier, 2015). For a more eclectic interpretation, see Louis Lo, 'Disappointment: Proust's *Un amour de Swann*', *Male Jealousy: Literature and Film* (London and New York: Continuum, 2008) and Frédéric Monneyron, 'Strindberg et Proust: deux écritures de la jalousie au tournant de siècle', *L'Écriture de la jalousie* (Grenoble: ELLUG, Université Stendhal, 1997).
2. Bersani, *Marcel Proust*, 17. Similarly, Bowie argues that jealousy is 'a slowly unfurling and all-enveloping analytic texture. Being between love and unlove is where the being of human beings comes into its own. It is more than a supreme piece of subject-matter for a fictional work: it is the condition of possibility for fiction itself'. Bowie, *Proust among the Stars*, 262.
3. Maurice Merleau-Ponty, *The Phenomenology of Perception*, trans. Colin Smith (London: Routledge & Kegan Paul, 1962), 378.
4. Merleau-Ponty, *The Phenomenology of Perception*, 378.

5. Merleau-Ponty, *The Phenomenology of Perception*, 378.
6. Peter Brooks, *Body Work: Objects of Desire in Modern Narrative* (Cambridge, MA: Harvard University Press, 1993), 96. Martin Jay offers a brief account of vision and Proust's scopophilia in *Downcast Eyes: The Denigration of Vision in Twentieth-Century French Thought* (Berkeley and London, The University of California Press, 1993), 108–10. Sight and vision are a frequently discussed subject in relation to Proust and emotion. See Mieke Bal, *The Mottled Screen: Reading Proust Visually*, trans. Anna-Louise Milne (Stanford: Stanford University Press, 1997); Suzanne Guerlac, 'Visual Dust: On Time, Memory, and Photography in Proust', *Contemporary French and Francophone Studies* 13, no. 4 (2009): 397–404; Katja Haustein 'Proust's Emotional Cavaties: Vision and Affect in *Á la Recherche du temps perdu*', *French Studies* 63, no. 2 (2009): 161–73.
7. Hägglund points out how the trace of temporality underscores the aporia of *Sa*. 'For Derrida, such an absolute knowledge is not impossible because of our human limitations; it is impossible because it would cancel out the condition of temporality that is the possibility for anything to be.' Hägglund, *Radical Atheism*, 154.
8. Brooks, *Body Work*, 97.
9. As when Swann begins to discern his jealousy for Odette, he notices that it had been 'the shadow of his love, [l'ombre de son amour]' (*S* 278; 271): now 'all the sensuous memories he carried away from her house were like so many sketches, "plans" [...] that allowed Swann to form an idea of the ardent or swooning attitudes she might adopt with other men [tous les souvenirs voluptueux qu'il emportait de chez ells étaient comme autant d'esquisses, de « projets » [...] qui permettaient à Swann de se faire une idée des attitudes ardentes ou pâmées qu'elle pouvait avoir avec d'autres]' (*S* 279; 272), generated by his jealousy, negating the possibility of a totalised version of Odette.
10. Masha Belenky, *The Anxiety of Dispossession: Jealousy in Nineteenth-Century French Culture* (Lewisburg, PA: Bucknell University Press, 2008), 20.
11. Belenky, *The Anxiety of Dispossession*, 41.
12. Ian Magedera, '*Seing* Genet, Citation and Mourning: A Propos *Glas* by Jacques Derrida', *Paragraph* 21, no. 1 (1998): 29–30.
13. Jacques Derrida, *Monolingualism of the Other; Or, The Prosthesis of Origin*, trans. Patrick Menash (Stanford: Stanford University Press), 24.
14. It would be remiss to consider Proust's conception of jealousy and the trace without mentioning Sigmund Freud. Freud notes in *Beyond the Pleasure Principle* (1920) that jealousy 'is rooted deep in the unconscious, it is a continuation of the earliest stirrings of the child's affective life', which defers its precise, present-able origin. Sigmund Freud, *The Standard Edition of the Complete Psychological Works of Sigmund Freud, Volume 18*, trans. James Strachey (London: Hogarth Press, 1953–75), 223. Toril

Moi observes that the 'little child's insatiable curiosity about sexuality', and its absolute uncertainty, is for Freud the root of any 'desire to construct intellectual hypotheses, to obtain knowledge, and to engage in philosophical speculation'. Toril Moi, *What is a Woman? And Other Essays* (Oxford and New York: Oxford University Press, 1999), 362. The link between sexuality, jealousy and knowledge – and all of the indistinguishable overlaps between these concepts – confronts the uncertainty of the always deferring trace: they are all projects of an impossible, traced *Sa*.

15. Jonathan Walsh, 'Jealousy, Envy and Hermeneutics in Prévost's *L'Histoire d'une Grecque moderne* and Proust's *À la recherche du temps perdu*', *Romance Quarterly* 42, no. 2 (1995): 69.
16. Bersani, *Marcel Proust*, 87.
17. Bersani, *Marcel Proust*, 87.
18. Bersani, *Marcel Proust*, 88.
19. Deleuze, *Cinema I*, 58.
20. Belenky, *The Anxiety of Dispossession*, 67.
21. Bowie, *Freud, Proust, and Lacan*, 64.
22. Sigmund Freud, *The Standard Edition of the Complete Psychological Works of Sigmund Freud, Volumes 4–5*, trans. James Strachey (London: Hogarth Press, 1953–1975), 321. In a notable reading of this important idea, Slavoj Žižek describes how these determinatives become part of 'the text of the dream, the dream in its literal phenoemenality' – as a kind of 'work (the mechanism of displacement and condensation, the figuration of the contents of words or syllables)', highlighting the role inscription plays in marking even the apparently 'latent' or 'transcendental' dream-content. Slavoj Žižek, *The Sublime Object of Ideology* (London: Verso, 1989), 4–5.
23. Miller, 'The Other's Other', 137–8.
24. Miller, 'The Other's Other', 138.
25. Christie McDonald reads this passage relating to Odette's lie as an example of the 'shifting sense of truth and the corresponding lack of definition in gender' in the *Recherche*. Odette's fiction is complicated by her incorporation of an 'innocuous – but also incongruous – truth' into her fiction: 'the recourse to truth, intended to authenticate the lie, marks its difference within the story', and unravels the lie's fictionality. McDonald, 'Literature and Philosophy at the Crossroads: Proustian Subjects', in *Writing the Politics of Difference*, ed. Hugh J. Silverman (Albany: State University of New York Press, 1991), 140.
26. Moncrieff offers a more direct translaton of this passage, noting that the suffering 'radiates through them to an infinite circumference a wistful melancholy'. Proust, *Remembrance of Things Past, Volume Two*, 628.

6. Grief: The Spectre and the Impossibility of Mourning (Writing)

ABSENTING LOVE – ABSENTING ABSENCE

When he looks back on his past romances, Swann emerges from his jealousy with a heart rich in memories like a showcase of priceless treasures. In the twilight of his life, he can finally appreciate these 'precious' artefacts for the emotional significance, and even beauty, that they offer him. But trapped within the dominion of his jealousy, their effect upon him is much different. In *Du côté de chez Swann*, the *restance* of jealous suffering (its existence across times, dispossessing each individual instant in which it might be overcome) places Swann in a cycle of unconquerable anguish. Odette's 'manner' towards him

> certainly caused Swann to suffer; but he was not aware of his suffering; since it was only gradually, day by day, that Odette had cooled towards him, it was only by comparing what she was now to what she had been in the beginning that he would have been able to fathom the depth of the change that had taken place. (S 324)

> certes Swann en souffrait ; mais il ne connaissait pas sa souffrance ; comme c'était progressivement, jour par jour, qu'Odette s'était refroidie à son égard, ce n'est qu'en mettant en regard de ce qu'elle était aujourd'hui ce qu'elle avait été au début, qu'il aurait pu sonder la profondeur du changement qui s'était accompli. (316)

Swann's desire, love, jealousy – his affective response to Odette – is only ever this remains, the *restance* of the trace that he can never present to himself distinctly, because it changes imperceptibly, 'gradually, day by day'. A dividual multiplicity, Odette is always perceived by Swann in constant, irreducible and imperceptible development. He cannot notice a change in her because of this constantly unfolding duration. This is an eminently Proustian trope: the inability of his characters to perceive change occur*ring*, and to notice it only after the fact, often when it is too late. But it also has profound implications for the novel's depiction of the intensive sense of *noēteon*. The flows of desire always lead Swann back to something which refers to Odette.

Knowing that he is inextricably tethered to his love and the suffering that it brings him, Swann hypothesises that physical distance would bring relief.

> No doubt Swann was sure that if he had now been living far away from Odette, she would in the end have become unimportant to him. (S 355)

> Sans doute Swann était certain que s'il avait vécu maintenant loin d'Odette, elle aurait fini par lui devenir indifférente. (347)

But at each moment that Odette shows him a hint of affection, or he discerns a version of her that loves him, he feels a pleasure he cannot do without. This insignificant, and often imaginary pleasure – derived from 'ostensible and deceptive signs of a slight renewal of feeling [ces signes apparents et menteurs d'un léger retour vers lui]' (S 355; 347) – greatly outweighs, in the instant at which it is perceived, the prospective relief of removing himself from this torturous love completely. The immediate satisfaction outweighs the long-term benefit:

> he would have been glad if she had left Paris for ever; he would have had the courage to remain; but he did not have the courage to leave. (S 355)

> Il aurait été content qu'elle quittât Paris pour toujours ; il aurait eu le courage de rester ; mais il n'avait pas celui de partir. (347)

Thus, Swann puts his faith in the abyss: he decides to allow time, forgetting and oblivion to do their work. Surely, to be freed from the *presence* of the person whose being appears to command, and instigate, a temporal circularity could then release him into the freedom of chronological time's passing? But Swann cannot free himself; hence, powerless, he conceives the desire for *her to leave him*.

His desperate imagination takes this resolution to its extreme.

> Sometimes he hoped that she would die in an accident without suffering, she who was outside, in the streets, on the roads, from morning to night. (S 357)

> Quelquefois il espérait qu'elle mourrait sans souffrances dans un accident, elle qui était dehors, dans les rues, sur les routes, du matin au soir. (349)

Swann's painful love has appropriated so much of his life that he hopes for his beloved's death. One would think that such a recurring (and iterative – 'Sometimes') desire for the beloved's death could not be a part of love. But because it is a nonnumerical multiplicity, Swann's love incorporates elements in a rhizome-like manner: these elements, as Deleuze and Guattari write, 'are not extensive qualities divisible by each other; rather, each is indivisible, or "relatively indivisible," in other words, they are not divisible below or above a certain threshold, they cannot increase or diminish *without their elements changing in nature*' (TP 30–1). The *restance* of Swann's love is so large that it can differentiate even opposing, contradictory values. There is no suggestion that Swann *hates* Odette: rather, he cannot extricate each, infinitesimal signifier from his rhizomatic perception of her. To recover his freedom, to renounce his pain, he hopes for Odette's absence, for ever.

The narrator tells us that Swann

> felt very close in his heart to Mohammed II, whose portrait by Bellini he liked so much, who, realizing that he had fallen madly in love with one of his wives, stabbed her in order, as his Venetian biographer ingenuously says, to recover his independence of mind. (S 357)

> sentait bien près de son cœur ce Mahomet II dont il aimait le portrait par Bellini et qui, ayant senti qu'il était devenu amoureux fou d'une de ses femmes, la poignarda afin, dit naïvement son biographe vénitien, de retrouver sa liberté d'esprit. (349)

In reality, though, this solution is illusory. The removal of the beloved's body, of their agency, cannot remove their *restance*.[1] If anything, absence presents to the grieving consciousness a ghostly presence, a simulacrum springing from even the most anodyne of foreign bodies. Swann discovers that, far from bringing relief, the absence of his beloved allows her to haunt him: to rest over all presen[ce]ts. The absent beloved is incorporated into the *agencement* of the lover's perception, tracing its way through each thought.

In Proust's description of absence, these relations are bound to memory's work through duration. Mourning is the coming to terms with the virtual *restance* of all of a person's absence[ ]. It is the *sumplokē* of memory that renders an absence ever-present: it does not simply await a correspondence, an 'involuntary' memory, but rather, it rests among them, interdependently colouring all of them, like the 'guest at the party' we encountered in Chapter 3, exiled from durational chronology, but bearing upon the sense of those distinctions nonetheless. As such, Swann's experience illustrates for us how mourning, as Derrida posits, 'is a question, in truth, of the impossible itself [. . .] it would have to fail in order to succeed'.[2] Mourning is pure aporia, which is why it is central to the multiplicity of Proust's literary *restance*.

In this chapter, then, I want to suggest a reading of mourning that emphasises the weaving of absence in Proust's fiction. The *Recherche* unravels the traces of absence in order to consider the aporia of mourning – which, Derrida would argue, is also the aporia of writing.

And even more than that: as Derrida asks, is 'not all work a work of mourning?' (G 86). We have seen that Swann's jealous consternation is a constant work of absences: he cannot fully present the *restance* of his love to himself in order to overcome it. And yet, it works over him in its haunting, ready to recalibrate any perception into the multiplying order it creates. In the same way, mourning cannot be spoken of as 'work', but speaks only after it 'comes to work over' the subject. '[W]hoever thus works *at* the work of mourning learns the impossible – [. . .] that mourning is interminable. Inconsolable. Irreconcilable', Derrida writes in *Specters of Marx* (SM 143). One can learn the impossible without presenting it; like the trace, or the abyss of *noēteon*, this lesson rests across the irreconcilable individuation of an absence. This is why Derrida insists on *le plus d'un* of mourning: it is the '*more than one*' that exists simultaneously with the '*no more one*' (SM xx).

This interplay of presence and absence is also the work of writing. Derrida frequently compares imagination, representation and writing to a kind of death and mourning.[3] He argues in *Of Grammatology* that imagination 'is at bottom the relationship with death', because both are '*representative and supplementary*': that is, 'the image is *a* death or (*the*) death is *an* image. Imagination is the power, for life, to affect itself with its own re-presentation' (OG 200). The work of 're-presentation' is a spectral imagination of *parousia* cloven from the self, from the signature, while inveterately bound to both. Because writing is '[c]onstituting and dislocating at the same time, [it] is other than the subject, in whatever sense it is understood. Writing can never be thought under the category of the subject' (OG 74). There is always a gap, a kind of irrecoverable dying, between the written and the writer. The *seing* or signature that seeks to sign for mourning, to write or imagine a death and its complications, confronts the literary impossibility of defining either a total absence or a total presence, in order to reify a death that this *seing* seeks to originate *and re*present, in the same movement.

It will be the work of this chapter to consider how Proust depicts mourning in his novel (that is, how his narrator writes life's understanding of death), of what or how to call death. In turn, the shadow of death, and its mourning, takes an important place in the history of critical interpretations of the *Recherche*. As early as his *The Image of Proust* (1929), Walter Benjamin asserts that Proust's illness made it possible for him to weave the horizon of his own death into the novel and its style: 'he very systematically placed [illness] in his service'.[4] In the chapter of *The Culture of Redemption* (1990) devoted to Proust and Melanie Klein, Leo Bersani argues that there are two contradictory interpretations of death and mourning in the *Recherche*: on the one hand, 'the possession of others is possible only when they are dead', but the beloved's death can also produce 'an irremediable loss of self', 'a radical separation of self from the world'.⁵ Responding to Bersani's reading, Scott Lerner has suggested that, 'if there is no successful mourning in the *Recherche*', if its mourning should instead be called '*abnormal* or *unsuccessful*', then 'perhaps these very terms need to be reevaluated'.⁶

Two other recent studies take up this task of re-evaluation: Jennifer Rushworth's *Discourses of Mourning in Dante, Petrarch and Proust* (2016), and Anna Magdalena Elsner's *Mourning and Creativity in Proust* (2017). Both critics undertake a Derridean reading of mourning in the *Recherche*, using the concepts of *demi-deuil* and *deuil impossible*, respectively. For Rushworth, Derrida's 'demi-deuil' enables a 'more unstable relationship with the deceased to be perpetuated [. . .] than is possible' in 'traditional psychoanalytical melancholia'.⁷ Elsner argues that mourning is essentially linked to Proustian creativity, and that it 'renders the impossibility of mourning' palpable by 'staging' the 'infinite fragmentation of both the self and the other', through Albertine's death.⁸ In making a connection between Proust's representation of mourning and literary representation or creation itself, Elsner touches on a common theme in discussions of Proustian mourning. As Alexander García Düttman notes, 'confronted with a work such as the *Recherche*, the reader is in much the same position as the narrator who has lost his beloved'.⁹ Jean-Michel Rabaté, similarly, likens the 'ghost of Albertine' in the novel to 'the penultimate trace of a writing that is full of pain but ineluctably haunting and haunted', while Malcolm Bowie attributes her persistence to the 'vigorous resurrectionist tendency of the narrator's imagination'.¹⁰ Building on the work of these and other critics, this chapter aims to consider how the portrayal of grief in the *Recherche* bears upon this question of textual or literary grief: the kinds of loss that inhabit all literary *restance*. As well as examining Proust's figuration of death and grief, I want to extend that reading to ask what the difficult representation of death and grief can tell us about the questions of presence, sense, time and becoming that have concerned me throughout this book.

Düttman points out that the status of the *Recherche* as a work of art introduces a strangeness into the idea of mourning. 'The dead awoken by the artist are neither the living whom death has spared so far nor creatures who have not existed before. There may well be a response to the *Recherche*, but there is no other Albertine behind the Albertine the narrator introduces.'¹¹ A related question guides my inquiry in what follows. Albertine's death can only be signed by 'Proust', by the artist who gives life to these imaginations yet does not re-present them: that is the reader's work. In turn, 'Proust' is the artist who can no longer sign for his death, but whose signature remains throughout the text. Thus, the *seing* of death is imagination, which is literature at its full living, or representative, limits of life. As Derrida writes,

> [t]he presence of the represented is constituted thanks to the addition to itself of that nothing which is the image, announcement of its dispossession in its proper representative [*représentant*] and in its death. The *property* [*le propre*] of the subject is nothing but the movement of that representative expropriation. (OG 200)

The *propre* of death, of literature, and of the self is the expropriation of signing, of the *seing*, which expires, always-already, in the act of giving itself.

THE SPECTRE

As Derrida has noted, a spectral understanding of absence – such as Odette's haunting of Swann, or 'Proust's' (*seing*'s) haunting of our reading of the *Recherche* – is one of the implications of classical phenomenology. In *Ideas III*, Husserl contends that when we make perceptual sense of an object, a tension arises between the object as an 'actually occurring experience in a definite sense', in which it 'authenticates itself as actually given' to us, and what, after '[c]arrying out eidetic focusing [. . .] we abstract from the existential positing of the actually occurring experience'.[12] This is the intuitive, synthetic operation of the subject, who must interpret the 'endless and manifold series of experience, ever new sides and properties' of the object as a material thing; thus, through the 'suspension of the experiential positing of their requirements, we are now free from all fetters which physics and chemistry could impose upon us'.[13] As opposed to the static material thing, the phenomenal object's adumbrative possibility, its potential disruption and integration of meanings, generates an 'endless and manifold' series of eidetic possibilities. As such, 'freely phantasying, we let the thing move, deform its shape in any way we like'. This phenomenal 'phantasy produces the most incredible deformities of things, the wildest physical spectre, scorning all physics and chemistry'.[14]

Husserl's image of a 'spectre' is suggestive here, especially as it is used to refer to the *possibility* latent in perceptions, in the absence of their physical referents. While 'the identity of sense, in so far as the objectivity presented' by an object 'is supposed to be able to appear as identical, univocal in itself',[15] manifest productions rely on experience, and thus memory, to interpret their sense. If 'we do not take care to respect the essential relation of real properties to real circumstances', then these circumstances are liable to collapse, and 'then the thing falls apart in manifolds of phantoms (sensuous schemata), [and the] flowing as manifolds that constitute real things simply cannot and may not flow'.[16] Husserl's 'care' is the eidetic levelling-off of the object, the acknowledgement of Albertine[ ] as Albertine. These 'phantoms' that flow through perception are akin to the limitless contingencies that Swann and the narrator contend with in their experience of love, jealousy and grief. In retaining the sense of an object's given-ness, of its actualisation, there exists the possibility for these phantastic elements, or possibilities, to remain latent upon the horizon of appearance and subsequent perception.

'What is *phenomenology*', Derrida asks in *Spectres de Marx*, 'if not a logic of the *phainesthai* and the *phantasma*, therefore of the phantom?' (*SM* 122). This 'logic of the phantom' is doubly determined, on the side both of the subject and the world: '(1) the phenomenological form of the world itself is spectral; (2) the phenomenological *ego* (Me, You, and so forth) is a specter' (*SM* 169). This double folds into itself in the unpresentable movement of its becoming: 'Number is the specter' (*SM* 168). Spectrality from this perspective is a nonnumerical multiplicity, one which *gives* the world without originally presenting it. Husserl's logical presentation of what exactly is '*extensive*' envelops and affirms the *restance* of phantoms. Phenomenology falls victim in this way to the infinite regress of the trace: because it is 'governed by the theme of presence,' Derrida writes, 'it participates in the movement of the reduction of the trace' (*OG* 67), which, because the trace is what *produces* spectrality, it cannot present. Thus, while phenomenology is 'the most radical and most critical restoration of the metaphysics of presence' (*OG* 53), it interprets the *presence of* phantoms in perception, but fails to consider their primary quality – their absence, or their trace, which is what gives experiential Being.

The idea of mourning is central to Derrida's account of memory in *Memoires: For Paul de Man* (1986). Derrida proposes the grieving memory as an example of how 'the being "in us" of the other, in bereaved memory, can be neither the so-called resurrection of the other *himself*', nor 'the simple inclusion of a narcissistic fantasy in a subjectivity that is closed upon itself or even identical to itself'.[17] The difficult ontological structure of the other's 'presence' renders their appearance confusing and often startling: the beloved is for the *first time* forever absent, but is also perennially, and retrospectively, absent by turns.

We are back to the question of Being and the law, at the heart of memory. If this experience of memory, of the memorial of the memorandum, and of memoirs encounters mourning, who could think that this would be accidental? This experience is mournful in its very essence; it gathers itself together, it assembles itself to contract alliance with itself, only in the impossible affirmation of mourning.[18]

The distinction between the self and the other, being 'already installed in the narcissistic structure' of subjectivity, resembles the indefinitely multiple versions of memory that try to make sense of the beloved's absence. Grief is installed in the heart of temporality, in perception and memory. It is for this reason that grief is the critical, finalising motif in Proust's temporal project, as the pure experience of deferral out of which presence is constituted. Grief renders present an absent being whose absence can never be satisfactorily decided upon, because of their having-been, the inscription of their constant, phantastic *restance*.

Just as metaphysics is bound by a jealous *Sa*, seeking to make present the trace that iteration renders ungraspable, it is also stricken by grief: it is always drawn to *re*present, to mourn, this absent origin. From Derrida's perspective, phenomenology is right to characterise the 'presence' of phantoms as intensive-extensive components of the Idea, but errs in seeking to present them. No thing is ever entirely present or absent, but, rather, the thing is traced along a memorial nexus, in which presence and absence mutually imply one another. The writing of mourning is always caught up in this aporia. As Derrida points out in *The Work of Mourning*, 'one should not be able to say anything about the work of mourning, anything about this subject, since it cannot become a theme, only another experience of mourning that comes to work over the one who intends to speak'.[19] So, too, the details narrated in the *Recherche* are structured around the deliquescent nature of presence 'becoming' absence and absence 'becoming' presence, a weaving which works over the narrative itself. And this work is itself spectral – it is a ghost.

The only way to explore such a difficult ontology is to ask why, and how, these ghosts may be able to haunt in this manner, and how one might describe living with them: to determine their 'hauntology'. When Derrida describes in *Specters of Marx* how one might 'learn to live', he specifies that the learning element 'remains to be done', and, as such,

> it can happen only between life and death. Neither in life nor in death *alone*. What happens between the two, and between all the 'two's' one likes, such as between life and death, can only *maintain itself* with some ghost, can only *talk with or about* some ghost. (*SM* xviii)

The a priori gap of differentiation is the spectral, that which '*is never present as such*' (*SM* xviii). In attempting to define the trace of the absent object, the subject entertains something actual, scattered and interspersed throughout the differentiation of the *noēteon*. Grief in the *Recherche* is subject to this spectral condition: the untimely, deferring/differing sense of the trace. There is an obvious temporal element to this aporia: as Derrida notes, the chiasm between time and selfhood is always haunted by forms of absence, by a ghost. A 'spectral moment, [is] a moment that no longer belongs to time, if one understands by this word the linking of modalized presents (past present, actual present: "now," future present)' (*SM* xx). Therefore, while it may *come from* a time, inasmuch as it comes from an instant that was previously lived by the conjurer of the spectre, its very apparition – to Derrida its *revenant* (returning, coming back again) – indicates an arrest of progressive, chronological temporality, and a breakdown of *le propre*. Logically, the absent Other can never contribute anything more to its now spectral existence, yet its spectrality interacts with the continual flow of the subject's perceptions. Subject and object interweave, already, or all-too-late. Proust's narrator hypothesises that,

> since the dead exist only in us, it is ourselves that we strike unrelentingly when we persist in remembering the blows we have dealt them. (*SG* 161)
>
> comme les morts n'existent plus qu'en nous, c'est nous-mêmes que nous frappons sans relâche quand nous obstinons à nous souvenir des coups que nous leur avons assénés. (156)

'Their' otherness takes up residence in our selves, blurring and *re*-insisting on the impossible distinction between *us* and *them*, over and again, every time – every time that, in '*re*calling', imagines a fixed past time in which the Other was other. Thus, for Derrida, when we enquire as to the spectre's spectrality, we

> are questioning in this instant, we are asking ourselves about this instant that is not docile to time, at least to what we call time. Furtive and untimely, the apparition of the specter does not belong to that time, it does not give time, not that one. (*SM* xx)

And yet, preserved as an imagined other within the self, the spectre haunts the unfolding of each new present. As Elsner points out, 'Derrida's provocative claim' about the impossibility of mourning asks:

> [w]hen we mourn, is it really the other that we mourn for? Or is mourning really mourning for the self – the self that experienced the other as part of the self or the self that fears the possibility of its own death?[20]

In this sense the temporality, the 'immanence', even the illegitimate perception or *phainesthai* (appearance) of the spectre, all ask something very intimate about ontology. How can a stable, unitary form – or idea, or name – be applied to multiple, differing impressions, particularly when their given stimuli remain absent? Just as jealousy writes schizophrenic narratives that present and absent a multiplicity of possibilities atop each other, so appearance is always-already too late to separate the spectral interweaving between grieving subject and grieved-for object. The '*phainesthai* itself (before its determination as phenomenon or phantasm, thus as phantom) is the very possibility of the specter' (*SM* 169). Grief is schizophrenic: the spectre *is* only *as* its multiplicity, which cannot be subsumed in any one, totalising definition, any single 'is'. Like the work of re-reading[ ] that Proust's text shows is never finished, never permanent, and never the same as the version we remember, so 'is' every percept being constantly, virtually, re-read. Rather than a perception of physicality, the spectre is the appearance within perceptions of interrelated ghosts of past perceptions, always evoking their appearance, but never realising it. In attempting to attribute form to the spectre, consciousness can only reach towards what it *once was*, enslaved to time: the memory of the object, which is not the spectre. The spectre

> becomes, rather, some 'thing' that remains difficult to name: neither soul nor body, and both one and the other. For it is flesh and phenomenality that gave to the spirit its spectral apparition, but which disappear right away in the apparition, in the very coming of the *revenant* or the return of the spectre. (*SM* 6)

The spectre '(re)arrives' at the very moment that knowing collapses; for Proust's lovers, this renders grief the apex of their affective project.

We remember that love and jealousy were both projects towards a kind of illusory and compelling knowledge, responding to the stimulus of the absent or untotalisable other. Similarly, the spectre is formally and temporally elusive, because it can come into existence only outside of knowledge, only outside of any eidetic reduction.

> *It is* something that one does not know, precisely, and one does not know if precisely it *is*, if it exists, if it responds to a name and corresponds to an essence. One does not know: not out of ignorance, but because this non-object, this non-present present, this being-there of an absent or departed one no longer belongs to knowledge. (*SM* 6)

The spectre signifies the vanishing of the beloved object. Spectral Albertine is not Albertine as such; her spectre appears only once she is absent, yet it could not come about without the *having been* of Albertine, of all the places, scents, days, tastes, laments, desires – haecceities – that extend outwards from her name like a network. The narrator can speak of a spectral apparition of Albertine, of the Albertine who is now dead, but he is only ever speaking of her spectre: *le plus d'un*. In speaking of a spectre, 'the Thing is still invisible, it is *nothing* visible [. . .] at the moment one speaks of it and in order to ask oneself if it has reappeared. It is still nothing that can be seen when one speaks of it' (*SM* 6). It is only ever the sense of an absence, the trace.

Hence the troubling 'quality' spectral grief acquires in the *Recherche*. With respect to Proust's representation of grief, as Elsner reminds us, it is important to note that

> Proust left no final version of the *Recherche* from *Sodome et Gomorrhe* onwards. The last three volumes of what we call the *Recherche* is really a patchwork taken from the unfinished manuscript, whereby Proust's text itself questions its origin. It is a work in progress staging the tragedy of the early death of its author.[21]

Not only does Proust's text always defer its origin, but that deferral is the endless work of the text, so much so that working (writing, correcting, staging) on mourning occupied Proust to the moment of his own death. In *La Prisonnière*, as we saw in Chapter 1, Bergotte is thinking about the posterity of his signature when he dies, immediately after having visited an exhibition of Vermeer's paintings. Compagnon notes the attention Proust paid to writing this scene, in the 'final period' of notebooks – 'Cahiers 59 through 62' – and points out that Proust himself visited an exhibition of Dutch painters at the Jeu de Paume in 1921. 'The novelistic in the *Recherche* is often the trace of life, of the present that happens after the fact'[22] – or, perhaps, the present that can only be deferred. In signing, marking oneself *over* and speaking *for* the work throughout it, the author works over the flow of its parts. Derrida notes that this constant 'inclusion of the whole in the part [. . .] subscribes oneself to mourning and even to mourning for oneself'.[23] The iterability of one's writing, of one's signature, leads to mourning: to write or say 'I have' or 'I know', is to disseminate, to dismantle the haecceity that utterance seeks to make present. When 'proper names' are signed, Derrida writes in *Glas*, they 'ring to call the work of mourning', which '*is called – glas*. It is always for/of the proper name' (*G* 86). Mourning wants to name its dead, but whatever name it applies will never capture the richness of the mourning, or the object[ ] that is mourned. Therefore, literature, which names or iterates ceaselessly – for naming, applying language to spectres, ideas, tracing traces, is its most appropriate property – mourns its absent origin, its absent creator whose proper name is a spectre. And let us not forget, having died without finishing these final novels, while mourning (in) them, Proust never signed them.

WRITING MOURNING WRITING

The grief that is described in Proust's work is similar to desire, and to love: it is an expression of the flows of sensible networks, tracing their *re*institution at every perception – tracing, but never presenting. To take an example, consider how the narrator attempts to fill the 'emptiness' of Albertine's absence by seeing other women, but finds that the vacuum of Albertine's absence haunts them, too (*PF* 521; *A* 138). Here we can note how Proust's application of literary *restance* – which never presents its subjects – works over this absence. None of these women offers the haecceities that constitute his love for Albertine, like speaking to him of Saint-Simon, of Vinteuil's music, of spraying themselves with too strong a scent, in short, things

> which take on importance because they seem to allow us to cradle the sexual act itself within our dreams and create an illusion of love. (*PF* 521)
>
> choses importantes parce qu'elles permettent, semble-t-il, de rêver autour de l'acte sexuel lui-même et de se donner l'illusion de l'amour. (*A* 138)

These 'dreams' – that are woven, like literature, like the *sumplokē* of discourse itself – allow any reading to forget the beloved in order to seek after her traces. The narrator finds nothing appealing in the faces of these other women, because they lack these searched-for impressions, that 'were part and parcel of [his] memory of Albertine and because she was the person whom [he] was hoping to find [elles faisaient partie du souvenir d'Albertine et que c'était elle que j'aurais voulu trouver]' (*PF* 521; *A* 138).

It is as if Albertine's spectre has possessed the Ideal bodies of other possible beloveds: not because she is reanimated in them, but because her absence is made present by them, by the correspondences that activate the narrator's memorial networks. Like literature itself, Albertine's spectre both is and is not real. The narrator is clear about this:

> The qualities that these women shared with Albertine made me feel more keenly what they lacked, which was everything, but an everything which could never exist again, since Albertine was dead. (*PF* 521–2)
>
> Ce que ces femmes avaient d'Albertine me faisait mieux ressentir ce que d'elle il leur manquait, et qui était tout, et qui ne serait plus jamais puisque Albertine était morte. (*A* 138)

Albertine traces the portrait of these other women. The narrator specifies that, whether or not these women are linked to Albertine via the correspondences of memory, in each instance they exhume the spectre and *re*iterate the sense of Albertine's absence, which is timeless precisely because it can 'never exist again'. And in reading, Albertine's absence shares the same form (language) as these women, yet is vitally different. 'Albertine' would remain only if her

> existence, isolated from the rest of [his] life, had been subject only to the play of [his] memories, to the actions and reactions of a psychology applicable to motionless states, and had not been sucked into a vaster system where souls move through time as bodies through space. (*PF* 522)

> existence, isolée du reste de ma vie, avait seulement été soumise au jeu de mes souvenirs, aux actions et réactions d'une psychologie applicable à des états immobiles, et n'avait pas été entraînée vers un système plus vaste où les âmes se meuvent dans le temps comme les corps dans l'espace. (*A* 138)

While a spectre retains its intra-instantaneous timelessness, it simultaneously plunges into this 'vaster system' that is the abyss and the *aiôn*. So, too, while the narrator's narration seemingly must submit to the 'motionless state' of writing – or having been written – its iterability *re*presents that state (and the 'play of [his] memories' woven into it), rendering the state far from immobile.

Derrida argues that a key element of mourning is 'always attempting to ontologize remains, to make them present, in the first place by *identifying* the bodily remains and by *localizing* the dead' (*SM* 9). For the narrator, Albertine's death prevents her 'remains' from being ontologised in this way, disseminating them as the traces, the memories that remain with him. Her spectre is everywhere and nowhere, eluding the materialising formula of the identifying copula verb, the 'is', altogether. For Derrida,

> [the] specter *appears* to present itself during a visitation. One represents itself to oneself, but it is not present, itself, in flesh and blood. This non-presence of the specter demands that one take its times and its history into consideration, the singularity of its temporality or of its historicity. (*SM* 101)

Spectral aporia, which binds phenomenology yet leads to the disseminating of presence in Derrida's work, challenges the stability of ontology, and of Being itself. In *Glas*, he links the aporia of death, its resistance to the standard categories of ontology, explicitly to the 'oscillation' of textual dissemination.

> Ideality is death, to be sure, but to be dead – this is the whole question of dissemination – is that *to be* dead or to be *dead*? The ever so slight difference of stress, conceptually imperceptible, the inner fragility of each attribute

produces the oscillation between the presence of being as death and the death of being as presence. (G 133)

Like 'Ideality', writing itself is dead: finite, formed and fixed in language, but haunted by iterability. Albertine, in being 'fixed' as dead, is as 'fixed' as infinitely iterable writing – that is, not fixed at all. Derrida's 'ever so slight difference of stress' mirrors the contradiction of mourning, in which the loved one leaves and returns in the same movement: how can one *be* dead, *be* not *be*ing? The intensity of this *sumplokē* is grief, and, specifically, the grief of literature. How, we might also ask, can language *be* resemblance (not *be*ing – to recall the Stranger's contention in the *Theaetetus*, which I discussed in Chapter 1)? Proust cannot rewrite his novel, but in (re-)reading (mourning) it, the novel takes on new forms – it dies again. The 'conceptually imperceptible' differen*t*iation between these forms of death, or the 'being' of death, is implied in the language that, in a present-less *restance*, cannot fix it, but stress*es* it. Literature is the *phainesthai* of this unpresentable death: the *rêve-n[é]ant*, and all of the possibilities that this *différance* implies – the dream of nothingness, the spectral re-coming of nothing, the abyss of a nothingness that is always, spectrally, something *having been* – the *aiôn*. Or, perhaps, it is a *rêven´ant* – a dream of a nothingness that haunts being, but which can never present the quality that makes it no-thing (that quality being the graphic *é*). This absence in turn implies the 'nothingness' of a dream – the full spectr[e]um of sensible traces that have no waking duration, and yet *were* – fully superimposed and real, as *Bilderschrift*, in the dream. In the *Recherche*, we oscillate between the imagined presence of death – Albertine's, Proust's, our own – as the work of reading.[24]

LE PLUS D'ALBERTINE

The spectral *restance* of grief in the novel hinges on the question: how can the 'being' of death (ostensibly not-being) be thought? Take this example: the narrator affirms that while 'Albertine existed in [his] memory only in the states in which she had appeared successively during her life, that is, subdivided into a series of temporal fractions, [his] thoughts, restoring her unity, reconstituted her as a person [Albertine avait beau n'exister dans ma mémoire qu'à l'état où elle m'était successivement apparue au cours de la vie, c'est-à-dire subdivisée suivant une série de fractions de temps, ma pensée, rétablissant en elle l'unité, en refaisait un être]' (*PF* 480; *A* 96), Albertine's absence seems to render a sense of her stable unity possible. But this possibility is constituted of fragmented, differing haecceities: in total absence, the narrator cannot give priority to any one of these – as with desire, he cannot let one *rest* at the 'frontispiece' (*FT* 298; 295) of his 'Albertine'. The narrator notes that, for those whom we love well but see infrequently, the 'image we retain of them is no more than a sort of vague composite of an infinite number of subtly different images [l'image que nous gardons d'elles n'est plus qu'une espèce de vague moyenne entre une infinité d'images insensiblement différentes]' (*FT* 156; 154): this 'infinite number' exists in the timeless space of forgetting. As such, each impression is superimposed upon the others, successively, in the compilation of *noēteon*. In a sense, this 'single person' never *was*, but rather is the virtual contraction, the 'vague average' of all of those selves which the narrator perceived Albertine to be. Because this Albertine exists across so many times, she is chronologically timeless, expressed fully only in the timelessness of haunting (the *aiôn*), which is, Derrida writes, 'historical, to be sure, but it is not *dated*, it is never docilely given a date in the chain of presents, day after day, in the instituted order of a calendar' (*SM* 3). This is the time of the narrator's grief: he felt himself

> still reliving a past that was no more than another man's story [. . .] rekindled every time that a spark passed the old current back through it, even when [his] mind had long since ceased to think of Albertine. (*PF* 498–9)

> je me sentais encore revivant un passé qui n'était plus que l'histoire d'un autre [. . .] brûlait encore à sa base chaque fois qu'une étincelle y refaisait passer l'ancien courant, même quand depuis longtemps mon esprit avait cessé de concevoir Albertine. (*A* 115)

Albertine will never be 'an Albertine' ever again, but rather 'Albertines' (the spectre can never be 'a' spectre: its timelessness means that its *revenant* is never present in 'a' place at 'a' time). Thus, the narrator resolves that to successfully overcome his grief he would have to wrest this composite Albertine apart. 'Each Albertine was attached to a moment, to a date where I was transported when I visualized her again [Chacune était ainsi attachée à un moment, à la date duquel je me trouvais replacé quand je la revoyais]' (*PF* 455; *A* 71). The spectre brings each of these Albertines, but only as Albertine[ ], not *an* Albertine. As he feels himself 'transported' to *a* past in the spectral apparition of Albertine, he realises that

> past moments do not stay still; they maintain in our memory the momentum which was driving them towards the future – towards a future which itself has already become the past – dragging us in their wake. (*PF* 455)

> les moments du passé ne sont pas immobiles ; ils gardent dans notre mémoire le mouvement qui les entraînait vers l'avenir, vers un avenir devenu lui-même le passé, — nous y entraînant nous-même. (*A* 71)

The spectre is dividual; it drags our future in its wake. While the *phainesthai* of 'countless Albertines' each produce specific, separate moments from the narrator's past, they are inextricably connected to the pasts and futures that these Albertines may not ever have known. Albertine's death – the apparent 'no more Albertine' – in fact produces more Albertines than if she were still alive: she *is*, in death, a composite and timeless *rêven´ant* Albertine[ ] – *le plus d'Albertine*. And these versions, being each an Albertine that has never exist*ed*, is the *revenant* of the spectre: always arriving outside of knowledge, inferring pasts and futures, but never capable of *giving* them in their fullness. At each *rêven´ant* the conjurer is drawn along towards the future – the conjurer *writes*, further into and of that future – and every other memory that has gone with it is drawn too, into the spectre's wake, producing more versions that can never be ratified. The narrator has 'long since ceased to think of Albertine' (*PF* 499), and never can again: she is *iteratively* timeless in every and any future. This Albertine both '*is* dead' and 'is *dead*', in Derrida's formulation. She *is* no longer, and yet she *no longer* 'is'. This perplicating 'difference of stress' renders Albertine's *literary* death a written nothingness, a reanimating remains *rest*ing among the traces of the signature – brought back to life (being) by *being* called.

But how, and by whom, can this written nothingness be signed? First, let us consider the consequences of Albertine's apparent non-being or non-thingness for the narrator. Having determined to 'form an overall judgment' (*PF* 480) regarding his jealous doubts – his jealous narrative writing – towards Albertine, the narrator begins to contemplate the nature of these doubts.

> My doubts! Alas, I had thought that I would be indifferent, even pleased, at the prospect of never seeing Albertine again, until her departure revealed my mistake. Similarly, her death had taught me how mistaken I was occasionally to believe that I would welcome her death and to suppose that it would liberate me. (*PF* 480)
>
> Mes doutes ! Hélas, j'avais cru qu'il me serait indifférent, même agréable de ne plus voir Albertine, jusqu'à ce que son départ m'eût révélé mon erreur. De même sa mort m'avait appris combien je me trompais en croyant souhaiter quelquefois sa mort et supposer qu'elle serait ma délivrance. (*A* 96)

Albertine's absence, far from rendering his jealous narratives immaterial, or expired, only succeeds in compounding them, because Albertine continues to be 'present' to the narrator, in a presence that is only ever potential. This is the spectral logic that utilises grief, the weaving of absence that comes to form part of the beloved's trace[ ], which arrests the progressive narrative possibility of jealousy and feeds it back into the timeless *rêven´ant*.

The absolution that both Swann and the narrator imagined their lover's death would bring them is a hypothesis that is doomed to refute itself. Considering the possibility that an accident befalling Albertine, leading to her death, might suppress his suffering, the narrator asks himself:

> Can I really have believed it, believed that death erases only what exists and leaves everything else in the state it was before, that it removes pain from the heart of the man for whom the existence of his partner is no longer anything but a cause of pain, that it removes pain and leaves nothing in its place? Suppression of pain! (*PF* 442–3)

> Ai-je pu vraiment le croire ? croire que la mort ne fait que biffer ce qui existe et laisser le reste en état ; qu'elle enlève la douleur dans le cœur de celui pour qui l'existence de l'autre n'est plus qu'une cause de douleurs ; qu'elle enlève la douleur et n'y met rien à la place ? La suppression de la douleur ! (*A* 58)

Grief is installed in the heart, but it is only ever coming *back* – the lover is always grieving for the beloved's iterability, the suppression of which is always deferred, like its origin. Unlike Swann, the narrator realises that to suppress such a grief would mean to supplement something in its place. The death of the beloved cannot simply recover the lover's freedom, though Swann, 'who was so refined and thought he knew himself so well, had believed it [Il l'avait cru, cet homme si fin et qui croyait se bien connaître]' (*PF* 443; *A* 58). 'How well', the narrator exclaims,

> I could have taught him a little later, had he still been alive, that his wish was as absurd as it was criminal and that the death of the woman he loved would have liberated him from nothing! (*PF* 443)

> Comme, un peu plus tard, s'il avait été encore vivant, j'aurais pu lui apprendre que son souhait, autant que criminel, était absurde, que la mort de celle qu'il aimait ne l'eût délivré de rien ! (*A* 58)

The *rêven'ant* of her death binds him further to the dream of absence, forgetting and nothingness: that Albertine *is*, dead.

While the strength of affective *agencement* remains intact, the absence of the beloved can only invite the subject to continue to render her present, but only as a web of potential narrative selves, as possible narratives. The narrator is left with the uncertainty that the chronological present, interacting with the future as it unfolds into it, modifies seemingly determined memories of Albertine each time they are remembered. At each *rêven'ant*, each returning, of the spectre Albertine, there emerges the infinity of memorial possibilities of the past, detached from any imaginable present which might have delivered it. The 'wealth' of these possibilities makes Albertine's death itself seem impossible:

Albertine was dead. It seemed that I had to choose between two facts and decide which was true, so blatantly did the death of Albertine – which arose for me out of a reality which I had not known, her life in Touraine – contradict all the thoughts that linked me to her, my desires, my regrets, my tenderness, my rage and my jealousy. Such a wealth of memories borrowed from her life's inventory, such a profusion of emotions evoking or involving her life, seemed to make it unbelievable that Albertine could be dead. Such a profusion of feelings, for while my memory preserved my affection it also preserved its whole variety. (*PF* 456)

Albertine était morte. Il semblait que je dusse choisir entre deux faits, décider quel était le vrai, tant celui de la mort d'Albertine – venu pour moi d'une réalité que je n'avais pas connue : sa vie en Touraine – était en contradiction avec toutes mes pensées relatives à Albertine, mes désirs, mes regrets, mon attendrissement, ma fureur, ma jalousie. Une telle richesse de souvenirs empruntés au répertoire de sa vie, une telle profusion de sentiments évoquant, impliquant sa vie, semblaient rendre incroyable qu'Albertine fût morte. Une telle profusion de sentiments, car ma mémoire, en conservant ma tendresse, lui laissait toute sa variété. (*A* 71)

Its 'whole variety': Albertine's death defers any final determination of her personality, her tastes, her desires, her lies – in short, her fictions. To reach an end to jealousy, the narrator would have to bring his

> affections up to date. But this was impossible, because they could locate their object, Albertine, only in memories where she still lived on. (*PF* 457)

> si seulement ma tendresse avait pu se mettre à jour. Mais c'est ce qui était impossible puisqu'elle ne pouvait trouver son objet, Albertine, que dans des souvenirs où celle-ci était vivante. (*A* 72)

The forever-absent beloved can never be totalised, or rendered totally dead or absent: the narrator can never locate *the* Albertine, because she is comprised of various, often contradictory times, latent on the perceptual horizon: *le plus d'Albertine*. The spiral of the narrator's jealousy obliges him to conjure a spectral *rêven´ant*:

> Since at any moment when I thought of her, I resuscitated her, her infidelities could never be those of a dead woman, for the moment when she had committed them became the present moment, not only for Albertine but also for whichever of my various selves was suddenly enlisted to contemplate her. (*PF* 457)

> Puisque, rien qu'en pensant à elle, je la ressuscitais, ses trahisons ne pouvaient jamais être celles d'une morte ; l'instant où elle les avait commises devenant l'instant actuel, non pas seulement pour Albertine, mais pour celui de mes moi subitement évoqué qui la contemplait. (*A* 72)

Albertine's death has rendered for the narrator a more terrifying possibility of uncertainty than the extensive and entropic future, one mysterious and cruel because

> it would unfold as far as [his] life itself, without [his] companion being there to alleviate the suffering that it caused. (PF 457)
>
> Il se déroulait aussi loin que ma vie elle-même, sans que ma compagne fût là pour calmer les souffrances qu'il me causait. (A 73)

Paradoxically, this life of future suffering depends upon a revival of the past, which is just as unknowable as the future, because it contains a 'reality that [he] had not known' – Albertine's 'life'. 'Her Past? [Son Passé ?]', the narrator protests:

> This is not the right term, since in jealousy there is neither past nor future, for what it imagines is always the present. (PF 457)
>
> C'est mal dire puisque pour la jalousie il n'est ni passé ni avenir et que ce qu'elle imagine est toujours le present. (A 73)

It *imagines* the present, like Derrida's *Sa*, but can never present it.

The only distinction that can be made is the one that seems the most difficult: the 'incredible' fact of the beloved's death. In going through this present of grief, and utilising jealousy's field, the narrator seeks to trace Albertine's life backwards, to go back to her earliest Balbec days, to seek information about her liaisons with other women. This very desire to discover 'a guilty act proven against Albertine [qu'un fait coupable à l'actif d'Albertine]' (PF 481; A 96) renders Albertine more alive in her death – more capable of haunting him – because her absolute silence can only ever bring uncertainty. He sends Aimé to discover what he can of Albertine's unknown life in Balbec, and receives a reply which describes a number of affairs with young women in the beachfront baths. And at once, the grief aroused by this 'certainty', this illustration of an undiscovered past, distributes itself among the narrator's sensible pasts, stored as the traces of forgetting. In attempting to construct, to know and make sense of these images of her guilt, which contravene what he *had* believed, he notes that

> these images had immediately been affected by [his] pain; an objective fact or an image is different according to the state of mind in which one approaches it. And pain is as powerful a modifier of reality as is intoxication. (PF 484)
>
> Mais aussitôt la douleur avait réagi sur elles : un fait objectif, tel qu'une image, est différent selon l'état intérieur avec lequel on l'aborde. Et la douleur est un aussi puissant modificateur de la réalité qu'est l'ivresse. (A 100)

Grief engulfs the whole complex of his perceptions and alters them according to its will. The suffering that knowledge of Albertine's infidelities brings changes the perceptions of that time into its own pattern: 'everything connected with Balbec now become fearfully permeated with that mystery [Ce mystère que j'avais jadis imaginé dans le pays de

Balbec [...] maintenant tout ce qui touchait à Balbec s'en imprégnait affreusement !]' (*PF* 484; *A* 100). So again 'Balbec' (and all of its varying haecceities, the cogs in its transversal *agencement*-machine), already so fecund with meaning and different perceptive forms, takes on yet another. But what use, he asks himself, is this knowledge, the baffling jealousy of a woman who, while still 'so alive within [si vivante en]' the narrator, 'was today stripped of the flesh that had enjoyed [aujourd'hui dépouillée de la chair qui en avait joui]' these infidelities, and 'was no longer capable of them or responsible for them [n'était plus capable, ni responsable, excitât en moi une telle souffrance]' (*PF* 456; *A* 72)? Aimé's revelations are meaningless, 'since Albertine would for evermore be unaware that he had told [puisque Albertine devait éternellement ignorer qu'il me l'avait appris]' the narrator, and his 'need to know was always surpassed by the need to show her that [he] knew [le besoin de savoir ayant toujours été surpassé, dans mon amour pour Albertine, par le besoin de lui montrer que je savais]' (*PF* 485; *A*101). This need to show Albertine his awareness of her prospective, past, or pretended infidelities, now that she can no longer be shown anything, revives her image for the narrator only to appease this need, impossible and absurd.

> How ever could I have wished so much that Albertine should know what I had heard about the shower room, when Albertine no longer existed! (*PF* 485–6)
>
> Avoir tant désiré qu'Albertine sût que j'avais appris l'histoire de la salle de douches, Albertine qui n'était plus rien ! (*A* 101)

But while it may be absurd in logic, it is precisely this aporia which *gives* Proustian grief.

> This was yet another of the consequences of our finding it impossible, when we have to analyse death, to imagine it in terms other than those of life. (*PF* 486)
>
> C'était là encore une des conséquences de cette impossibilité où nous sommes, quand nous avons à raisonner sur la mort, de nous représenter autre chose que la vie. (*A* 101)

Just as the essential quality of thought or of *le propre* denies a possibility of nothingness, it is impossible, the narrator posits here, to make sense of death. We can only inscribe it – even as absence, as loss – further in the 'hollow' of our being, to be taken up, re-read and rewritten as we go on living. How can we imagine the absolute absence, not only our own living consciousness – '[w]hen we try to figure out what will happen after our death, are we not mistakenly still projecting the image of our living selves which we have at that moment?' [Quand nous raisonnons sur ce qui se passe après notre propre mort, n'est-ce pas encore nous vivant que par erreur nous projetons à ce moment-là ?]' (*PF* 486; *A* 102) – but that of another whom we constantly recall in our memories, about whom we phantasise in our most basic perceptions? Death cannot be *present*ed. In turn, neither can the death of the signatory be presented in the literary work – the work whose origin (the signatory) is dead, even as the flow of its dissemination continues. Death, and literature as death, is the *rêven´ant*: we can never 'imagine it in terms other than those of life' – and yet the image, the re-presentation, is death 'itself'.

It is in this context that the narrator raises the impossibility of expropriating an appropriation that is expropriated from the start.

> For we exist only through what we possess, and we possess only what is actually present, since so many of our memories, moods and ideas leave us and travel to faraway places, where we lose sight of them! Then we can no longer enter them into the accounting system whose sum is our whole being. But they find secret ways of returning within us. And some evenings, having fallen asleep hardly missing Albertine any longer – we can miss only what we remember – I awoke to find that a whole fleet of memories had sailed into my clearest consciousness and had become marvellously distinct. Then I wept for the things which I saw so well and which for me the day before had been utterly absent. Albertine's name and her death had changed their meaning; her betrayals had suddenly resumed their old significance. (*PF* 454–5)

> On n'est que par ce qu'on possède, on ne possède que ce qui vous est réellement présent, et tant de nos souvenirs, de nos humeurs, de nos idées partent faire des voyages loin de nous-même, où nous les perdons de vue ! Alors nous ne pouvons plus les faire entrer en ligne de compte de ce total qui est notre être. Mais ils ont des chemins secrets pour rentrer en nous. Et certains soirs m'étant endormi sans presque plus regretter Albertine – on ne peut regretter que ce qu'on se rappelle – au réveil je trouvais toute une flotte de souvenirs qui étaient venus croiser en moi dans ma plus claire conscience, et que je distinguais à merveille. Alors je pleurais ce que je voyais si bien et qui, la veille, n'était pour moi que néant. Puis, brusquement, le nom d'Albertine, sa mort avaient changé de sens ; ses trahisons avaient soudain repris toute leur importance. (*A* 70)

In this passage, we find gathered together many of the themes that have concerned me throughout this book. In one sweeping, disseminating paragraph, the narrator raises the concepts of *le propre* ('what we possess'), its deferring abyss ('travel to faraway places'), ab-sense ('until we lose sight of them'), the problem of *parousia* ('we possess what is actually present'), the dividual (the productive, multiplying 'sum which is our whole being'), iteration ('had changed their meaning'), and the *sumplokē* of 'returning secret ways'. In this account, the traces that are the 'secret ways' of the Proustian novel come to possess the writing itself, resting across the unconscious, absent, intensive work of sleep. The grief that the narrator describes in this excerpt is the work of the trace, seemingly some*thing* that can be possessed, but which disseminates at the juncture of consciousness, form and language. When the narrator awakes, the work of mourning has reiterated the directions of his sufferings: like the roots of arborescent *agencement*, the traces constitute an affect-machine, flowing on as the marks of grief – these 'memories' which sail into the narrator's consciousness. But they can never be dug through to present their prior, racinating function – the trace, which produces and recalibrates the machine. Proust's novel, in staging the dissemination of this 'possession', casts light on the sense given by the trace, felt so acutely in the *seing*, the always-already, of Proustian affect.

How can we forget forever anything that we have lived? By writing it? Grief, in forcing a subject to engage with a possibility that cannot be perceived, opens up the final, inviolable rupture between subjectivity, affect, presence and literature. If affect is the *phainesthai* of the *phainesthai* itself, then to appropriate, to speak or write for or of the experience of grief, one must sign oneself 'in' what remain(s) *between* the spectre and its *phainesthai*: the trace and/of the *seing*. In the passage quoted above, the narrator teases us with objective facts regarding psychological logic: 'we can miss only what we remember', he inserts, axiomatically, into his thesis, but then proceeds to unravel the certainty of any such claim. He does not 'possess' these memories of Albertine (this much he makes clear in the hundreds of pages that follow, those that uncertainly ferret through every trace revived by the name Albertine); he does not remember them, and therefore cannot regret them, or suffer for them. But while he cannot remember them – that is, he cannot sign for his memory – he *can* sign his text, if always only provisionally. Literature *is* mourning, and mourning literature. There can be no other 'secret way' about it. From out of the primordial *already* of the abyssal *seing* ('the accounting system whose sum is our whole being'), forgotten memories can always emerge, now rendered 'marvellously distinct'. To appropriate memories is to possess them, to sign them, to sign *one*self, a self that wouldn't disseminate. This 'sum' of our '*whole* being' can never be total, because it disseminates at every new signing – deferring a grief for one's memories that, for Proust, has never finished beginning.

NOTES

1. As Swann discovers; immediately after the narrator teases us with the possibility that Swann might simply forget Odette, noting that he 'felt absolutely calm, and almost happy [se sentait absolument tranquille, presque heureux]' (S 375; 367) because she had been absent from Paris for nearly a year, Swann meets Mme Cottard on a bus, who tells him that Odette adores him. This immediately forges Odette's 'transformation [transformation définitive]' back into that version of her 'loved with a peaceful attention [aimée d'affection paisible]' (S 378–9; 370–1) – a year's absence collapsed by a phrase.
2. Derrida, *The Work of Mourning*, trans. and ed. Michael Naas and Pascale-Anne Brault (Chicago and London: University of Chicago Press, 2001), 144.
3. Colebrook explains Derrida's reasoning: 'We can only have the notion of the origin or the presence that lies before language from the productions of language. It is only with the notion of language *as fallen from presence* – only with the process of language as mourning – that an "original" presence is effected.' Claire Colebrook, *Irony* (London and New York: Routledge, 2004), 98.
4. Walter Benjamin, *Illuminations*, trans. Harry Zohn (New York: Schocken Books, 1969), 213–14.
5. Leo Bersani, *The Culture of Redemption* (Cambridge, MA: Harvard University Press, 1990), 7.
6. Scott L. Lerner, 'Mourning and Subjectivity: From Bersani to Proust, Klein and Freud', *diacritics* 37, no. 1 (2007): 48.
7. Jennifer Rushworth, *Discourses of Mourning in Dante, Petrarch, and Proust*, 98.
8. Anna Magdalena Elsner, *Mourning and Creativity in Proust*, 45.
9. Alexander García Düttmann, 'Separated from Proust', *Angelaki* 9, no. 3 (2004): 89.
10. Jean-Michel Rabaté, *The Ghosts of Modernity* (Gainesville: University Press of Florida, 1996), 13; Bowie, *Proust among the Stars*, 290.
11. Düttmann, *Separated from Proust*, 90.
12. Edmund Husserl, *Ideas Pertaining to a Pure Phenomenology and to a Phenomenological Philosophy, Third Book*, trans. Ted E. Klein and William E. Pohl (The Hague: Nijhoff, 1980), 26.
13. Husserl, *Ideas III*, 26.
14. Husserl, *Ideas III*, 26.
15. Husserl, *Ideas III*, 26.
16. Husserl, *Ideas III*, 27.
17. Derrida, *Memoires: For Paul de Man*, trans. Cecile Lindsay, Jonathan Culler and Eduardo Cadava (New York: Columbia University Press, 1986), 21–2.
18. Derrida, *Memoires: For Paul de Man*, 31–2.

19. Derrida, *The Work of Mourning*, 143.
20. Elsner, *Mourning and Creativity in Proust*, 19–20.
21. Elsner, *Mourning and Creativity in Proust*, 2. Ortega y Gasset begins his 'Time, Distance, and Form in Proust', published after Proust's death but before the publication of the *Recherche*'s final volumes, by noting that 'death, in mowing down another's life, has in passing cut off our own pleasures'. Ortega y Gasset, 'Time, Distance, and Form in Proust', trans. Irving Singer, *The Hudson Review* 11, no. 4 (1958): 504. Cano cites a letter from Proust to his publisher only months before his death to indicate that the *Recherche* is, as imagined by its author anticipating his own death, 'an unfinished work'. Cano, *Proust's Deadline*, 83.
22. Compagnon, *Proust between Two Centuries*, 109.
23. Derrida in Hillis Miller, 'Derrida and Literature', 77.
24. As well as, of course and especially, the hardest work of the multiplying *re*-s of *re*-reading[ ].

Conclusion: Sign: Ending Text

SIGNING THE TEXT(,) AS IS

With the *Recherche*, Proust used writing to develop a fictive universe that is always different from itself. He created a text that encourages the most evocative of fictive expressions (his poetical descriptions of the sensory and conceptual world overflow with detail), yet masterfully never settles on any. As we have seen, this equivocation is often attributed to specific elements of the narrative – the narrator's uncertainty regarding his perceptions, often influenced by affect, is a regularly cited cause of this textual openness. Attempts to portray the *Recherche* on film throw this quality of textual undecidability into relief. Adaptations like Volker Schlöndorff's *Un amour de Swann* (1984) and Raúl Ruiz's *Le Temps retrouvé* (1999) seem, in comparison to the novel, one-dimensional. How can one settle on a specific age for the narrator in the scene in which Charlus ridicules him for his youth, for his 'wearing that bathing-costume with anchors embroidered upon it [celui d'avoir des ancres brodées sur votre costume de bain]' (*YG* 347; 334)? This is the narrator who, on the next page, emits a sophisticated critical opinion on the different periods of de Musset's oeuvre (*YG* 348; 334–335). Proust's narrative is deliberately elusive when it comes to specific, quantitative details (such as ages, dates, clock-times), but never shies away from inordinate information when it comes to qualitative ones (names are valued only for their dividual intensity; such is the case with the narrator's persistent interest in genealogy, for instance). The novel opens out onto the multiplicity, and contradictions, that are always sensible in perception.

This book has argued that this transversal unattainability in Proust's *Recherche* is an effect of its literary form, Proust's radical reinterpretation of textuality. It has suggested that Proust upturns the generic expectations of the novel – such as the presence of a unified, identifiable narrator, and the limits of a coherent, organised narrative arc – and in doing so promotes his own, virtuosic image of thought. We saw in Chapter 1 that Proust's novel unravels the critical desire to tie the novel's 'narrator' down to a static, iterable 'character', eschewing in the process the presentational logic of traditional metaphysics. Chapter 2 traced the deferring movement of sensation as Proust portrays it in the *Recherche*, arguing that the virtual 'property' of dividual multiplicity is a constant interest of the novel, which shows how percepts retain the trace[ ] of varied sensations while they change qualitatively – by always producing a new, virtual *noēteon*. By implementing a temporality removed from standard chronology, Proust portrayed the virtual contraction inherent in every percept – its way of opening out onto a multiplicity of variant, often contradictory traces.

The final four chapters then sought to apply this reading of Proust's text (as offering an image of thought freed from presentational logic) to the depictions of affective experience in the novel. Chapter 3 argued that desire is the abyssal production of the lack of lack *ad infinitum*, a *without* without *without* that is aroused by a sense of place always too large for its total presentation. Hence, desire seeks to trace the impossible deferral of desire itself, in an expropriating-appropriating movement of the trace that lacks only (always) another productive lack. Chapter 4 offered a conception of Proustian love as motivated by the black hole/white wall system of the beloved's faciality. The beloved is sensed as the cyclic movement of the black hole of the lover's subjectivity across the white wall of the beloved's signification. This leaves the lover constantly seeking to level off this a priori intersection between self and other, in the infinitive movement of love. Chapter 5 described jealousy as writing narratives that are necessarily prior to language, that take the shape of dreamlike, hieroglyphic 'determinatives', or *Bilderschrift*, because they must remain open to contradictory multiplicities, even in the real-world of chronological perception. Finally, Chapter 6 considered how grief operates in Proust's text, and problematised the relationship between writing and death. Writing grief seeks to appropriate a death that, as writing, it already *is*, yet in its iterability (as with the iterability of a 'literary death' such as Albertine's, who cannot be 'literally dead' without being brought back to a 'literary life') is always living, becoming and deferring anew in the vital movement of inscription.

In concluding this book, before I sign it, I would like to briefly consider this aporia of the 'life' of literary writing signed by Proust. If literature is mourning, if a text is inanimate or dead, what does it mean to sign it? What is it to sign one's personal reading of it, or to sign a critical 'reading' of it, such as this one you are reading now? And how does one sign for the signs made, or rather sensed, that *become* the *restance* of the literary work? In turn, as the signature itself is iterative, as that constant dying of the signatory disseminates (the version of yourself who began reading this book has been replaced by the version reading now, and so on), ~~there~~ rests the remains of that subject, the whole that this dissemination goes towards in deferring away from. In never totally appropriating its signatory, the signature is only ever its own abyssal resemblance: to use the formulation that I introduced in Chapter 2, the signature is, as. The signature as much as the signatory, in constantly 'dying', is constantly becoming; it is the iterability of textual *restance*, opening out towards the intensities of the *aiôn*. 'Even if we could reconstitute, morsel by morsel, a proper name's emblem or signature,' Derrida writes, 'that would only be to disengage, as from a tomb someone buried alive', the text that the signatory would never have succeeded in signing (G 169–70). In the inexhaustible abyss that constitutes the citational work going on not only above (throughout this book), but also throughout Proust's, Deleuze's or Derrida's reality or fiction[ ], the *sumplokē* weaves its way through the inexhaustibility of these traces – the becoming of iterability itself. The signature of such a text – the *bricolage* of citations, the *bricolage* of *re*iterating a word, of citing (it) again – disseminates before it is signed, and thus signs before it is signed, as well. Is it signed by the author, the reader, or by *Aiôn*? The passage quoted from *Glas* above continues:

> That text is what makes a hole in the pocket, harpoons it beforehand, regards it; but also sees it escape the text, bear its arrow away to unknown parts. This text here (or *glas*) no more reduces to a reading of Genet [or Proust, or Derrida himself, for that matter] – that forms neither its example nor its essence, neither its case nor its truth than this text here allows itself to be reassembled or arrowed, with others, by my paraph. (G 170)

Whose paraph is this? Or, if we consider the infinite mirroring of the abyss of appropriation: who *is* paraph *as* this? Who is it that is becoming 'their' text? Potentially anyone who writes, who absents – dies – into their literature, which *means* me, now, writ*ing*. The text constitutes itself, but in *primarily* filling and emptying the hollow that it gives, that it *is*, it escapes itself: it rests as its own *restance*, but that *restance* is dividual, and thus the text is always more than itself, more than it ever *presents* – more than it was signed *as is*. The paraph (the flourish in a written signature that verifies its *singularity*, or identity) is intense in its singular iterability. It 'must be singular each time, and must run its risk uniquely' (G 170), signing *for* one who is never present in their own literature, or who – which amounts to the same thing – remains.

So how do we 'have' a text, or how can we speak of 'a' text, this text? What is the reply to these seemingly unanswerable questions? That aporias like these defer, potentially *seeking* an answer, but only an answer that is itself becoming, itself deferring. 'Such' an aporia multiplies in Proust's writing. Not only must we contend with this problem of the paraph textually sign*ed*, but throughout this elaborating, forgettable hollow of a text, we contend with the multiplying signature of multiplying tense[ ], knowledge[ ] and trace[ ], all indicating multiplying narrators. It is not possible for all these narrators to sign their textual remains. If they were to do so, they would be signing over, *instead of*, the text.[1] In the book you have almost finished reading, I have tried to show how those ~~voices~~ whose signatures rest throughout Proust's novel come to have their paraph iterated. Albertine signifies inexorably, and yet she can never sign. Never, at least, until after she is *dead*, at which point she *is* dead (in the terms of Derrida's 'ever so slight difference of stress'), and thus signs incessantly (G 133).

In a moving sequence of *Albertine disparue*, the narrator's jealous *Bilderschrift* comes to an abrupt, insensible conclusion. On the same page, after having manically postulated a series of feints and subterfuges to coax Albertine back, the narrator foreshadows Albertine's death in an uncanny *sumplokē* of distinctly fluctuating temporality. His plotting descends the abyss, from compromise to complete self-effacement: in losing all sense of the power or pride he had sought the previous moment to assert, he 'abandoned all pride concerning Albertine, [he] sent her a desperate telegram asking her to return on any terms [Je laissai toute fierté vis-à-vis d'Albertine, je lui envoyai un télégramme désespéré lui demandant de revenir à n'importe quelles conditions]' (*PF* 443; *A* 58). But the next moment, he pauses, and directs his narrative outside of itself in one short sentence which breaks apart any pretence towards linearity. 'She never returned [Elle ne revint jamais]' (*PF* 443; *A* 58). This is a kind of prolepsis – the narrator foreshadows Albertine's death, and not for the first time – but more arrestingly, he works this certainty into the absolute uncertainty of her *literary* death. The brevity of this sentence attracts, but passes over, its temporal supererogation: Albertine never returns. Never return*ed*. But from where, or *when*, can a narrator speak for her *never* return*ing*? As we read on, the name – and thus the imagined, *literary* entirety – Albertine appears hundreds of times. This sentence seems to want to speak for the future of the narrative, of any other narrative it might give, and yet, seems to disqualify itself as the narrative, nonetheless, continues.

> Ah! It was not the suppression of suffering that the first two lines of the telegram produced in me: 'My poor friend, our little Albertine is no more, forgive me for having to tell you this terrible thing, knowing that you loved her so much. She was thrown against a tree by her horse whilst out riding. We did everything we could, but could not revive her. Would that I had died in her place!' No, not the suppression of suffering, but a previously unknown kind of suffering, that of learning that she would not return. But had I not told myself several times that she might not return? (*PF* 443)

> Ah ! ce ne fut pas la suppression de la souffrance que produisirent en moi les deux premières lignes du télégramme : « Mon pauvre ami, notre petite Albertine n'est plus, pardonnez-moi de vous dire cette chose affreuse, vous qui l'aimiez tant. Elle a été jetée par son cheval contre un arbre pendant une promenade. Tous nos efforts n'ont pu la ranimer. Que ne suis-je morte à sa place ! » Non, pas la suppression de la souffrance, mais une souffrance inconnue, celle d'apprendre qu'elle ne reviendrait pas. Mais ne m'étais-je pas dit plusieurs fois qu'elle ne reviendrait peut-être pas ? (*A* 58–9)

Knowing that Albertine 'never returned', perhaps this telegram should have been anticipated by the reader. But the iterability of Albertine's white wall is such that the narrator never trusts any of her disseminating signs, and yet this text received from her aunt, Mme Bontemps, is so unequivocally trusted that its message is accepted immediately. Albertine's death is signed, its/it's *seing*, always-already.[2] In so far as 'events extend further than the moments in which they happen' (*PF* 371), here the narrator weaves the sensed premonition of Albertine's death, the event of his discovering it, and its disseminat*ing* ramifications, into less than a page of a novel thousands of pages long. He accepts Albertine's death as though it has already occurred. The textual *sumplokē* Proust weaves here is especially interesting because it spreads over, cancelling out, the sign that ostensibly signifies it. Amid the direct, causal narration that apparently confirms Albertine's 'never returned[-ing]' is the reminder that this confirmation had been made by the narrator, by and to himself, 'several times' – this wearied certainty can only ever be woven into the iterations that are the deeper, virtual textuality of its iteration. Her death is undecidable, and always productive, like the text itself.

How can one narrate an event of such gravity? And if it can be done, how can it hold – what is its *restance*, short of bringing that person back to life? Proust defers the dramatic answer to such questions: he weaves the certain utterance of Albertine's death into an undecidable discourse of *Bilderschrift*, of the contingencies Albertine's absence continues to arouse, as though the definitive, irreversible event of Albertine's *becoming dead* – once, and irreversibly – cannot be uttered. This is a claim that is doubly underlined in the text. Firstly, Albertine's death can only be cited in the form of quoted speech *sign*ed by Mme Bontemps (which awkwardly trails off without her signature). Secondly, in the same paragraph (*PF* 443–5; *A* 58–60) Proust begins weaving one of his most complex paraph-machines: he receives and quotes two telegrams from Albertine, one affecting compliance with the narrator's feigned desire to marry Andrée (a ruse designed to compel Albertine to return of her own accord), and the other professing a hasty, fretful desire to return. The narrator's anxiety about the multiplicity of Albertine's variant desires remain in his text, while *her* text[ ], that is, these telegrams, further multiplies her possible desires. (Could she be writing more? To whom? Or why not? And where are they?)

Amid the multiplication of Albertine's desires, one should ask: why does the narrator accept, without interrogation, the content of Mme Bontemps's telegram? It is *the* event of the novel, and yet it is washed over by a paragraph that assumes its effects and translates them without so much as a pause for contemplation. Albertine's death can eventually be contemplated, but the singular event that signs it can never be signed *for* (by Mme Bontemps, Albertine, the narrator, Proust, or even the reader), because such a definitive death is not something that the novel allows. Albertine's resemblance, clearly, goes on living throughout the novel. Her resemblance is real in the resemblance of the real that is fiction (that is, resemblance). Or rather, it remains in what remains. This is why Proust inserts Albertine's death within a flowing paragraph that *also* cites her ~~voice~~ in the form of these telegrams. Mme Bontemps's telegram is reproduced in the text, and then, by the following paragraph, the narrator's grief for Albertine's 'death' is being contemplated as a certain fact. The death of the woman who was always in motion, always inspiring an extra doubt between two doubts, is made into an inarguable certainty by an unsigned letter from an unreliable source. Albertine's death *itself* is signed, *seing*, always-already. The certainty of Albertine's death is signed by the text itself. The text is responsible for her death because the text itself is the paraph that guarantees its credibility, its certainty, its *is*: each contention of absence *rest*ing in the text, each seemingly unnecessary excursus by the ~~voice~~ is the necessary, non-forgeable weave of the paraph that guarantees Albertine's death.

And as though more evidence were required for the verification of this paraph, to guard against its forgery, Proust returns later in the uncompleted, posthumous (that is, unfinished and unsigned by Proust) *Albertine disparue*, to Albertine's signature. The narrator is finally in Venice, aloof, though sometimes sensing that the

> Albertine of former times, although invisible, was none the less locked deep inside [him], as if in the lead-lined cells of some inner Venice. (*PF* 603)

> Albertine d'autrefois, invisible à moi-même, était pourtant enfermée au fond de moi comme aux plombs d'une Venise intérieure. (*A* 219)

Returning to the hotel, he receives a telegram, which reads:

> 'DEAR FRIEND YOU BELIEVE ME DEAD, MY APOLOGIES, NEVER MORE ALIVE, WOULD LIKE TO SEE YOU TO DISCUSS MARRIAGE, WHEN DO YOU RETURN? AFFECTIONATELY, ALBERTINE.' (*PF* 605–6)

> « Mon ami vous me croyez morte, pardonnez-moi, je suis très vivante, je voudrais vous voir, vous parler mariage, quand revenez-vous ? Tendrement, Albertine. » (*A* 221)

This spectral writing takes the porous form of an abyssal *propre* – is it a hoax, an anachronism or the writing of a ghost? This *Unheimlichkeit* streams forth from the signature itself, which de*sign*ates this absolutely reproducible text (it is a telegram, its signature is typed, and for that reason it bears no paraph) as a *restance* intensified by its iterability. And again, the narration treats the content of this sign as its/it's *seing*, an undecidable always-already: the narrator does not stop to contemplate Albertine's death, or *re*surrection, because he has never *present*ed either. His narration passes directly into the effect of her non-death.

> Now that Albertine was no longer alive in my thoughts, the news that she was alive did not bring me the joy that I would have expected. (*PF* 606)

> Maintenant qu'Albertine dans ma pensée ne vivait plus pour moi, la nouvelle qu'elle était vivante ne me causa pas la joie que j'aurais cru. (*A* 221)

Albertine *is* dead; Albertine *was* alive. The conjunction that overwhelms this sentence is like the *sumplokē* of Proust's signature grief, or rather, the grieving of Proust's signature. In the same unsigned statement, Albertine is dead and alive, signed into an absolute simulacrum – her text indicates to the narrator her simultaneous living and *being* dead, and all because 'her' *signature* exhumes her literary Being: its brings her back to a life that never left her. But this complicit belief hinges on the narrator's understanding that 'Albertine had been for [him] but a bundle of thoughts [Albertine n'avait été pour moi qu'un faisceau de pensées]' (*PF* 606; *A* 221). Can Albertine ever be alive or dead? Or rather, *was* Albertine ever alive or dead? She is a bundle of thoughts, generated from a mass of words, or *re*iterable language – both in the literature that we read and have read, and to the narrator, who has only *read* of her death and resurrection. The life of the narrator's Albertine is, here, the same as our Albertine's – the 'present certainty' of a text, the verification of a signature. And yet there is a proper hold, a contiguity that *re*turns the differen*ti*ation of Albertine to the narrator, and to us, as solid as stone or a statue. She *rests* throughout the literature, throughout memory, and throughout *re*production: the virtual work of her properties is the paraph of her virtual (unsigned) signature.

The narrator, all of a sudden, experiences a transversal flash of insight: this ghostly telegram was not from Albertine at all, but rather, it 'was from Gilberte'. The 'rather factitious originality [originalité assez factice]' (*PF* 619; *A* 235) of Gilberte's signature, or its self-disqualifying paraph, enacts exactly what such a disqualifying expression implies: it disseminates its *propre* as it's becoming *propre*. The paraph, and even the signature, is supposed to single out its signatory, to identify that *it is verifiably* that person (Gilberte), and no other. And yet, for the narrator, it instantly identifies, and belongs, to someone else (Albertine). Let us remember, too, that the narrator first reads this signature as a telegram – that is, transcribed into paraph-less, typed text. As the paraph is the complex, inimitable sign of individuality (or the *weaving* of the signature; that which inscribes this diffe*rence*), it *signs as* the graphic transcendence of language. In this virtual, multiplying *sumplokē* of differen*c*iation becoming differen*t*iation and vice versa, the *aiôn* envelops the literary form. Albertine's spectre is given *and* not taken away, *while* being effaced – *re*named – because 'her' bundle of thoughts becomes a *revenant* from the enveloping paraph of a differing signature. Gilberte's paraph has disseminated what her signature properly defines: the properly verifying property presented in absence, always-already. This is logically assembled as an abnormality, but this is nothing new, any more than an absent origin of literary becoming, as Derrida suggests.

> Everything is played out, everything and all the rest, – that is to say, the game – is played out in the *entre* [. . .] When this undecidability is marked and re-marked in *writing*, it has a greater power of formalization, even if it is 'literary' in appearance, or appears to be attributable to a natural language, than when it occurs as a proposition in logicomathematical form, which would not go as far as the former type of mark. (*D* 222)

This paraph has a 'greater power of formalization' than its form itself, because of the intensity of its undecidability. We inject this greater power into the paraph, the literary mark, just as we inject a greater power into the mark[ ] 'Albertine', which is nothing more than a mixture of letters or a bundle of thoughts (for us as well as for Proust), but that inscribes itself on our understanding of desire, love, jealousy, grief – indeed, of the very lives we are living.

Because of the disseminating work done by Gilberte's paraph, the narrator notes that 'it was natural enough that a telegraph clerk [il était tout naturel que l'employé du télégraphe]' should have misinterpreted

Gilberte's signature. But to translate it *exactly* into 'Albertine' – notwithstanding the narrator's equivocations that 'her G [...] had the appearance of an *A* in gothic script [Quant à son *G*, il avait l'air d'un *A* gothique.]' (*PF* 620; *A* 235–26) – seems fanciful, or rather forced, artificial, *unnatural*. It is not natural, or not real, but rather a resemblance of the real. As if to qualify either the clerk's or his real non-reality, the narrator considers the sanctity of a 'correct' reading, and the literary complications of the always deferred, absent origin of a meaning that means what it means.

> How many characters in each word does a person read when his mind is on other things and when he is already sure that he knows who the letter is from? How many words in each sentence? We guess as we read, we invent; everything stems from one initial error; those that follow (and this not only in reading letters and telegrams, not even only in all acts of reading), however extraordinary they may seem to someone who does not share the same starting-point, are natural enough. Thus it is that a great deal of what we believe to be true, not to mention the ultimate conclusions that, with equal perseverance and good faith, we draw from it, results from an initial misconception of the premiss. (*PF* 620)

> Combien de lettres lit dans un mot une personne distraite et surtout prévenue, qui part de l'idée que la lettre est d'une certaine personne ? combien de mots dans la phrase ? On devine en lisant, on crée ; tout part d'une erreur initiale ; celles qui suivent (et ce n'est pas seulement dans la lecture des lettres et des télégrammes, pas seulement dans toute lecture), si extraordinaires qu'elles puissent paraître à celui qui n'a pas le même point de départ, sont toutes naturelles. Une bonne partie de ce que nous croyons (et jusque dans les conclusions dernières c'est ainsi) avec un entêtement et une bonne foi égales vient d'une première méprise sur les prémisses. (*A* 236)

This conceiving misconception is the work of literature itself. To sign is simply to give up the pretence of meaning, the original mistake made by the signatory, to the *différante* mistakes made by the reader. Each 'mistake' is the work of reading, of writing, of creation – of signing – and as such, we should not call the work of creation a mistake, or even an interpretation, but rather the becoming of signing, of a making-semblance of the real, which is more natural in its resemblance.

Literature speaks with an absent ~~voice~~ – a voice that, bearing a signature as the very reason for (haunting) its absence, can never be natural. There is every chance that Proust's signature is not the one we have read – and not only because his final signature is absent from his uncompleted novel. So, whose signature do we supplement in its place? Because the *Recherche* is the furthest possible thing from a 'purely descriptive literature', it is in-between each of its words that we find *our own* signature – departing the moment we think we can present it.

NOTES

1. Bowie describes how this transversal selfhood facilitates the creativity of a work of art such as Proust's: 'This interlacing of optics, astronomy and music, which is also an indefinite sequence of displacements between small and vast, not only promises no selfhood to the artist and to those who follow his example, it presents selfhood as an impediment to creative perception. The only conception of self that can usefully remain is that of a discontinuous itinerary, leading towards but never reaching that moment of plenitude at which the entire range of possible forms would stand revealed and realized.' Bowie, 'Proust's Narrative Selves', 141.
2. This is an undecidable *seing*: the narration both treats *seing* as the *seing* that belongs to it, its *proper seing*, and it treats the content of the *seing* as it is 'a' *seing*, a signature (even its own) that is always-already signed. It does not prioritise either form.

Bibliography

Alliez, Éric. *Capital Times: Tales from the Conquest of Time.* Trans. Georges Van Den Abbeele. Minneapolis: University of Minnesota Press, 1996.
——. *The Signature of the World, or, What is Deleuze and Guattari's Philosophy?* Trans. Eliot Ross Albert and Alberto Toscano. London and New York: Continuum, 2004.
Attridge, Derek. *The Singularity of Literature.* London and New York: Routledge, 2004.
Attridge, John. 'Episodic Trust: Self, Society and Sociology in *À la recherche du temps perdu*.' In *Incredible Modernism: Literature, Trust and Deception.* Ed. John Attridge and Rod Rosenquist, 199–213. Farnham: Ashgate, 2013.
Bal, Mieke. *The Mottled Screen: Reading Proust Visually.* Trans. Anna-Louise Milne. Stanford: Stanford University Press, 1997.
Balsamo, Gian. 'The Fiction of Marcel Proust's Autobiography.' *Poetics Today* 28, no. 4 (2007): 577–606.
Barbaras, Renaud. *Desire and Distance: Introduction to a Phenomenology of Perception.* Trans. Paul B. Milan. Stanford: Stanford University Press, 2006.
——. 'Life, Movement, Desire.' Trans. Jen McWeeny. *Research in Phenomenology* 38, no. 1 (2008): 3–17.
——. 'The Phenomenology of Life: Desire as the Being of the Subject.' Trans. Darian Meacham. In *The Oxford Handbook of Contemporary Phenomenology.* Ed. Dan Zahavi, 94–112. Oxford: Oxford University Press, 2012.
Baross, Zsuzsa. 'Deleuze and Derrida, by Way of Blanchot: An Interview.' *Angelaki* 5, no. 2 (2000): 17–41.
Barthes, Roland. 'Une idée de recherche.' In *Recherche de Proust.* Ed. Gérard Genette and Tzvetan Todorov, 34–9. Paris: Éditions du Seuil, 1980.
——. *New Critical Essays.* New York: Hill &Wang, 1980.
——. *Œuvres complètes.* Paris: Éditions du Seuil, 2002.
Bayard, Pierre. *Le Hors-Sujet: Proust et la digression.* Paris: Minuit, 1996.
Beckett, Samuel. *Proust.* New York: Grove Press, 1931.
Beckman, Frida. *Between Desire and Pleasure: A Deleuzian Theory of Sexuality.* Edinburgh: Edinburgh University Press, 2013.

Belenky, Masha. *The Anxiety of Dispossession: Jealousy in Nineteenth-Century French Culture*. Lewisburg, PA: Bucknell University Press, 2008.
Benhaïm, André. 'Preamble.' In *The Strange M. Proust*. Ed. André Benhaïm, 1–11. London: Legenda, 2009.
Benjamin, Walter. *Illuminations*. Trans. Harry Zohn. Ed. Hannah Arendt. New York: Schocken Books, 1969.
Bergson, Henri. *Creative Evolution*. 1907. Trans. Arthur Mitchell. New York: Holt, 1911.
——. *Matter and Memory*. 1986. Trans. Margaret Paul and W. Scott Palmer. London: Allen & Unwin, 1912.
——. *Time and Free Will: An Essay on the Immediate Data of Consciousness*. 1889. Trans. Frank Lubecki Pogson. London: Allen & Unwin, 1910.
Bersani, Leo. *The Culture of Redemption*. Cambridge, MA: Harvard University Press, 1990.
——. 'Déguisements du moi et art fragmentaire.' In *Recherche de Proust*. Ed. Gérard Genette and Tzvetan Todorov, 13–33. Paris: Éditions du Seuil, 1980.
——. *A Future for Astyanax: Character and Desire in Literature*. 1976. New York: Columbia University Press, 1984.
——. *Marcel Proust: The Fictions of Life and Art*. New York: Oxford University Press, 1965.
Bowie, Malcolm. *Freud, Proust, and Lacan: Theory as Fiction*. Cambridge and New York: Cambridge University Press, 1987.
——. *Proust among the Stars*. London: Harper Collins, 1998.
——. 'Proust and the Art of Brevity.' In *The Cambridge Companion to Proust*. Ed. Richard Bales, 216–29. Cambridge: Cambridge University Press, 2001.
——. 'Proust's Narrative Selves.' In *Moy qui me voy: The Writer and the Self from Montaigne to Leiris*. Ed. George Craig and Margaret McGowan, 131–46. New York: Oxford University Press, 1989.
——. 'Reading Proust between the Lines.' In *The Strange M. Proust*. Ed. André Benhaïm, 125–34. London: Legenda, 2009.
Bray, Patrick M. 'Deleuze's Spider, Proust's Narrator.' *Contemporary French and Francophone Studies* 16, no. 5 (2012): 703–10.
——. *The Novel Map: Space and Subjectivity in Nineteenth-Century French Fiction*. Evanston: Northwestern University Press, 2013.
Brooks, Peter. *Body Work: Objects of Desire in Modern Narrative*. Cambridge, MA: Harvard University Press, 1993.
Brown, Stephen Gilbert. *The Gardens of Desire: Proust and the Fugitive Sublime*. New York: State University of New York Press, 2004.
Cano, Christine. *Proust's Deadline*. Urbana and Chicago: University of Illinois Press, 2006.
Carbone, Mauro. *The Thinking of the Sensible: Merleau-Ponty's A-Philosophy*. Evanston: Northwestern University Press, 2004.
——. *An Unprecedented Deformation: Marcel Proust and the Sensible Ideas*. Trans. Niall Keane. Albany: State University of New York Press, 2010.
Carter, William C. *Proust in Love*. New Haven: Yale University Press, 2006.

Chardin, Philippe. *L'Amour dans la haine, ou, La Jalousie dans la littérature moderne: Dostoïevski, James, Svevo, Proust, Musil*. Geneva: Droz, 1990.

Cisney, Vernon. *Deleuze and Derrida: Difference and the Power of the Negative*. Edinburgh: Edinburgh University Press, 2018.

Colebrook, Claire. *Gilles Deleuze*. London and New York: Routledge, 2002.

——. *Irony*. London and New York: Routledge, 2004.

——. *Understanding Deleuze*. Sydney: Allen & Unwin, 2002.

Compagnon, Antoine. 'Le narrateur en procès.' In *Marcel Proust 2: Nouvelles directions de la recherche proustienne*. Ed. Bernard Brun, 309–34. Paris: Minard, 2000.

——. *Proust between Two Centuries*. Trans. Richard E. Goodkin. New York: Columbia University Press, 1992.

——. 'Writing Mourning.' Trans. Sam Ferguson. *Textual Practice* 30, no. 2 (2016): 209–19.

Cornell, Drucilla. 'Where Love Begins.' In *Derrida and Feminism: Recasting the Question of Woman*. Ed. Ellen K. Feder, Mary C. Rawlinson and Emily Zakin, 161–206. New York and London: Routledge, 1997.

Décarie, Isabelle. 'Tentations proustiennes.' *Études françaises* 38, no. 1–2 (2002): 189–205.

Deleuze, Gilles. *Bergsonism*. 1966. Trans. Hugh Tomlinson and Barbara Habberjam. New York: Zone Books, 1988.

——. *Cinema I: The Movement-Image*. 1983. Trans. Hugh Tomlinson and Barbara Habberjam. London and New York: Bloomsbury, 2013.

——. *Cinema II: The Time-Image*. 1985. Trans. Hugh Tomlinson and Robert Galeta. London and New York: Bloomsbury, 2013.

——. *Desert Islands and Other Texts: 1953–1974*. Trans. Michael Taormina. London and Cambridge, MA: MIT Press, 2004.

——. *Difference and Repetition*. 1968. Trans. Paul Patton. London: Athlone Press, 1994.

——. *Essays Critical and Clinical*. 1993. Trans. Daniel W. Smith and Michael A. Greco. London and New York: Verso, 1998.

——. *The Logic of Sense*. 1969. Trans. Mark Lester with Charles Stivale. New York: Columbia University Press, 1990.

——. *Proust and Signs*. 1964. Trans. Richard Howard. Minneapolis: University of Minnesota Press, 2000.

——. *Two Regimes of Madness: Texts and Interviews, 1975–1995*. Trans. Ames Hodges and Mike Taorima. Ed. David Lapoujade. London and Cambridge, MA: MIT Press, 2006.

Deleuze, Gilles, and Guattari, Félix. *Anti-Oedipus: Capitalism and Schizophrenia*. 1972. Trans. Robert Hurley, Mark Seem and Helen R. Lane. Minneapolis: University of Minneapolis Press, 1983.

——. *A Thousand Plateaus: Capitalism and Schizophrenia*. 1980. Trans. Brian Massumi. Minneapolis and London: University of Minneapolis Press, 1987.

——. *What is Philosophy?* 1991. Trans. Hugh Tomlinson and Graham Burchill. London and New York: Verso, 1994.

de Man, Paul. *Allegories of Reading: Figural Language in Rousseau, Nietzsche, Rilke, and Proust*. New Haven and London: Yale University Press, 1979.
Derrida, Jacques. *Acts of Literature*. Ed. Derek Attridge. London and New York: Routledge, 1992.
———. 'At This Very Moment in This Work Here I Am.' 1980. Trans. Ruben Berezdivin. In *Re-Reading Levinas*. Ed. Robert Bernasconi and Simon Critchley, 11–50. Bloomington and Indianapolis, IN: Indiana University Press, 1991.
———. 'Biodegradables: Seven Diary Fragments.' Trans. Peggy Kamuf. *Critical Inquiry* 15, no. 4 (1989): 812–73.
———. *Dissemination*. 1972. Trans. Barbara Johnson. London: Athlone Press, 1981.
———. *Glas*. 1974. Trans. John P. Leavey Jr. and Richard Rand. Lincoln and London: University of Nebraska Press, 1986.
———. *Of Grammatology*. 1967. Trans. Gayatri Chakravorty Spivak. Baltimore: Johns Hopkins University Press, 2016.
———. *Limited Inc.* Trans. Samuel Weber and Jeffrey Mehlman. Evanston: Northwestern University Press, 1988.
———. *Margins of Philosophy*. 1972. Trans. Alan Bass. Brighton: Harvester Press, 1982.
———. *Memoires: for Paul de Man*. Trans. Cecile Lindsay, Jonathan Culler and Eduardo Cadava. New York: Columbia University Press, 1986.
———. *Positions*. 1972. Trans. Alan Bass. London and New York: Continuum, 1981.
———. *The Post Card: From Socrates to Freud and Beyond*. 1980. Trans. Alan Bass. Chicago and London: Chicago University Press, 1987.
———. *Signéponge/Signsponge*. 1976. Trans. Richard Rand. New York: Columbia University Press, 1984.
———. *Specters of Marx: The State of the Debt, The Work of Mourning, and the New International*. 1993. Trans. Peggy Kamuf. New York and London: Routledge, 1994.
———. *Speech and Phenomena: And Other Essays on Husserl's Theory of Signs*. 1967. Trans. David B. Allison. Evanston: Northwestern University Press, 1973.
———. *Spurs: Nietzsche's Styles/Éperons: Les Styles de Nietzsche*. Chicago and London: University of Chicago Press, 1978.
———. 'The Time of a Thesis: Punctuations.' 1980. Trans. Kathleen McLaughlin. In *Philosophy in France Today*. Ed. Alan Montefiore, 34–50. Cambridge: Cambridge University Press, 1983.
———. *The Work of Mourning*. Trans. and ed. Michael Naas and Pascale-Anne Brault. Chicago and London: University of Chicago Press, 2001.
———. *Writing and Difference*. 1967. Trans. Alan Bass. Chicago: University of Chicago Press, 1978.
Deschamps, Nicole. 'La voix proustienne.' *Inconvenient: Revue littéraire d'essai et de creation* 11 (2002): 15–24.

Descombes, Vincent. *Proust: Philosophy of the Novel*. Trans. Catherine Chance Macksey. Stanford: Stanford University Press, 1992.
Dosse, François. *Gilles Deleuze and Félix Guattari: Intersecting Lives*. Trans. Deborah Glassman. New York: Columbia University Press, 2010.
Doubrovsky, Serge. *Writing and Fantasy in Proust: la place de la madeleine*. Trans. Carol Mastrangelo Bové with Paul A. Bové. Lincoln: University of Nebraska Press, 1986.
Dowd, Garin. 'Apprenticeship, Philosophy, and the "Secret Pressures of the Work of Art" in Deleuze, Beckett, Proust and Ruiz; or Remaking the *Recherche*.' In *Beckett's Proust/Deleuze's Proust*. Ed. Mary Bryden and Margaret Topping, 89–103. Basingstoke: Palgrave Macmillan, 2009.
Düttmann, Alexander García. *The Gift of Language: Memory and Promise in Adorno, Benjamin, Heidegger, and Rosenzweig*. Trans. Arline Lyons. London: Athlone Press, 2000.
——. 'Separated from Proust.' *Angelaki* 9, no. 3 (2004): 89–90.
Dutton, James. 'Life Stories: How to Write Remains.' *Symploke* 28, no. 1–2 (2020): 313–30.
Ellison, David. *The Reading of Proust*. Oxford: Basil Blackwell, 1984.
Elsner, Anna Magdalena. *Mourning and Creativity in Proust*. New York: Palgrave Macmillan, 2017.
Ffrench, Patrick. 'Proust and the Analysis of Gesture.' In *Proust and the Visual*. Ed. Nathalie Aubert, 47–68. Cardiff: University of Wales Press, 2013.
Finch, Alison. 'Love, Sexuality and Friendship.' In *The Cambridge Companion to Proust*. Ed. Richard Bales, 168–82. Cambridge: Cambridge University Press, 2001.
Flieger, Jerry Aline. 'Becoming-Woman: Deleuze, Schreber and Molecular Identification.' In *Deleuze and Feminist Theory*. Ed. Claire Colebrook and Ian Buchanan, 38–63. Edinburgh: Edinburgh University Press, 2000.
Freed-Thall, Hannah. *Spoiled Distinctions: Aesthetics and the Ordinary in French Modernism*. New York: Oxford University Press, 2015.
Freud, Sigmund. *The Standard Edition of the Complete Psychological Works of Sigmund Freud*. Trans. James Strachey. London: Hogarth Press, 1953–75.
Fülöp, Erika. *Proust, the One, and the Many: Identity and Difference in À la recherche du temps perdu*. London: Legenda, 2012.
Fülöp, Erika, and Philippe Chardin, eds. *Cent ans de jalousie proustienne*. Paris: Classiques Garnier, 2015.
Gasché, Rodolphe. 'Deconstruction and Hermeneutics.' In *Deconstructions: A User's Guide*. Ed. Nicholas Royle, 137–51. Basingstoke: Palgrave, 2000.
——. *Inventions of Difference: On Jacques Derrida*. Cambridge, MA and London: Harvard University Press, 1994.
——. *The Tain of the Mirror: Derrida and the Philosophy of Reflection*. Cambridge, MA: Harvard University Press, 1986.
Genette, Gérard. *Narrative Discourse: An Essay in Method*. Trans. Jane. E. Lewin. Oxford: Basil Blackwell, 1980.
Girard, René. *Deceit, Desire, and the Novel: Self and Other in Literary*

Structure. Trans. Yvonne Freccero. Baltimore: Johns Hopkins University Press, 1965.
Graff Zivin, Erin. *Anarchaeologies: Reading as Misreading*. New York: Fordham University Press, 2020.
Grande, Per Bjørnar. 'Proustian Desire.' *Contagion: Journal of Violence, Mimesis, and Culture* 18 (2011): 39–69.
Grosz, Elizabeth. *Chaos, Territory, Art: Deleuze and the Framing of the Earth*. New York: Columbia University Press.
Guerlac, Suzanne. 'Visual Dust: On Time, Memory, and Photography in Proust.' *Contemporary French and Francophone Studies* 13, no. 4 (2009): 397–404.
Hägglund, Martin. *Dying For Time: Proust, Woolf, Nabokov*. Cambridge, MA: Harvard University Press, 2012.
——. *Radical Atheism: Derrida and the Time of Life*. Stanford: Stanford University Press, 2008.
Haustein, Katja. 'Proust's Emotional Cavaties: Vision and Affect in *À la recherche du temps perdu*.' *French Studies* 63, no. 2 (2009): 161–73.
Husserl, Edmund. *Cartesian Meditations: An Introduction to Phenomenology*. 1931. Trans. Dorion Cairns. The Hague: Nijoff, 1960.
——. *Ideas: General Introduction to a Pure Phenomenology*. 1913. Trans. W. R. Boyce Gibson. London: Allen & Unwin, 1932.
——. *Ideas Pertaining to a Pure Phenomenology and to a Phenomenological Philosophy, Third Book*. 1952. Trans. Ted E. Klein and William E. Pohl. The Hague: Nijoff, 1980.
——. *The Phenomenology of Internal Time-Consciousness*. 1928. Trans. James Churchill. Bloomington, IN: Indiana University Press, 1964.
Jay, Martin. *Downcast Eyes: The Denigration of Vision in Twentieth-Century French Thought*. Berkeley and London: The University of California Press, 1993.
Kemp, Gary. 'Proust on the Art and Value of Living.' *European Journal of Philosophy* 15, no. 2 (2007): 270–82.
Kubala, Robbie. 'Love and Transience in Proust.' *Philosophy* 91, no. 4 (2016): 541–57.
Lacoue-Labarthe, Phillip. *Typography: Mimesis, Philosophy, Politics*. Ed. Christopher Fynsk. London and Cambridge, MA: Harvard University Press, 1989.
Lambert, Gregg. 'The Philosopher *and* the Writer: A Question of Style.' In *Between Deleuze and Derrida*. Ed. Paul Patton and John Protevi, 120–34. London and New York: Continuum, 2003.
Ladenson, Elizabeth. *Proust's Lesbianism*. Ithaca and London: Cornell University Press, 1999.
Landy, Joshua. *Philosophy as Fiction: Self, Deception, and Knowledge in Proust*. Oxford: Oxford University Press, 2004.
Lecercle, Jean-Jacques. *Badiou and Deleuze Read Literature*. Edinburgh: Edinburgh University Press, 2010.

Lerner, Scott L. 'Mourning and Subjectivity: From Bersani to Proust, Klein and Freud.' *diacritics* 37, no. 1 (2007): 41–53.
Lo, Louis. *Male Jealousy: Literature and Film*. London and New York: Continuum, 2008.
Lucey, Michael. *Never Say I: Sexuality and the First Person in Colette, Gide, and Proust*. Durham and London: Duke University Press, 2006.
Lyotard, Jean-François. *The Inhuman: Reflections on Time*. Trans. Geoffrey Bennington and Rachel Bowlby. Cambridge: Polity, 1991.
Magedera, Ian. 'Seing Genet, Citation and Mourning: A Propos *Glas* by Jacques Derrida.' *Paragraph* 21, no. 1 (1998): 28–44.
Matz, Jesse. *Literary Impressionism and Modernist Aesthetics*. Cambridge: Cambridge University Press, 2001.
McDonald, Christie. 'Literature and Philosophy at the Crossroads: Proustian Subjects.' In *Writing the Politics of Difference*. Ed. Hugh J. Silverman, 135–44. Albany: State University of New York Press, 1991.
Merleau-Ponty, Maurice. *The Phenomenology of Perception*. 1945. Trans. Colin Smith. London: Routledge & Kegan Paul, 1962.
———. *The Visible and the Invisible*. 1964. Trans. Alphonso Lingis. Evanston: Northwestern University Press, 1968.
Miller, J. Hillis. 'Derrida and Literature.' In *Jacques Derrida and the Humanities: A Critical Reader*. Ed. Tom Cohen, 58–81. Cambridge: Cambridge University Press, 2001.
———. 'The Other's Other: Jealousy and Art in Proust.' *Qui Parle* 9, no. 1 (1995): 119–40.
Milly, Jean. 'Phrase, Phrases.' In *Marcel Proust 3: Nouvelles directions de la recherche proustienne 2*. Ed. Bernard Brun, 197–216. Paris: Minard, 2001.
Moi, Toril. *What is a Woman? And Other Essays*. Oxford and New York: Oxford University Press, 1999.
Monneyron, Frédéric. *L'Écriture de la jalousie*. Grenoble: ELLUG, Université Stendhal, 1997.
Moss, Howard. *The Magic Lantern of Marcel Proust*. London: Faber, 1963.
Murphy, Michael. *Proust and America*. Liverpool: Liverpool University Press, 2007.
Naas, Michael, *Taking on the Tradition: Jacques Derrida and the Legacies of Deconstruction*. Stanford: Stanford University Press, 2003.
Nicole, Eugene. '"Quel Marcel!" (And Other Oddities of the Narrator's Designations in *Á la recherche du temps perdu*).' In *The Strange M. Proust*. Ed. André Benhaïm, 36–44. London, Legenda, 2009.
Nussbaum, Martha. 'The Ascent of Love: Plato, Spinoza, Proust.' *New Literary History* 25, no. 4 (1994): 925–949.
———. *Love's Knowledge: Essays on Philosophy and Literature*. Oxford and New York: Oxford University Press, 1990.
Ortega y Gasset, José. *On Love: Aspects of a Single Theme*. Trans. Toby Talbot. London: Cape, 1967.

———. 'Time, Distance, and Form in Proust.' Trans. Irving Singer. *The Hudson Review* 11, no. 4 (1958): 504–513.
Parker, Jo Alyson. *Narrative Form and Chaos Theory in Sterne, Proust, Woolf, and Faulkner*. New York: Palgrave Macmillan, 2007.
Patton, Paul. *Deleuzian Concepts: Philosophy, Colonization, Politics*. Stanford: Stanford University Press, 2010.
———. *Political Deleuze*. London and New York: Routledge, 2000.
Patton, Paul, and John Protevi. 'Introduction.' In *Between Deleuze and Derrida*. Ed. Paul Patton and John Protevi, 120–34. London and New York: Continuum, 2003.
Plato. *The Dialogues of Plato*. Trans. Benjamin Jowett. Oxford: Clarendon Press, 1875.
Proust, Marcel. *Albertine disparue*. 1925. Paris: Éditions Gallimard, 1989.
———. *À l'ombre des jeunes filles en fleurs*. 1919. Paris: Éditions Gallimard, 1988.
———. *Du côté de chez Swann*. 1913. Paris: Éditions Gallimard, 1988.
———. *Le Côté de Guermantes*. 1920/1921. Paris: Éditions Gallimard, 1988.
———. *Finding Time Again*. 1927. Trans. Ian Patterson. London: Penguin Modern Classics, 2003.
———. *The Guermantes Way*. 1920/1921. Trans. Mark Treharne. London: Penguin Modern Classics, 2003.
———. *The Prisoner* and *The Fugitive*. 1923/1925. Trans. Carol Clark and Peter Collier. London: Penguin Modern Classics, 2003.
———. *La Prisonnière*. 1923. Paris: Éditions Gallimard, 1989.
———. *In the Shadow of Young Girls in Flower*. 1919. Trans. James Grieve. London: Penguin Modern Classics, 2003.
———. *Remembrance of Things Past*. Trans. C. K. Scott Moncrieff. Ware, Hertfordshire: Wordsworth Editions, 2006.
———. *Sodom and Gomorrah*. 1921/1922. Trans. John Sturrock. London: Penguin Modern Classics, 2003.
———. *Sodome et Gomorrhe*. 1921/1922. Paris: Éditions Gallimard, 1989.
———. *Le Temps retrouvé*. 1927. Paris: Éditions Gallimard, 1990.
———. *The Way by Swann's*. 1913. Trans. Lydia Davis. London: Penguin Modern Classics, 2003.
Protevi, John. 'Love.' In *Between Deleuze and Derrida*. Ed. Paul Patton and John Protevi, 183–94. London and New York: Continuum, 2003.
Rabaté, Jean-Michel. *The Ghosts of Modernity*. Gainesville: University of Press of Florida, 1996.
Riccardi, Alessia. *The Ends of Mourning: Psychoanalysis, Literature, Film*. Stanford: Stanford University Press, 2003.
Rivers, Julius. *Proust and the Art of Love*. New York: Columbia University Press, 1983.
Rogers, Brian. 'Proust's Narrator.' In *The Cambridge Companion to Proust*. Ed. Richard Bales, 85–99. Cambridge: Cambridge University Press, 2001.
Roloff, Volker. 'Desire, Imaginary, and Love: Erotic Readings of the *Recherche*.'

Trans. Jane Kuntz. In *Proust in Perspective: Visions and Revisions*. Ed. Armine Kotin Mortimer and Katherine Kolb, 157–71. Urbana and Chicago: University of Illinois Press, 2002.

Rushworth, Jennifer. 'Derrida, Proust, and the Promise of Writing.' *French Studies* 69, no. 2 (2015): 205–19.

———. *Discourses of Mourning in Dante, Petrarch, and Proust*. Oxford: Oxford University Press, 2016.

Scheler, Max. *The Nature of Sympathy*. 1923. Trans. Peter Heath. London: Routledge & Kegan Paul, 1979.

Segal, Alexander. 'Demarcating the *Recherche*: Joshua Landy's *Philosophy as Fiction: Self, Deception, and Knowledge in Proust*.' *Journal of the Australasian Universities Language and Literature Association* 116 (2011): 99–119.

Shattuck, Roger. 'Lost and Found: The Structure of Proust's Novel.' In *The Cambridge Companion to Proust*. Ed. Richard Bales, 74–84. Cambridge: Cambridge University Press, 2001.

———. *Marcel Proust*. Princeton: Princeton University Press, 1974.

Simon, Anne. 'The Formalist, the Spider, and the Phenomenologist: Proust in the Magic Mirror of the Twentieth Century.' In *The Strange M. Proust*. Ed. André Benhaïm, 23–35. London: Legenda, 2009.

———. *Proust ou le réel retrouvé: le sensible et son expression dans* À la recherche du temps perdu. Paris: Presses universitaires de France, 2000.

———. *Trafics de Proust: Merleau-Ponty, Sartre, Deleuze, Barthes*. Paris: Hermann, 2016.

Sloterdijk, Peter. *Spheres, Volume 1: Bubbles: Microspherology*. Trans. Wieland Hoban. London: Semiotexte, 2011.

Stiegler, Bernard. *The Neganthropocene*. London: Open Humanities Press, 2018.

———. *States of Shock: Stupidity and Knowledge in the 21st Century*. Cambridge: Polity, 2015.

Suprenant, Céline. 'Freud and Psychoanalysis.' In *Marcel Proust in Context*. Ed. Adam Watt, 107–14. Cambridge and New York: Cambridge University Press, 2013.

Tadié, Jean-Yves. *Proust et le roman*. Paris: Gallimard, 1971.

Topping, Margaret. 'Errant Eyes: Digression, Metaphor and Desire in Marcel Proust's *In Search of Lost Time*.' In *Digressions in European Literature: From Cervantes to Sebald*. Ed. Alexis Grohmann and Caragh Wells, 106–17. New York: Palgrave Macmillan, 2011.

Vernant, Jean-Pierre. *Myth and Thought among the Greeks*. London: Routledge & Kegan Paul, 1983.

Walsh, Jonathan. 'Jealousy, *L'Histoire d'une Grecque moderne* and Proust's *À la recherche du temps perdu*.' *Romance Quarterly* 42, no. 2 (1995): 67–81.

Watt, Adam. *The Cambridge Introduction to Marcel Proust*. Cambridge: Cambridge University Press, 2011.

Wilson, Emma. *Sexuality and the Reading Encounter: Identity and Desire*

in Proust, Duras, Tournier and Cixous. Oxford: Oxford University Press, 1996.
Žižek, Slavoj. *Organs without Bodies: On Deleuze and Consequences*. London: Routledge, 2012.
——. *The Parallax View*. Cambridge, MA: The MIT Press, 2006.
——. *The Sublime Object of Ideology*. London: Verso, 1989.

Index

abyss, 6, 11, 12, 35–6, 38, 40–1, 47, 58, 65, 70, 71, 95, 124, 133, 138, 168, 173, 184, 198
affect, 15, 54, 63, 125, 193
  as intensive, 92
agencement/assemblage, 126, 127, 136, 142n, 148, 174
aiôn, 14, 46, 64–9, 70, 72–5, 82, 85n, 91–2, 96–7, 112, 116n, 128, 137, 160, 161, 162, 163, 167, 168, 184, 185, 186, 198
aisthesis, 59, 61, 69
Alliez, É., 56
antonomasia, 12
Attridge, D., 3, 17n
Aufhebung, 9

Balsamo, G., 26
Barbaras, R., 115–6n
Baross, Z., 19n
Barthes, R., 3, 17n, 24, 115n
Beckett, S., 143n
Beckman, F., 142n
beginnings, 47
Belenky, M., 152, 161
Benhaïm, A., 25
Benjamin, W., 175
Bergson, H., 55, 56, 60, 83n, 85n, 107
Bersani, L., 115n, 116n, 140, 145, 158, 175
  WORKS
  The Culture of Redemption, 175
Bilderschrift, 162–4, 166, 185, 199, 200
black hole/white wall system, 129–31, 135, 136, 139, 153, 157, 159, 200
Bois du Boulogne, 88–90, 91, 92, 98
Borges, J.-L., 69
Bowie, M., 23, 86n, 115n, 138, 143n, 161, 169n, 176, 205n
Bray, P., 11, 12, 13, 85n
Brentano, F., 125
Brooks, P., 147, 149

Cano, C., 17n, 195n
Carbone, M., 46, 64–6, 68–9, 72, 74, 161
catachresis, 41
chronology 51, 64, 66, 73, 82, 107, 125, 173, 180
chronos, 64, 66
Cocteau, J., 25
Colebrook, C., 5, 20n, 84n, 114n, 115n, 194n
Compagnon, A., 1–2, 17n, 54, 83–4n, 118, 182
contrariety, 71, 127
Cornell, D., 84–5n

Décarie, I., 13
Deleuze, G.
  and Derrida, 6–7, 18n
  and literature, 11
  love, 118
  nomadology, 59
  plane of immanence, 10–11
  writing on Proust, 10–11
  WORKS
  Anti-Oedipus (with Guattari), 87, 91, 92

A Thousand Plateaus (with
    Guattari), 59, 119, 129, 142n
Bergsonism, 51
Cinema I, 54
Cinema II, 83n
Difference and Repetition, 50
Proust and Signs, 10, 121, 165
The Logic of Sense, 65
What is Philosophy? (with Guattari),
    83n
de Man, P., 30
Derrida, J.
    and Deleuze, 6–7, 18n
    and literature, 11–12
    biodegradability, 10
    critique of presence, 28
    parasitism, 10, 29, 41
    writing on Proust, 9–10, 18n
    WORKS
    'Biodegradables: Seven Diary
        Fragments', 10
    Dissemination, 30
    'Force and Signification', 9
    'Freud and the Scene of Writing',
        162, 163
    Glas, 10, 147, 154, 161
    Memoires: For Paul de Man, 178
    Monolingualism of the Other, 154
    Of Grammatology, 7, 22, 175
    Signsponge, 95
    Specters of Marx, 175, 179
    The Post Card, 97
    The Work of Mourning, 179
    Writing and Difference, 130
Descombes, V., 1, 13, 20–1n, 117
desire, 87, 88, 90–112, 117–20, 167,
    172–3
    and/for place, 87, 88, 90, 98, 101–3,
        105, 110, 111
    and/for the trace, 94, 96, 97, 102–3,
        104, 105, 108, 110
    aporetic temporality, 99
    becoming *restance*, 108–9
    exceeding origin, 90–1, 108
    lacking lack, 92, 97
    mimetic, 94
    schizophrenic, 87, 91, 93, 95–7, 101,
        105, 111
    triangular, 95–6

without object, 87, 90, 95, 97, 100,
    102, 103, 116n
writing, 112, 116n
desiring-machines, 100
différance, 5, 10, 28, 42
differenciation, 62, 69, 74, 107, 119,
    127, 162
    and Oedipal triangulation, 95
differentiation, 62, 63, 70, 74, 75, 77,
    81, 82, 91, 97, 100, 119, 138,
    162, 166, 174, 180, 185
dividual (the), 6, 46, 53–4, 59, 63, 67,
    70, 89, 94, 107, 130, 166, 172,
    187, 198
dissemination, 30–1, 42
Dowd, G., 143n
dreams, 73–9, 82, 160–2
    extra-sensibility of, 75
    virtuality, 77
    writing, 161, 171n; see also
        Bilderschrift
Duns Scotus, 127
duration, 48, 51–2, 53, 54, 82, 83n
Düttmann, A., 142n, 176

Ellison, D., 33
Elsner, A. M., 20n, 47n, 176, 180, 182
engainement 14, 53, 82
epoché, 56, 68, 84n

face, 117, 129, 130, 134, 139
    of God/Yahweh, 135
    shattering of, 134–5
faciality, 130–3, 135, 137, 139, 141
Ffrench, P., 116n
Flieger, J. A., 143n
forgetting, 66–8, 75, 164, 186
    and narration, 37–41, 99
    as *sumplokē*, 67
    outlines of, 129
Foucault, M., 91–2, 114n
Freed-Thall, H., 143n
Freud, S., 55, 96–7, 114n, 161–2,
    170n
    WORKS
    Beyond the Pleasure Principle,
        170n
    The Interpretation of Dreams, 161
Fülöp, E., 13

Gasché, R., 17–8n
Genette, G., 25, 38
ghost(s); *see* spectre
Girard, R., 94
Grande, P. B., 96, 114n
grief, 63, 174, 176, 179, 181, 188–90,
    193, 202
  and absence, 174, 187–8
  aporia of, 191
  iterability, 188
  literary, 176, 185
  sumplokē of, 185
Grosz, E., 84n

haecceity, 127–9, 131, 133–4, 135,
    182, 183, 185, 191
Hägglund, M., 13, 24, 116n, 170n
hauntology, 179
Hegel, G. W. F., 9
Heidegger, M., 28
hieroglyph, 161–2
Husserl, E., 46, 56, 59, 84n, 126, 177
  WORKS
    *The Phenomenology of Internal
    Time-Consciousness*, 56, 57

immanence 50,
implex, 32–3, 37, 40, 41, 48, 49, 52,
    57, 70, 77, 81, 89, 123, 132
individuation, 106, 127, 133, 134,
    139, 141, 168
infinity, 65, 130–1, 138, 149
inscription, 8, 9, 15, 50, 53, 55, 80, 82
  and *agencement*, 136–7
  of our pasts, 52
intensity, 46, 65, 71–2, 74, 82, 91–2,
    99–100, 128, 140, 162
iterability, 5, 11, 23, 29, 34–5, 37–8,
    54, 62, 93, 99, 112, 118, 137,
    182, 184, 198, 200, 202

Jammes, F., 75
Jay, M., 170n
jealousy, 80, 145–63, 165–9, 172,
    189–91
  and love, 145, 146, 149, 167
  and possession, 152–3, 154–5, 168
  as epistemology/knowledge, 145,
    146–51, 156–7, 158, 162, 181
  as supplementarity, 145
  dream(s), 161
  dream-writing; see *Bilderschrift*
  for the trace, 145, 148, 151, 154–5,
    156, 157, 159, 160–1, 168
  hatred, 151
  ideological function, 152
  implex of, 150
  language's, 155
  narrative impulse, 156–8, 160–1,
    162, 165, 167, 181, 187
  signature of/as, 145, 154
  'staircase', 156–7
  temporality of, 154, 165, 172

Kemp, G. 27
Klein, M., 175

Lacoue-Labarthe, P., 114n
Laing, R. D., 92
Lambert, G., 19n
Landerson, E., 144n
Landy, J., 13, 24–5, 115n, 116n,
    144n
Lecercle, J., 11
Lerner, S., 176
Lethe (river), 68, 69, 74, 138, 151
lies/lying, 128, 144n, 162–6
  as invention/discovery, 162–3
love, 76, 117–9, 121–6, 128–33,
    135–41, 146–7, 149–50, 172–3,
    181
  and desire, 117, 118–9
  and/for the trace, 117–8, 125
  as dividual, 121, 130
  as inscription, 124, 135–6
  as need for possession, 150
  exceeding origin, 125
  groups/grouping, 121,
  iterability of, 118, 121
  packs, 121–2, 133, 142n
  virtual contraction, 132, 133
Lucey, M., 23
Lyotard, J.-F., 7, 55

McDonald, C., 171n
Magedera, I., 154
'Marcel', 23–7, 35, 41, 99
Matz, J., 21n

Merleau-Ponty, M., 46, 64, 68, 69, 82, 146, 154
Miller, J. H., 23, 34–5, 162
Mnemosyne, 68, 69
Moi, T., 171n
mourning, 174–6, 178, 182–3
  as/of writing, 175, 179, 183–5, 193, 197–8
  contradiction of, 185
  le plus d'un of, 175, 182
  strangeness of, 176
  work of, 175, 179
multiplicity, 53, 57, 64, 65, 66, 70, 73, 90, 111, 119, 164, 196
  as love, 122–3
  nonnumerical, 54–55, 56, 77, 89, 95, 106, 129, 166, 173, 178
Murphy, M., 143n
'mystic writing pad', 55

Naas, M., 20n
Neoplatonism, 83n
noēteon, 59–61, 63, 64, 65, 66, 67, 68, 70, 72, 73, 75, 77, 78, 79, 81, 82, 90, 93, 99, 109, 121–3, 126, 128, 138, 161, 173, 175, 180, 186
  and epistemology, 149
noēton, 60, 73, 78, 79, 82

Ortega y Gasset, J., 142n, 195n
paraph, 198–9, 201, 202–3; *see also* signature
  intensity of, 203

Parker, J. A., 37
parousia, 28, 33, 52, 56, 113, 115n, 147, 175
Patton, P., 84n, 114n
perception, 50, 53, 55, 61, 82, 177–8
  implex of, 105
phainesthai, 57, 178, 181, 185, 187, 193
Phantasievorstellung, 56–8
phantom, 178, 181; *see also* spectre
pharmakon, 6
phenomenology, 46, 55–9, 177, 178, 179
  concern with absence, 177
  intentionality, 56, 57, 66, 69, 125

transcendental/immanent distinction, 91, 94
Plato, 33
property/*propre*, 12, 27, 29, 152, 177, 180, 202–3
  as abyssal, 36, 40, 155
Protevi, J., 118
Proust, M.
  and Bergson, 85n
  as philosopher, 1, 13,
  contradiction, 25
  death, 182
  irony, 76
  'narrator', 22–3, 27, 199
  nuance, 143n
  opinion of prefaces, 47
  place-names, 103
  'preformationism', 9
  signature, 4, 176–7, 182–3
  WORKS
    Albertine disparue, 28, 199
    À l'ombre des jeunes filles en fleurs, 37
    Du côté de chez Swann, 88
    Jean Santeuil, 26
    La Prisonnière, 28, 136, 150
    Le Côté de Guermantes, 126, 146
    Le Temps retrouvé, 2
    Sodome et Gomorrhe, 167
Pseudo-Dionysius, 83n
pseudo-iterative, 39

Rabaté, J.-M., 176
realism, 2
rebus, 161–2
restance, 23, 31–7, 40, 41, 47, 63, 65, 69, 71, 72, 73, 75, 82, 89, 99, 109–10, 124, 132, 134, 149, 162, 166–7, 172, 174–5, 179, 183, 185, 198, 200, 202
  desire for, 100
revenant (the), 5, 180, 181, 187, 203
rêven'ant, 185, 187, 188, 189, 192
Rogers, B., 27
Rosita and Doodica (Barnum's circus twins), 138
Rousset, J., 9
Ruiz, R., 196
Rushworth, J., 176

Sa (*Savoir Absolu*/Absolute knowledge), 147–9, 151, 152, 153, 155, 156–7, 163, 165–6, 179, 190
Scheler, M., 125–6
Schlöndorff, V., 196
Segal, A., 24, 26
seing, 154–5, 157, 163, 168, 175, 193, 200–2, 205n
   of death, 177
sense/sensation, 6, 11, 14, 46, 50–82, 99, 141, 166, 174, 177, 196
   being of, 71
   of music, 107, 131–2
   of place, 88, 90, 98, 116n
   in dreams, 163
   vagueness, 130
sight/seeing, 147, 163, 170n
   as epistemology, 147
signature, 12, 23, 35, 154–5, 163, 168, 175, 197–8, 199, 202–3, 204
Simon, A., 14, 16, 19n, 86n, 113n
sleep, 47–8, 61–2, 72–4, 162, 192–3
   Albertine's, 139, 144n
   sommeil de plomb, 72
   time of, 73
   unconscious as, 79
Sloterdijk, P., 83n
Socrates, 33
spectre (the), 177–8, 179, 180–9, 203
   as trace, 182
   multiplicity, 181
   temporality, 180, 186
speed(s), 127–8
Stiegler, B., 6
subjectivity, 24, 78, 82, 140, 179
   abyssal, 109
   and death, 180, 184–5
   dispersal of, 48, 153
   multiplicities of, 65
sumplokē, 5, 23, 34–41, 47, 53, 56, 57, 58, 71, 75, 91, 92, 104, 110–1, 122, 123, 134, 135, 152–3, 156, 157, 165, 167, 174, 198, 200
   drive as, 155
synecdoche, 12, 34–5
synthesis 49, 50–1, 57, 158
   and sleep, 74
   love as, 122
   of memory in narrative 39

Tadié, J.-Y., 23, 27, 37
time/temporality, 2, 7, 46
   contraction of, 49–51
trace (the), 15, 28, 29, 56, 58, 61, 65, 66, 71, 79, 82, 90, 92, 98, 100, 110, 125, 139, 141, 148, 163, 172, 175, 178, 182
   and/as infinity, 130–1
   in sleep, 72–3
   resistance to ambiguity, 102
   writing, 113, 120, 139
transcendence/transcendental, 50, 96
   memory, 59
transversality, 11, 22, 49, 59, 91, 138, 196, 205n

undecidability, 203

Vermeer, J., 35–6
Vernant, J.-P., 65
virtual (the), 4, 6, 49–50, 52–3, 55, 56, 58, 64, 71, 78–9, 81, 82, 83n, 103, 127, 133–4, 193, 197, 203
voice, 10, 31

Walsh, J., 157
Watt, A., 22
weaving, 3, 14, 33, 35, 36–7, 41, 55, 70, 153, 174
   love as, 124
   spectral, 179
'*without* without *without*', 97, 102
   and place, 103

Zivin, E., 8
Žižek, S., 7, 124, 171n

EU representative:
Easy Access System Europe
Mustamäe tee 50, 10621 Tallinn, Estonia
Gpsr.requests@easproject.com

www.ingramcontent.com/pod-product-compliance
Lightning Source LLC
Chambersburg PA
CBHW052049220426
43663CB00012B/2505